ZAMBIA UP CLOSE AND PERSONAL

BY

MOIRA COOKE

Published by New Generation Publishing in 2017

Copyright © Moira Cooke 2017

First Edition

The author asserts the moral right under the Copyright, Designs and Patents Act 1988 to be identified as the author of this work.

All Rights reserved. No part of this publication may be reproduced, stored in a retrieval system or transmitted, in any form or by any means without the prior consent of the author, nor be otherwise circulated in any form of binding or cover other than that which it is published and without a similar condition being imposed on the subsequent purchaser.

www.newgeneration-publishing.com

DEDICATION

To my husband Bob . . .

friend and fellow traveller

who put up with all my foibles

and without whom, none of it would

have been possible!

INTRODUCTION

For the record, I never actually said there would be a third book about our experiences in Zambia. Yet even as the second book was released in 2011, people were asking when a third book would appear . . . is there perhaps an avid audience out there eager to read yet more of our escapades in darkest Africa?

In 2011, during my longest trip to Africa since leaving in 1976, an idea began germinating that what remained was the untold story of our personal life in Zambia. Yes, unbelievably, we managed a life apart from the roller coaster of charity work and this is what 'Zambia Up Close and Personal' is about.

Though this manuscript has been dabbled with and put aside many times over recent years, the time has finally come for it to see the light of day. It is dedicated to Bob, my long suffering husband and travel companion, without whom none of this would have been possible.

May you once again laugh and cry along with us, as we face yet more trials and adventures, this time getting 'up close and personal' with both people and animals in Zambia, as well as battling with vehicles and scary situations that at times defy description, all the while watching our family grow and enter a third generation in Africa.

Happy reading!

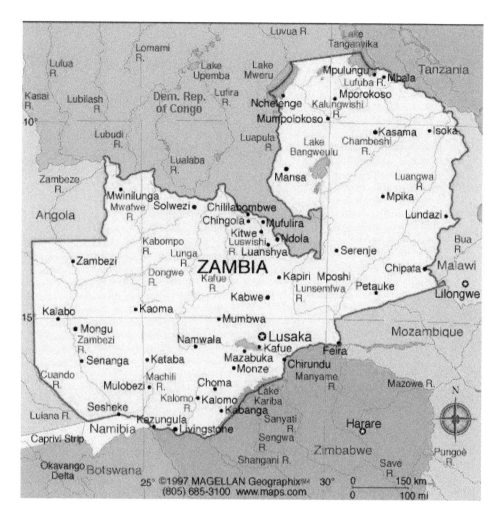

Zambia Map

PART ONE:

DECEMBER 2002 - > JANUARY 2003

A TRIP DOWN MEMORY LANE

CHAPTER ONE: A RUDE AWAKENING
Thursday December 12th & Friday December 13th 2002

Sunrise on Thursday December 12th, 2002. As the aeroplane lands, we have our first glimpse of Africa for more than twenty-five years. The surge of emotion is so great, I'm tempted to imitate the former Pope, John Paul II, who used to kneel and kiss the blessed earth of each country he arrived in. Yet such a move would doubtless embarrass my husband, not to mention amuse fellow passengers, as well as ground staff clustered around the foot of the aeroplane steps, smiling faces beaming upwards like black sunflowers waiting to welcome the sun.

Our daughter arrived in Zambia in June of this year to spend two years here as a VSO volunteer. Now we plan to spend three weeks accompanying her on a grand tour of old haunts recollected from when we lived here in the 1970s, but also, hopefully, discovering a few new ones along the way. Three weeks in and out, then back to our comfort zone. We left Africa in 1976, swearing never to return, an oath we've adhered to rigidly. So what possible difference can one short trip make?

And if these well-laid plans are dispelled in the first forty-eight hours when we come face to face with hardship and suffering caused by poverty combined with the HIV AIDS crisis in twenty-first century Zambia, at least at 6am on the morning of our arrival, we're blissfully unaware these hazards lie strewn along the pathway ahead, just waiting to blow up in our faces like unexploded landmines.

Much to Bob's relief, I don't kneel to kiss the ground. Instead I battle with a tumult of emotion as we queue in sweltering heat for entry visas, then wait interminably for bags to appear on the rickety conveyor belt which creaks ever louder in protest with every revolution, while overhead a single fan attempts to stir up the tropical soup that passes for air.

"First impressions?" Bob asks as everyone else's suitcases bar ours appear.

"Everyone's black," I mutter darkly.

"Hardly surprising since they now run the country!" he responds.

When we first arrived in Zambia in the late 1960s, the country was still taking its first teetering steps along the road to independence. Many old colonials and diehards had already departed for pastures new where they could still wield power and influence, making way for a new breed of whites like ourselves, arriving by the plane load, anxious to lend expertise in persistently infertile fields such as medicine, education and engineering.

Fast forward thirty years and all has changed. There are Zambian airport controllers, ground staff and immigration officers. Zambian policemen and policewomen in smart khaki uniforms with knife edge trouser pleats man checkpoints along the road into town, keeping a watchful eye out for small money to be made from traffic infringements real or imaginary.

Despite a lack of sleep and the unexplained presence of a young Zambian called Alex in our daughter's car, I peer out fascinated at passing scenes of Africa waking to greet another day, searching for something recognisable.

It's the rainy season so, not surprisingly, it looks as if it might rain. Everywhere is lush and green and verdant. Tulip trees dazzle with their brilliant vermilion flowers, while ripening mangoes hang heavily from laden branches in the humid air. Inhaling deeply, the faint whiff of last night's charcoal fires mingles with the heady scent of frangipani. I sigh with relief: Africa still smells the same.

"Do you recall when we first arrived in December 1968?" Bob as ever is right about dates.

Closing my eyes, I recall peering out the plane, eager for that first glimpse of Africa, perhaps expecting to see elephant, giraffe, lion littering the plains below. Yet there was nothing but endless bush as far as the eye could see. Zambia seemed deep, dark and impenetrable. Nothing relieved the monotony of endless bush, except for the occasional ribbon of red earth winding its way seemingly into oblivion.

Even flying on up to Ndola on the Copperbelt to take up teaching posts in Mufulira, first impressions weren't great. So, are they any different thirty years on? Hmmm, hard to say yet!

Later that afternoon, we take a taxi to a safari company on Cairo Road. Cairo Road is Lusaka's main road, running as it does from north to south and dissecting the city in two, trading areas and high-density townships on one side and government enclaves and affluent suburbs on the other.

It looks vaguely familiar. The same buildings, albeit some crumbling into disrepair, still mark the southern end of Cairo Road. The northern end however has seen development with newer buildings and offices. Yet the Lonely Planet Guide to Zambia now warns against thieves and pickpockets thronging Cairo Road. Best perhaps not to linger too long there!

The safari company is located in a modern office block near the north end of town. Plucked at random from the guidebook, it will hopefully soon speed us on our journey down memory lane by providing a vehicle within budget yet nevertheless suited to hammering over dirt roads. To date no actual vehicle has been specified.

Formalities completed and budget finalised, we discover an immense Toyota Hilux Surf awaits in the car park. Not only is it built like a tank but, if Jeremy Clarkson is to be believed, it will take us anywhere. Indeed, he once tested one under the most gruelling conditions and pronounced it indestructible. Time and Zambian roads will prove whether he was right.

"A four-wheel drive!" Bob exclaims gleefully. "*This* will go anywhere!"

That is supposing he can get it out of the car park. The Hilux is an automatic and doesn't respond readily to a mere man trying to tell it what to do. Try as he might, he can't get it into reverse.

"I thought the idea of automatics was they did things automatically," I murmur unhelpfully as the engine protests loudly enough to make even Jeremy Clarkson wince.

"Maybe we should drive around some quieter streets till I get the hang of it," Bob concedes. "It's certainly the largest vehicle I've ever driven."

But that is supposing these days there are any quieter streets in Lusaka. As he edges out into Cairo Road, traffic swarms past and on up Church Road where Alex, again inexplicably along for the ride, directs us. Blue and white minibuses crammed with passengers, career around like demented dodgems, pulling out in front with no warning, while yet more 4x4s generally massive and mainly brand new try to force us off the road.

Eventually, after several tentative circuits around tree-lined avenues, Bob announces, "Right, I've got the hang of it now."

I pray he has because, if driving in this traffic is challenging, then being a passenger is nerve-wracking. Most of the vehicles, even though brand new, are conceivably not being driven by their owners but rather by lunatics hellbent on destroying them. Yet scattered amongst the shiny 4x4s and the crowded blue and white taxi buses, are other vehicles looking as if they've come from the local dodgem track. These vie for road space along with clapped out lorries barely able to trundle along, their tyres bald as an old man's head and belching noxious clouds of exhaust fumes.

Mastery asserted over the monster, we head back into the mêlée of Cairo Road. We need to change precious dollars into Zambian kwachas. Apparently, Alex is also in the know about such things. Maybe that's why he's been assigned to accompany us on this first sortie back into Zambian society. While we might have stuck with recognisable banks such as Barclays or Standard Chartered, not so Alex, who makes a beeline for one of many shady exchange bureaux that have sprung up along Cairo Road.

"Er, is this wise? We don't want to be ripped off on our first day back!" I try feebly.

It's already too late. A security guard brandishing an AK-47 leaps forward to usher us into a parking space reserved for clientele. Goodness, what do they suppose we're after, gold bullion? We step out nervously onto Cairo Road.

"The guidebook does say this is a no-go area for tourists flaunting bum-bags, backpacks or handbags," I remind Bob. And what are we carrying but bum-bags, backpacks and a handbag stuffed with more $US dollars than a bank vault!

But why so fearful? No sooner are we out the car than the same security guard, AK-47 now dangling carelessly by his side, takes us under his wing like a clucking mother hen. Does he perhaps imagine we're loaded? And does it also explain why that same gun is now pointing at my back?

Once inside, he leads the way not into the front office but into a darkened back room, perhaps where dodgier deals take place. Sweating buckets, not just from the humid December afternoon, but also from cold trickles of fear coursing down from armpits to groin, we step inside.

"If we get out of this alive, I'll eat my hat!" I hiss at Bob.

"Talk about baptism by fire," he responds. "Al Capone doesn't have a look in!"

Nervously we part with three hundred and fifty crisp, new US dollar bills, receiving in exchange not gold bullion but grubby, much-thumbed Zambian kwachas notes. Instantly we become kwachas millionaires. I stuff K1.7 million into my secret body purse. The bulge is so large it's an instant giveaway for any potential pickpocket. I shift the telltale bulge around the front in the hope, even at fifty-seven, I might look six months pregnant. *Some hope!*

We emerge into blistering tropical sunshine. All trace of rain has vanished along with the armed guard. Even though we're now loaded and ripe for the plucking, he's inexplicably lost all interest. All he wants is our parking space for the next loaded customer. We dive for the vehicle, only escaping after Bob once more does battle with reverse.

"There never used to be traffic like this thirty years ago," Bob says, nosing his way into the never-ending river of vehicles.

No, there didn't, but isn't it just adding to the fun of discovery!

Next day Alex, now identified as a former street kid turned personal bodyguard by appointment of our daughter, proves invaluable at locating anywhere and everywhere in the vastly expanded and ugly sprawl of Zambia's capital. Not only does he know every shortcut through Lusaka's bewildering streets, he also knows his way round a Toyota Hilux Surf which still stubbornly refuses to respond to almost everything Bob expects it to do.

Alex even directs us into the depths of Kalingalinga township for a meeting with Tresford, a part-time gardener where our daughter works. Tresford is also HIV positive and the newly set up Tanworth[1] Starfish Fund has begun funding treatment with ARVs to control his HIV AIDS. This harrowing meeting, along with explicit revelations about Alex's own chequered background, opens up our minds to the startling realisation that perhaps we are here for some reason other than simply a stroll down memory lane.

---

[1] Initially known as Starfish Fund, only when it became a registered charity did it become The Tanworth Starfish Fund.

"Truly, you two people have become like parents to me," swears Tresford, grasping our sweaty palms between his cold clammy ones in the gloomy confines of his family home in the depths of Kalingalinga township.

Then later, "Already you have become like parents to me!" Alex's voice chokes with emotion as he steers us around Lusaka's small botanical gardens, stopping in front of a bed of zinnias. "May I please call you Mum and Dad?"

But that's one step too far for less than forty-eight hours' acquaintance. Heavens, we only came here for a holiday, not to acquire an adopted family, nor to become entangled in Zambia's many problems. Yet the first forty-eight hours have so assaulted our senses, that all we can do is crawl into bed praying that tomorrow, as we head northwards out of town, this initial rude awakening can be put behind us.

So, what are we waiting for, let the sentimental journey back through time finally commence . . .

CHAPTER TWO: THE ROAD LESS TRAVELLED...
Saturday December 14th and Sunday December 15th, 2002

On Saturday morning, we head northwards on our epic journey. A holiday it may well be, yet Bob and I are still struggling to process disturbing images twenty-first century Zambia has thrust in our faces since arriving forty-eight hours ago.

"Let's hope we see more than just the desperate plight of orphans, street kids and AIDS victims on our travels," I say as the dust and grime of Lusaka recede into the distance.

"Try living with it all the time!" observes Ali drily. "Anyways, I'd like to forget about work for the next three weeks and discover something of the country where I'm spending the next two years."

"And all we want, is to enjoy a sentimental journey back in time!" Bob puts his foot down and feels the Hilux respond accordingly. Finally, these two are learning to get along with each other.

As the car speeds northwards, I reflect how many times we made this journey thirty years ago in a little red Honda 600, heading south from the Copperbelt to Lake Kariba or Vic Falls, or else into Rhodesia, even as far as Mozambique. There seemed no limit to the distances we covered in that tiny car.

Back then, bush lining the sides of the road was dense, impenetrable, featureless. The story was told of someone who fell asleep at the wheel, spun his car round and, without realising, travelled back in the direction from which he'd come. The highlight of the entire five hundred miles up and down to Lusaka, was spotting a troupe of baboons warming their backsides on the side of the road. Yet how things have changed...

For the first fifty miles out of Lusaka vast farms growing grain and rearing cattle now border the sides of the road. The bush has been stripped right back to be replaced by massive ranches and fertile fields with not a baboon baring its backside in sight.

Further north, rustic stalls constructed from rickety poles bound together with rope line the road. Stallholders are selling melons, tomatoes, cabbages, sweet potatoes and onions. Women wearing brightly coloured 'chitenges', sometimes children in rags step forward to thrust a live chicken or a bag of bush fruits towards the car even...

"Wasn't that a rat?" I swivel round for a second look, but Bob has sped past, confident at last in his mastery of the Hilux. Bet he wouldn't swap this for a tiny Honda 600!

"Why would anyone want to buy a rat?" I muse.

"Possibly to eat it," suggests Ali.

This unappetising thought takes time to digest, till I spot a goat's leg, bloody and swarming with flies. Hmmm, this journey gets more interesting by the minute.

One thing at least hasn't changed. Charcoal sellers still abound, even though this practice is supposedly banned because of deforestation. Try telling that to the charcoal sellers, who have stuffed sacks brimful of charcoal, then tied the tops with elaborate nets of twine, causing the overfilled sacks to wobble to attention at the roadside like drunken soldiers on parade.

Correction two things remain unchanged . . . there are still only two stopping places on the entire road between Lusaka and Ndola. Reaching the first, Kabwe, we crawl through appreciating how much it has grown from a one street straggle to a town abuzz with petrol stations and stores selling everything from groceries to car parts, clothing to sewing machines. People with small money to spend now throng the streets, while high speed buses ply the route between the Copperbelt and the capital, stopping both here and in Kapiri Mposhi.

Ah, Kapiri Mposhi, second stop on the road northwards and from which the road north to Tanzania and Dar es Salaam branches off. The Hell Run as it was formerly known, because it used to be littered with the detritus of vehicles that never made it all the way. And no, that's one road we never risked in a little Honda.

"All I remember of Kapiri Mposhi was a disgusting, unusable toilet," recalls Bob.

Yet Kapiri Mposhi, like Kabwe, now bustles with people. A veritable market has grown up where the high-speed buses stop. Women balancing bowls on their heads stuffed full of ripe to bursting bananas, grilled mealies or cheap sweeties ply their trade alongside waiting buses. For the princely sum of K300 there's even a proper flush toilet with toilet paper. Times really have changed!

We make good time to Ndola, administrative capital of the Copperbelt. Kitwe being larger, is arguably more important, yet Ndola has now grown large enough to merit a by-pass. Out of town we search for the road to Mufulira, which must be here somewhere. Suddenly I spot a signpost pointing round a roundabout instead of a right turn as it was before. "Aha, that's it."

"Are you sure?" Bob hesitates. "Only there's no other traffic turning off here."

"We could ask somebody," suggests Ali, "even though there isn't actually anyone around to ask."

"Well, there never *was* much along this road," I say, "except the occasional anthill or dambo. No signs for farms or other habitation and, since the road runs parallel to the Congo border, anything along here is as likely to be in the Congo as in Zambia."

7

And do we want to end up in the Congo? No, we do not!

For sure there's nothing now but endless bush, in places encroaching onto the road with grass sprouting from the tarmac. Eventually I voice what we're all thinking. "Should we actually be taking this road?"

Bob isn't as confident as before. "Let's get to Mufulira as quickly as we can and not hang about on the way."

For which read: *Let's get out of here . . . fast!*

Some years later in conversation with a Zambian, we mention taking this road today.

"Ah, you were not knowing a minibus was held up on that very road?" She shrieks in horror at our stupidity. "Even thieves forced all the passengers out of the bus at gunpoint. They stripped them not only of their valuables, but also of their clothes, then drove off in the minibus leaving the hapless passengers naked on the roadside."

Meanwhile today, in blissful ignorance, we continue wending our way to Mufulira, albeit with mounting unease. In hindsight, we can only think that, since we have lived to tell the tale, God was on our case that day.

Instead of heading straight for Kitwe where we're staying for two nights, we're making a detour via Mufulira, the town where we lived from late December 1968 until August 1971.

"So what was Mufulira like?" Ali asks when eventually it appears we may get there clothed and alive, rather than stark naked or in a coffin.

"It used to be a thriving mining town with a large expatriate community working in the mine as well as in schools and local government offices," I tell her. "White-washed schools, churches and houses stood in shady tree-lined streets. Okay, maybe it wasn't exactly the epicentre of Zambia, let alone of the universe, but it was a pleasant town."

"What on earth did you do there?" asks Ali.

"There was a cinema, theatre, outdoor swimming pool, library, golf course, boating dam, though the town itself had nothing of interest, apart from the copper mine. Yet the expats certainly knew how to enjoy themselves."

"I've heard it's become a ghost town since the mine stopped working in the eighties, so goodness knows what we'll find there today."

Indeed, an air of dereliction is immediately apparent. Mufulira is a town where time has stood still. There's no sign of recent development apart from straggling shanty towns springing up on its outskirts, no sign of any effort to maintain what was once one of the Copperbelt's smaller but pleasanter towns. Once neat red-brick bungalows, where mine managers lived surrounded by well-irrigated lawns and lush tropical plants, have become ramshackle buildings stranded on dusty, arid plots and inhabited by squatters with tribes of ragged children, numbers swollen by Zambia's burgeoning orphan crisis.

"According to my reckoning, the next road on the right is Lumumba Avenue. Why don't we show Ali where we used to live?" I suggest eagerly.

However, there's no way into Lumumba Avenue. A solid concrete block bars all access from the main road. We end up doing an about-turn, going up another road, then doubling back before eventually entering Lumumba Avenue from the other end. We crawl down it, trying not to draw attention to ourselves. So far, there's not been another white face in town.

"Well 56A Lumumba Avenue is still there," I announce triumphantly.

The car stops and we gaze dejectedly at what was once our home. It used to be a neat semi-detached bungalow, just the right size for a couple with their first baby. Now it's a dilapidated dump, the house number daubed untidily in whitewash on the wall. The plot is surrounded by chicken wire fencing in a state of collapse, dividing the drive overgrown with weeds in two. The tin roof badly needs stripping and re-painting.

Maybe we should have left Mufulira there and then. But no, instead we try to locate the church where our son was christened. The only building remotely resembling it is now a beer hall. Mufulira High School, where Bob once taught, is still there, but no longer the pristine establishment it once was, while Ross Avenue Primary School where I taught, is now Pamodzi Girls High School, secreted like a prison camp behind six feet high walls with barbed razor wire on top.

"I've seen enough," I announce dejectedly.

"At least let's find the swimming pool?" Bob perhaps recalls lazy afternoons spent there when afternoon school activities didn't beckon.

Yet try as we might, we cannot locate it. We do however find the mine hospital where our son was born, which bucks me up sufficiently to suggest a photo of the hospital would be nice. One for the album perhaps? Is it perhaps illegal to take photos of Zambian hospitals? Bob's camera immediately attracts the attention of the gun toting guard on the gate. Never one to miss a shot, Bob slips the camera to me for a quick one before roaring off faster than a bank robber leaving a crime scene in a cloud of dust.

We turn into Mufulira's main street, once filled with bustling shops. The same buildings are there, but that's all. Solankis has gone along with the fruit and vegetable shop on the corner where the queue would stretch around the corner whenever a delivery of apples arrived. Bata shoes is the only shop still there. Shops further down the street are mere empty shells with doors and windows barred and shuttered.

Bob swings into Mufulira's one garage. Thankfully that at least is still there, because one thing this car does, is drink petrol by the gallon. A smiling young Zambian sporting the distinctive red and grey Total colours comes out to serve us. It is the same garage from which the Honda 600 came all those years ago.

"You are visitors to Mufulira?" guesses the petrol pump attendant. For sure there can't be many white people still living here because we still haven't seen one white face.

"We used to live here many years ago," reveals Bob.

"Ah me, I am born here in the mine hospital," announces the petrol pump attendant sensing an opening wider than the Nile Delta.

Since the mine hospital was a private hospital, you could only be born there if your father worked on the mine, or if you paid privately. The alternative was too ghastly to contemplate. Stories were rife of babies being delivered on the floor of government hospitals.

"Our son also was born there," Bob shares magnanimously.

"Even my Mom used to work in Solankis!" The petrol pump attendant ups the stakes.

Solankis was the one shop of *any* size in town and much patronised by expatriate ladies as a source of dress material. If you weren't into dressmaking when you arrived in Mufulira, you certainly were by the time you left. In the seventies, there was nowhere in the whole of Zambia to buy suitable, let alone fashionable, clothes.

"Ah but Solankis is no longer there." The young man shakes his head. "Which is why I am unable to take up my place in college because there is no-one now to support me. So, if you could just give me your email address?"

This may not be a good idea, yet there's no holding Bob. Out comes pen and paper to write down his email address. It might as well be his chequebook, since doubtless his details will be passed on to everyone within a thirty mile radius of Mufulira.

"In fact I am hoping to go to England on a scholarship. Maybe I can contact you?"

But this again is one stage too far, like the unexpected acquisition of sons. Bob hands over a fistful of kwachas for the petrol and we escape, having parted with nothing more incriminating than an email address.

"You must stop doing that, Dad," chides Ali who, in six short months, has the new Zambia sussed. "He'll keep pestering you for money. Once they've got contact details, they never leave you alone."

With that sobering thought we leave Mufulira for Kitwe, passing en route Mufulira Teachers' College which, like all colleges here, now trains teachers faster than you can say its name, simply to replace those dying of AIDS.

Not surprisingly Mufulira offers nothing by way of accommodation. Kitwe therefore is where we are to spend two nights at the Edinburgh Hotel. Apart from mine stacks continually belching smoke, this towering salmon pink relic of colonial days is the only notable feature marking Kitwe's skyline. According to the internet, the Edinburgh Hotel now boasts a swimming pool. This of course is pure fiction. The towels are verging on grey and neither of our rooms boasts a full complement of either light bulbs or working plug sockets.

The restaurant however comes up trumps. At the close of the meal a young chef called Florence, clad in whites so dazzling they put the room towels to shame, asks if we enjoyed our meal. Florence is highly articulate. Soon Alison involves her in discussion regarding HIV testing and resources for workers at the hotel. Unwittingly, Florence may have just become peer educator for the entire staff of the Edinburgh Hotel.

"Is this a holiday or a recruitment drive?" I ask later.

"Never miss an opportunity in the fight against AIDS!" Ali responds.

"Tomorrow should be right up your street then, a visit to a Christian Aid partner organisation that operates in the field of HIV testing and counselling. Just a quick visit, naturally, and on our way. This is a holiday after all," we joke, little knowing how, after that same visit, things were destined to turn out very differently indeed.

CHAPTER THREE: BUSH HAPPY
December 16th -> 18th, 2002

"So, how was it, returning to the Copperbelt after so many years?" asks Ali as we leave Kitwe on Monday morning.

"It was good taking a trip down memory lane, but yesterday's meeting at Chep . . ." I shudder at what it revealed about the desperate plight of orphans and vulnerable children.

"Just try to put it behind you for now!" After six months here, Ali may be rather more adept at this than two greenhorns could ever hope to be.

Leaving behind Kitwe's smoke shrouded skyline, we're heading for the little known Kasanka Game Reserve. This involves retracing our route back to Kapiri Mposhi, before turning onto the once infamous Hell Run which may now be resurfaced, but could it also have lost some of its former allure?

Previously one of our favourite pastimes was spending time in the bush. The bush can be a scary place, full of unexpected dangers, yet it's also exhilarating and the unexpected doesn't always happen, especially if you're careful or lucky or both. Certainly we were 'bush happy' on many an occasion.

But will the bush still hold the same allure some twenty-six years on?

In no time we reach Kasanka Game Reserve where, driving along sandy roads to reach camp, the car scatters yellow baboons and flocks of helmeted guinea fowl. Wasa Camp is basic, just a cluster of mud-baked rondavels washed in ochre paint and decorated with black silhouettes. It overlooks a dambo with a small lake in the centre where herds of puku graze and where hippo are occasional visitors.

However, Kasanka's main attraction lies in the millions of fruit bats, which arrive annually in November and December. Each evening at dusk they swarm in their thousands into the evening sky, creating what experts claim is the largest mammal movement in the world. Conservative estimates rate each nightly flight as containing between 2.5 million and eight million bats.

Definitely not the place for anyone suffering from bat phobia!

On the first evening Rod, here on a post university gap year, and Clifford, resident bird and flower expert, take us in the Landrover to see the bats, stopping en route at a hide to view rare and shy sitatunga. Reaching the hide entails climbing an almost vertical pole ladder up to a viewing platform high in the treetops and causing rickety knees to creak in protest. Getting down proves far worse!

"Perhaps we should mention your neck and my balance problems?" I suggest. "These activities could be risk averse for the likes of us?"

"Doubtless there's worse to come," Bob predicts. Correctly as it turns out, since reaching trees where fruit bats are nesting involves trekking on foot through dense bush and snake, scorpion and lizard infested jungle, before ploughing through waist-high grasses and reeds. God alone knows what else is in there; I can only pray He's on the case. And all this to see . . . *bats!* Maybe we're bats, because all they're doing is hanging upside down like bits of shredded black bin bag. And there's still the trek back through dense bush.

What was that about being bush happy?

Back at the Landrover, darkness falls as we watch the silent spectacle of millions of bats taking to the air silhouetted against the darkening sky, creating one of those magical Africa moments that lasts a lifetime. Since this sight so completely overwhelms both of us, Alison quite rightly fears her parents may finally be losing the plot.

Showering before dinner is problematical. The shower consists of a two-gallon bucket suspended behind the chalet. A little man runs along in the dark filling each bucket with hot water from the fire. By which time the water is not only lukewarm, but also runs out mid-shower.

After dinner, more civilised than expected in darkest Africa, we sink into bed and switch off the lights. Unfortunately, in the bush it's not possible also to switch off the sound effects. Under the velvet cloak of darkness, crickets whirr excitedly, courting frogs clink-clunk one to another, while a lone hippo honks in the distance, proving there really is one out there somewhere.

"What if a snake gets in under the door in the night?"

"You've got a torch, haven't you?" Does Bob mean hit it or dazzle it?

"And if a scorpion gets inside our trainers?"

Across the darkness Bob sighs, weary for the curtains of sleep to close. "Just remember to bang your shoes together before you put them on."

"But just about anything could be hidden in the thatched roof, deadly spiders, even a python . . ."

"Why don't you just go to sleep?"

So I do, but still switch the torch on several times during the night to check for spiders, scorpions, snakes or whatever else is keeping us company.

Who said being in the bush was fun?

Next day at 5.30am we stand outside admiring the first golden streaks of an African dawn piercing the sky. Oh, the delights of game viewing at the crack of dawn! Why do animals choose such an ungodly hour for grazing, hunting or early morning socialising?

After tea and biscuits, we set off for the same hide reached by the same treacherous ladder in order to spot rare sitatunga, puku, as well as a marsh harrier and spurwing geese. On the way back more puku, wattled cranes, vervet and blue monkeys and guinea fowl scatter from the approaching vehicle before someone makes a meal out of them.

Breakfast is late. As we wait on the veranda, the hippo making all the noise last night begins plodging in and out of the reeds in the marshy centre of the dambo. Infuriatingly, just as Bob has him in focus, down he ducks into the water, reluctant to have his photo taken. Yet soon after, a second hippo arrives and the two begin racing each other from one end of the dambo to the other. Suddenly all is quiet until, without warning, one hippo charges out the reeds and onto the grass in front of the chalets where it races full pelt from one end to the other before grinding to a halt like an armoured tank running out of steam.

"Maybe something spooked him in the water," suggests Clifford. "A larger male, even a water snake perhaps."

That afternoon another treat lies in store . . . a walk in the bush! Clifford, the Zambian guide, and Saskia, a Dutch volunteer, accompany us. Regulations dictate one must go in front and one behind with the rest of us staying bunched together at all times in order to present a united front and making wild animals less likely to attack.

Wise advice indeed!

We set off skirting the dambo. Since the hippo disappeared during lunch, no-one is sure whether it returned to the water or is still out on dry land. En route Clifford points out birds, flowers and insects. Half way round we startle a herd of puku, which skitter away, even more jittery than I'm feeling. Suddenly Clifford halts, pointing at huge prints in the soft earth. "Fresh hippo prints!" he exclaims. Since the footprints are the size of dinner plates, we'd worked that out already.

"So where is the hippo right now?"

"In fact, you should never get between a hippo and water," he reveals. "However, since it is mid-afternoon, maybe he is in the water. Generally, they spend daytime in the water sleeping and night-time on land grazing." This gives little comfort, especially when Clifford adds, "In fact hippo are more dangerous than lion or elephant. Even they are reputed to kill more people."

We press on, praying we're not currently between the hippo and the water. Or if we are, that our guards will protect us. Not that slender Saskia has anything to protect anyone with, other than a stick to beat off snakes, while gentle giant Clifford is armed with nothing more threatening than a wild flower and bird guidebook.

Just then someone notices the sky. "Ah, it looks a bit like rain." An understatement, since this is the height of the Zambian rainy season when thunderstorms of tropical dimension abound. As if to enforce the point, lightning rents the darkening sky in two.

"Actually, this is the highest point on our circuit," Saskia informs us, "meaning we're exactly halfway round."

So, if the hippo doesn't get us, maybe the lightning will. I start counting seconds between each searing flash and the subsequent thunderclap only to find the gap between them is narrowing. Time for a prayer we will not meet our end out here in the middle of nowhere. As the heavens open, we plod on around the circuit. In seconds, we're drenched through. Tropical rain may be warm, yet that doesn't make getting soaked any pleasanter. Yet because we're going straight out on a game drive in an open vehicle, we don't bother changing.

Bad mistake! Following the rainstorm, the temperature plummets leaving us atop an open vehicle shivering in damp clothes and struggling to work up enthusiasm for the largest mammal movement in the world. In the gloom following the rainstorm, the fruit bats are barely visible against the grey sky. Spotting waterbuck and bush pig on the way back fails to dispel the gloom. Even the novelty of using a spotlight to spy out animals' eyes gleaming like red rubies in the darkness falls flat. What we need is a hot bath and a comfy bed, not a dribble from a bucket and an iron bedstead in a chalet with unwanted nocturnal companions.

Dinner is potato soup, followed by lamb chops with gem squash, sweet potatoes and mashed potato, followed by apple crumble tart. Quite how staff here produce this so far from civilisation is amazing. Soon ease and warmth begin to dispel gloomy spirits . . . until the owner of the camp wanders in barefoot to warn everyone to take care on the way back to the chalets; he's just spotted a puff adder, one of Zambia's deadliest snakes, out back of the dining area. Instead of slithering away like most snakes, puff adders lie unmoving until stepped on, then seek revenge by biting and injecting deadly poison. Victims of a puff adder bite rarely survive to tell the tale.

"What are you doing?" From his bed Bob watches me rooting around in the corners of the chalet.

"Checking the puff adder isn't in here." Satisfied, I climb into bed only to climb straight back out again to spread a bath towel along the foot of the door. "That should stop it getting in," I say.

"Unless it's already inside, in which case it can't now get out!" I fling the towel at him and retire to bed. This is the bush after all. Either it's in here or it isn't. I settle down with a fervent prayer to the Almighty that the latter is indeed the case.

The night is not peaceful. Although the puff adder doesn't appear, food and diet begin doing their worst. And today a canoe trip down a crocodile infested river is on offer.

"What if I need the loo?" I say through gritted teeth.

"There's always the bush," responds Bob.

If things can't get better, they certainly can get worse!

Today Timothy is driving the Landrover, while Clifford sits up front armed not with a bird book but with an impressive looking gun.

"That's a mighty big gun," I point out. "Big enough to shoot a crocodile perhaps?" But Clifford is giving nothing away. Does he imagine we haven't worked out the gun is a precaution against any twelve-foot croc fancying a mid-morning snack?

Luwombwa Camp lies in the remote reaches of Kasanka, one hour's drive from Wasa Camp. Although road access is closed in the rainy season, Clifford reckons we can reach the camp by crossing a small river by pontoon, even though the *small* river is currently in flood and there are crocs in the water. We reach the pontoon that crosses the croc infested river, its waters swollen dramatically by recent heavy rain. Raft might be a better description since the pontoon consists of two wooden boards nailed onto oil drums.

"Today is only my second time making the crossing by pontoon," announces Timothy. This doubtless explains why he still appears to be practising and makes several abortive attempts to negotiate all four wheels onto the wooden boards. We wait anxiously on the bank, praying no crocs lurk concealed amongst dense, head high reeds bordering the riverbank.

Safely on the other side, we pass bushbuck, reedbuck, yellow baboons and a magnificent dark-skinned sable antelope standing guard over his females and young, before arriving at the camp on the remote reaches of the Luwombwa River. Since the canoes aren't ready, staff serve tea and scones underneath a bamboo and thatch 'nsaka' while we chat with the camp's current residents. One lady, bizarrely clad in an afternoon tea dress, lazes in a hammock. Maybe she simply forgot to pack bush clothes in beige, brown or green. Since she's surrounded by Bible study notes and various editions of the Bible, I hazard, "Ah, you're a Christian?"

"Indeed, though I've no connection with any church." Watery blue eyes gaze from pallid features never kissed by the tropical sunshine. "I've never felt becoming a church member necessary to connect with God."

It might be interesting to pursue the point as to whether one can call oneself a practising Christian without being a part of Christ's body, the church. However, the canoes are now ready. We leave her communing with her own private God in favour of canoeing downriver.

Both canoes are not only small, they also sit low enough in the water for a reasonable sized croc to successfully board or else take a sizeable chunk out of one of the boat's occupants. I am in pole position, while Bob is in the middle, camera poised for the photo of the century. *Wife overboard perhaps?* Meanwhile Clifford occupies the rear complete with gun slung across his knee and paddle to hand. Alison is in a second canoe along with another guide.

As Clifford pushes off from the shore, the boat slides seamlessly into murky brown water that mid-stream turns into thick pea green soup where a croc could easily escape notice until it was too late. I watch warily for anything slinking silently into the water ahead. Yet nothing disturbs the river as we slip slowly past an African python lying prone on the bank, followed by a great white egret, then an owl motionless amongst dense foliage watching. A magnificent fish eagle, national bird of Zambia, observes our passing, as well as pied and malachite kingfishers. The glassy river is incredibly peaceful, nevertheless, it's a relief to pull ashore without encountering . . . a sudden thrashing in the water shatters the silence. Has the croc finally caught up with us? But it's only a huge monitor lizard, scary enough since its whip-like tail can snap an arm or leg in two.

It's a slow journey back to camp with the canoes on the roof of the Landrover scraping every overhanging tree branch. Suddenly Clifford yells, "Stop!" The vehicle lurches to a halt. Nerves already in tatters, what deadly menace has he spotted this time?

But Clifford is out the vehicle, leaping off like a gazelle into the bush. He returns clutching two enormous mushrooms the size of small umbrellas. For the rest of the journey he sits in the back holding one in each hand, grinning like the cat that got the cream.

"For the vegetarian 'mzungu'," he exclaims, meaning our daughter.

"Ah, but not for me," I warn him.

"Ah, you are not liking mushrooms?" His face falls.

"Allergic," I explain, praying he grasps the need for caution when cooking them lest the mushroom succeeds where the croc failed.

Back at camp, we haul ourselves one last time up another rickety ladder to watch the sun sink in splendour. As if on cue bats rise once more into the orange streaked sky. Even a lone sitatunga on the far side of the dambo arrives to complete the spectacle.

After a dinner of Mediterranean potato cakes, followed by lasagne and spotted dick pudding, we're too tired to do anything but collapse exhausted into bed.

"Haven't you forgotten your nightly inspection for snakes, scorpions, rats, spiders . . ." mumbles Bob sleepily.

"I'm too tired to care!"

"Ha, more like bush happy again!" he gloats.

Quite possibly I am once more bush happy, yet barely one week into the trip is a bit soon to own up to it. Heavens, next we'll be talking about coming back again, and we wouldn't want to do that, now would we?

CHAPTER FOUR: NOT FOR THE FAINT-HEARTED TRAVELLER!
December 19th & 20th, 2002

All too soon it's time to leave bat watching and head for north-western Zambia. Thirty years ago reaching this remote region involved a thirty miles heart-in-the-mouth dash across the Congo Pedicle before re-entering Zambia on the far side of this oddly shaped stretch of land that pokes its way into Zambian territory like a painfully in-growing toenail.

However, by 2002 crossing the Congo Pedicle has become too dangerous even to contemplate. Instead a brand new tarmac road soon speeds us the 250 miles to Luapula Province in under three hours.

Approaching the fast flowing Luapula River, dense bush gives way to verdant grassland, which in turn gives way to the Bangweulu Wetlands, an area of abundant wetness where bird life thrives. Oriels, weavers and long tailed whydah birds abound as well as birds of prey soaring high into the sky, scouring the ground below in search of prey. Here also the traditional mud and thatch huts of central Zambia give way to houses made of kiln-fired red mud bricks.

The town of Samfya is as much Zambia by the sea as is possible in this landlocked country. Blistering white sandy beaches border a seemingly vast and limitless inland lake. The temptation to swim may be irresistible, however, enormous crocs populate these waters. Not to mention the risk of contracting bilharzia, a parasitic infection which, if left untreated, can prove fatal. Bilharzia enters the human body when it comes in contact with infected water where snails, part of the parasitic cycle, lay their eggs.

On entering Samfya, signs point encouragingly to Bangweulu Lodge which looks vaguely familiar, albeit empty of clients. Staff there appear surprised by our arrival. Nevertheless, a receptionist shows us a two bed-roomed chalet containing iron bedsteads, skimpy faded curtains at the windows and not a lot else. Not just basic, but downright shabby.

"You have a letter of reservation?" The receptionist's tone suggests it's a long time since she saw guests here.

I hand over the booking receipt from the same safari company that arranged the vehicle hire.

"Ah, you are not booked here but at the Samfya Beach Lodge." She indicates a newer development across the road, which is exceedingly honest of her, since she could have just collared our custom. My only hope is management there are expecting us, since they don't even look open for business.

As we head over, I take a second look at the email confirmation. "I don't understand, the email says we're booked in at Bangweulu Lodge, the dump where we've just been."

Bob scrutinises the e-mail. "So which one *are* we staying at?"

"Search me! First let's see whether this other place is expecting us." They are, which is just as well because none of us fancies returning to the decrepit Bangweulu Lodge. However, yet more confusion lies ahead.

"These are our accommodation rates." The receptionist slides across a paper showing room rates.

"But we've already paid the safari company in Lusaka for everything."

A lengthy pause ensues during which she ponders whether to believe us.

"Look, it says $40 per night for a luxury two bed-roomed chalet," I explain, well aware this means luxury by Zambian standards. "A chalet with one bedroom en suite and a second with private bathroom plus a living room and an additional $8 per person for breakfast payable in kwachas."

Is this perhaps information overload?

"Is that so!" Though whether this is a question, or mounting disbelief, confirming earlier suspicions they don't see many tourists up here, who can say. Yet can she sort out the confusion?

She shows us to a luxury chalet where luxury is indeed by Zambian standards. The living-room is dominated by a plush velvet three-piece suite, guaranteed in a tropical climes to provide a nesting place for every bug around. Bedrooms likewise contain unsuitably padded divan beds, impossible to move let alone sweep underneath.

Yet the beach in front of the chalet is as blisteringly white as ever. Barely a ripple breaks the glassy surface as water gently and invitingly laps the shore. Bliss, except for a stark warning nailed to a tree: *Crocodile infested area, swimming at own risk.* Even the beach bears fresh imprints where immense reptilian tails have recently swept aside sand as their owners lumbered clumsily down for a swim.

Swim here? *Somehow, I don't think so!*

Later we try for dinner.

The receptionist's eyes widen in alarm. "Let me see what I can do." With these uninspiring words, she disappears for some time.

Eventually she returns. "We have fish."

Did they perhaps send somebody out in a boat? "And?"

"You want something *with* the fish?" Her astonishment knows no bounds.

"Chips would be good," I suggest hopefully.

"I will see what I can do," she responds stiffly.

"And I'd like something vegetarian," puts in Ali.

"Aieeh!" the receptionist shrieks. *Why would someone who can afford meat and fish, not want to eat it?*

"Actually 'nshima' and vegetables are okay," Ali offers.

The receptionist grins widely. At least one of us is making life easier. 'Nshima' with vegetables is the staple diet of most rural Zambians. Vegetarian food the receptionist may not comprehend, but local, no problem.

The food arrives at 19.00, not 19.30 as requested, because the entire staff of receptionist plus chef is knocking off. Apparently a night guard is on duty, yet she advises parking the car out of sight close to the chalet.

"Are you suggesting somebody might steal it?"

"Ah no, they can't steal it," she titters nervously. "However, when people here have been drinking, sometimes they throw stones at vehicles."

Actually, it would be a shame if somebody did pinch it or stone it. It was so lovingly 'bathed' earlier by an old guy using a filthy rag and buckets of lake water. He washed it till it shone, then we drove back up the dirt road to Samfya making it dirty all over again.

Dinner consists of enormous fresh local bream so large they spill over the edges of the plates and accompanied by cold, greasy chips. Ali receives bowls of 'nshima' with Zambian style cabbage and baked beans. There is no starter, no dessert, not even a piece of fruit. As for a drink, forget it! Leaving the food to congeal further, we toddle over to Bangweulu Lodge to eat humble pie and buy two beers and one lemonade.

Yet Bob complains at what he considers are short rations, before tucking into an enormous bream. Since most Zambians only eat one meal a day, perhaps he fears returning to UK a mere shadow of his former self.

"Well, there's far too much for me!" Plate in hand Ali heads for the door where doubtless a starving guard waits outside.

"I doubt your leftovers will make him guard the car any better," I quip.

"No, but he might sleep better on a full stomach!"

Again, after only six months here, our daughter is streets ahead of us in comprehending the way of things, while we're still wallowing in the mire of learning. The new Zambia may have moved on in some ways, yet in others it's positively stepped backwards. Thirty years ago, there was food enough for everyone. If anyone fell on hard times, the extended family looked after them. Yet that was before the arrival of AIDS combined with large scale famine and poverty. Now the extended family system is bursting at the seams and no longer coping.

Meanwhile outside, the guard tucks into Ali's leftovers, instead of guarding the car. But let's not spoil the holiday contemplating less fortunate mortals! Heavens, we might even get drawn into doing something about it!

Did one of us actually mutter that thought aloud? I don't think so yet . . . *how many a true word is spoken in jest!*

What with mosquitoes buzzing for blood and bedbugs feasting ravenously, both leaving copious bites as evidence of their nocturnal activities, we sleep fitfully. There are no mosquito nets and we forgot to plaster on Deet before retiring.

At least after his bounteous meal, the guard stays sufficiently awake to guard the expensive hired vehicle from night-time marauders. However, during the night another disaster strikes.

"Yuk, our emergency rations are crawling with ants!" Dropping the food bag from which ants scatter by the dozen, I leap about stamping on the unwanted invaders.

"Don't worry, we'll wash the fruit." Ali is ever the optimist, just like her father.

"Well you can't wash cake and biscuits!" I dump the bag in the bin from where, doubtless, staff will later rescue the food and eat it.

With this unappetising thought, we head for breakfast. What to expect, since everything so far has been hit and miss? But no, plates of eggs, beans and sausage sit on the table congealing in the fat in which they were cooked. There's not a sign of anything else.

"Let's eat these before they get cold," I suggest. "Correction, they're cold already!" We demolish them anyways, then just as we finish, bowls of cornflakes arrive.

"What do we eat them with?" Bob looks around for large spoons but sees only teaspoons. He demands a *big* spoon and is given a soupspoon. "Excuse me . . ." he calls feebly after the body scuttling back to the kitchen before he demands anything more outrageous than a *big* spoon. Yet before we finish, not one but three dessertspoons arrive plus one jug of milk, one tumbler of milk and one glass of milk. Ali pushes her bowl aside.

"Is the milk off?" I ask.

"No, I just can't stand the stuff. And, before you say it, it's nothing to do with not having been breastfed as a baby!"

All three of us collapse in giggles just as a kettle appears containing not quite boiling water for tea and coffee along with six teaspoons but no cups. As to whether the water is safe to drink . . .

"How are you enjoying your stay?" A large Zambian alpha male explodes onto the scene, mobile phone glued to one ear. His face falls. "Ah, you are not liking your cornflakes?" The latter is directed at Ali.

We attempt to control ourselves and nod weakly. We did get everything in the end, even if teacups are this very minute appearing from behind his expansive back.

"We are so glad you are staying with us, not at that place over there." He nods towards Bangweulu Lodge. "It won't be long before it closes down and the guy running it moves on."

This news provides little comfort since, spartan as it is, staff over there may make a better job of serving breakfast than staff here who give the impression they're still practising.

Today we plan a boat trip into the Bangweulu Wetlands. The Lonely Planet Guide, along with the receptionist, assures us boats can be hired from Twingi, which is not far. Strange then that we drive for two hours deep into the heart of undiscovered Zambia where they rarely see white faces. At each sign of habitation, barefoot children wearing rags race after the car shouting, "Mzungus! Iwe! How are you?"

Not only children, but also dogs, chickens, goats stray freely in front of the car. People wobble precariously on bicycles. Women waddle by weighed down with bales or bowls of washing balanced on their heads, unable to decide which direction to leap as the mzungus' immense vehicle thunders past creating clouds of choking dust.

Twingi is the end of the line. The road, which has threatened to give out for some time, finally peters out on the shore of Lake Kumpolombo. As the vehicle halts, curious children surround it, cheering and smearing small fingers in its dusty coating.

"Boat?" we ask hopefully. "Is there a boat from here?"

"Port," they point down a barely discernable track. Delightedly, they shepherd the vehicle down the track to the 'port'. At first glance the port looks promising. Nestling amongst the reeds, are four boats pulled up onto the shore. All we need is a man plus engine and we're away. But how to communicate this? Get the eldest boy to nip off sharply and tell Dad manna is indeed falling from heaven: three mzungus are willing to pay more than he earns in a month merely to travel in his fishing boat out into the wetlands.

We wait but no-one appears.

"Maybe this isn't such a good idea," I suggest.

"Let's wait a bit longer," the other two confer.

"Look, even if someone comes, are we seriously going to leave an expensive hired vehicle in the middle of nowhere while we sail off with someone we don't know, in a boat we have no idea is safe, not knowing whether we'll come back in one piece?" As ever I am the lone voice of reason.

"Where's your sense of adventure?" they counter as one.

Where indeed!

"You two are so alike," I snort. "Just tell me, who even knows we're here? Why am I the only one smelling danger?"

They concede the point. Absolutely *no-one* knows we're here. So instead we head for Mapunto where yet more ragged children jostle to have pictures taken, posturing shamelessly for the camera. Nearby people are bathing in the river. One, naked black skin sleekly dripping water droplets, dashes for cover at our unexpected arrival.

"Look, a boat out on the river!" I point excitedly, but the boat is on a far more important mission, ferrying two velvet armchairs in stately style downriver. The boatmen stubbornly ignore calls for attention.

There's nothing for it but to head back to base with the hope of a boat trip on the lake this afternoon. However dark clouds loom ominously overhead, eventually settling into a relentless downpour by early afternoon. Nothing remains then, but the prospect of another dinnertime.

Tonight dinner arrives at ten to seven. Staff are knocking off early again. Immense T-bone steaks struggle to stay on the plates alongside enough potatoes to feed the entire Zambian army.

"There's far too much again," groans Ali gazing at a mountain of 'nshima' and vegetables. But fear not, the night guard is already hovering outside anticipating a repeat of last night's bounty.

What Ali doesn't bargain on, as she opens the door, is the equally ravenous cloud of midgies and mozzies, roused to life by this afternoon's rainstorm and now eagerly swarming inside. She slams the door shut, leaving those outside beating their wings furiously against the neon strip-light, while those that make it inside, spend the rest of the night devouring us in gratitude.

Ah Zambia, with its ravenous hordes of both people and insects, and its abortive sorties into the heart of nowhere. Right now, it's proving frustrating to the extreme and definitely *not* for the faint-hearted traveller.

CHAPTER FIVE: THE LAKE OF THE 'LOYAL' CROCODILE
December 21st & 22nd

In the southern hemisphere, today is the longest instead of the shortest day. Except, so close to the equator, night and day remain more or less twelve hours long all year round anyways. And on this longest day, we're heading north once more on the Great North Road.

First stop is Mpika, last town of any size before the Tanzania border post. Since the town still resembles a last trading post where trekkers might be spotted hitching up ox wagons, it's perhaps not the best place to boost meagre food supplies before a spot of self-catering. Nevertheless, we set off in search of basic foodstuffs along Mpika's one street, while Ali plunges into the depths of the African market seeking fresh fruit and vegetables to replace those lost to ants at Samfya.

Later en route we spy women selling giant mushrooms at the roadside.

"How do you know they're not poisonous?" I mutter darkly. "I don't fancy returning minus the pair of you."

Do they heed this dire warning? No, they don't. Thus the unappetising aroma of raw mushrooms pervades the remaining ninety kilometres before turning off onto a dirt road leading to Shiwa Ngandu, otherwise known as 'The Africa House.'

In the sunset years of the British Empire, Lt. Col. Sir Stewart Gore-Browne created a feudal paradise in this remote northern corner of what was then Northern Rhodesia. It comprises a sprawling country estate complete with redbrick country mansion in the style of an English country house. Like many hard-up owners of country piles in the UK, its present owners have opened it up to the public. Since it costs a small fortune to stay in the house itself, we're staying in self-catering lodges at nearby Kapishya Hot Springs.

Once inside the estate, the road rapidly deteriorates, yet this doesn't deter Bob who rattles along at breakneck speed, convinced the faster he drives, the less passengers feel the bumps and ridges. His passengers don't necessarily agree.

"Whoah, stop!" Ali yells from the back seat as he thunders over a speed hump. The vehicle shudders to an abrupt halt. I bounce upwards off the front seat cracking my head on the roof while Ali, along with most of our provisions, slithers off the back seat, landing with a bump on the floor.

"What's up?" asks Bob.

"You've just shot past the first view of the lake that inspired Gore-Brown to build here!" Ali's no old colonialist, just quoting from the trusty guidebook.

Yet, since darkness here falls with remarkable regularity, Bob is more focused on reaching our destination and drives on regardless. In his haste almost missing the first view of the big house as well.

He doesn't get away with that and we stop long enough to marvel at the bizarre spectacle of an English country mansion in the middle of the African bush. The magnificent redbrick building, bedecked with stone balconies, balustrades and carvings as well as belfreyed coach house, is surrounded by verdant lawns, neatly clipped privet hedges, stately cypresses and towering eucalyptus trees.

Kapishya Hot Springs lie a further twenty kilometres from the main house. Here four rustic lodges are set on manicured lawns dotted with rusted iron statues of crocodiles and stags in a tranquil riverside setting conveniently adjacent to the hot springs.

"And that's exactly where I'm going!" Bob dumps the assorted bags and baggage which are increasing daily in number, thrusts on his swimming trunks and heads for the hot springs, pretty much as Gore-Browne and company must have done in days gone by.

"Do you suppose they enjoyed dips in the altogether?" Ali and I join him, sitting on the pure white sandy bottom of the pool, soaking up to our necks in aquamarine water while steam gently rises around us.

"Whatever, this certainly is the life!" And even a taste of it for us, since staff are on site to do all our cooking. However, they require some instruction as to how to concoct a meal from pork chops, potatoes, one giant mushroom and a bunch of wilting rape.

Let's hope they understand the necessity of cooking the mushroom separately!

No worries, the meal is excellent, sitting later under the velvety cloak of darkness in front of a blazing brazier. But there's always something to spoil the idyll . . .

After dinner the chef-cum-waiter serves one last titbit with a nervous smile. "We advise you to shut yourselves in your lodge during the night."

"What, not come out at all?"

"Exactly! If anything should disturb you, simply shout loud and long, then an armed guard will come to your assistance."

"So what exactly *might* disturb us?" I ask apprehensively.

"Perhaps a passing crocodile." He hesitates. "Crocodiles in the river nearby are *very* large." Another significant pause, "Or maybe thieves might come." With this, he departs leaving us alone for the night.

"It certainly beats chocolates on the pillow!" I comment wryly. "Perhaps you'd rather sleep in with us?" I put to Ali.

"I'll be fine," she insists.

So with the comforting thought that if deadly mushrooms or hungry crocs don't get us, then an armed thief might, we retire for the night.

Yet again, Africa has come just a bit too close for comfort!

Yet neither crocs nor robbers disturb the night. Or else we don't hear them, alone in the heart of the bush where the darkness is impenetrable.

By 6.30am, having decided any nocturnal dangers are now past, Bob and I stroll over to the open thatched dining area where hot water is available for tea. We sit drinking tea by the river, sharing how lucky we are to return to Africa and enjoy all this . . . *though just for this one trip, naturally!*

After breakfast of a mammoth pot of porridge that exhausts our three days' supply of Jungle Oats, accompanied by orange squash instead of orange juice and toast instead of croissants, we travel twenty kilometres back to visit the main house at Shiwa Ngandu.

The name Shiwa Ngandu means 'lake of the royal crocodile', though locals insist on pronouncing 'royal' as 'loyal.' Inside, the house is everything one expects of an English country house, rooms beautifully furnished and maintained as far as possible as in the days of Gore-Browne, even if wearing a little shabby at the seams.

"Did such a grand scale building go down well with locals?" I ask the guide. "After all, it's considerably bigger than the average mud hut."

"Maybe not so well," he concedes.

"Yet building it must have created opportunities for employment?"

"Even so, there was much opposition locally. However, undeterred, Gore-Browne pushed the project through. This earned him the nickname locally of 'chipembele' or rhino."

However, not all was doom and gloom. Once established here, Gore-Browne went into politics and did much to steer Northern Rhodesia towards becoming independent Zambia, thus earning him the respect of other political giants of the time such as Sir Roy Welensky, last governor of Northern Rhodesia, and Dr Kenneth Kaunda, Zambia's first president.

"Even Dr Kaunda still comes here," the guide says proudly. And why not, since the place is eminently suited for hosting past presidents.

Upstairs in the library, we encounter John Harvey, youngest son of the Harvey family that inherited the house from Gore-Browne.

"Sadly my parents were murdered here on the estate," he reveals. "My brother and I, grandsons of 'chipembele', now run the place."

No-one would have blamed them for scarpering, given the place's tragic history. Yet white Africans, going back generations, are made of sterner stuff. But I keep this to myself, asking instead, "So who murdered them?"

"Poachers we believe, though it was never proven. If you like, the guide will take you to visit their graves, also the grave of my grandfather."

Outside we follow a gravel track up a small knoll to reach the site of the graves. Gore-Browne had already selected the site, though perhaps not expecting his daughter and son-in-law to take up residence beside him quite so soon or quite so tragically.

"What a stunning view of the lake!" I exclaim, reflecting it's a pity those buried in the graves can't fully appreciate it. Lt. Col. Gore-Browne, his daughter, known as Lorna II, and his son-in-law occupy pride of place, while at a discreet distance stand graves of lesser mortals.

A short game drive round the estate takes us closer to the 'lake of the loyal crocodile'.

"Are there actually any crocs in the lake?" It's always best to know these things.

"For sure," responds the guide. "In fact, not long ago a young couple came here on honeymoon. In the evening the young lady unfortunately consumed too much alcohol and went swimming in the lake."

Do I really want to hear this?

"Her screams were heard all over the estate. She emerged from the lake, dripping with blood from where a crocodile had bitten her head. Luckily for her it was a young crocodile . . ."

Does luck even enter into this? Apparently it does!

"Indeed, if it had been a big crocodile, it would have taken off her head!"

Hmmm, some honeymoon that must have been!

Heading back to the hot springs, we pick up three young women plus a young boy, all laden with bags and bundles. Goodness knows where they're walking to. Two of them squeeze onto the back seat beside Bob, while the others sit on the floorboards at the rear.

As we bump and grind along, suddenly the young girl next to Bob throws up her breakfast of cold lumpy 'nshima'. True, she catches most of it in the lap of her 'chitenge'. Nevertheless, some inevitably splatters onto the seat and onto Bob as well. We pull off the red dirt road in the middle of nowhere and carry out a hasty mop-up job before carrying on.

Back at base Bob is stoical. "Accidents happen!" Or words to that effect!

Not me, my brain's in overdrive. "You should strip off, put your clothes in the wash, then scrub yourself down with soap and antiseptic."

"Whatever for? The poor kid was car sick, probably never even been in a car before."

"But what if she's HIV positive?"

"For heaven's sake . . ." He falters. "She was a kid, not even in her teens . . ." Silence falls as he recalls what we were told at Chep in Kitwe about young girls being particularly vulnerable to abuse by men with HIV AIDS in the belief that, by having sex with a young virgin, they will be cured.

"Fact: body fluids are the main means by which infection is spread. Fact: she certainly shared hers along with her breakfast with you."

Reluctantly Bob strips off and soaps himself down, yet unbelievably *still* protesting, "There aren't any cuts on my body anyways."

I send up a silent prayer that the girl was indeed merely anxious or carsick. That she was not a virgin who'd been raped by someone HIV positive. That none of her bodily fluids have harmed Bob. And above all,

Lord, that our guardian angel was with us today. It was a sobering experience.

Lunch is a somewhat silent affair. Afterwards Ali departs on a guided walk to reach a waterfall. Meanwhile Bob and I opt for the lazy alternative: reading, writing, bathing in the hot springs while the sky darkens menacingly and thunder rolls overhead.

Later Bob strolls down towards the river, yet returns after a few minutes at a sharp trot. "Snake, down there!" His breath emerges in short bursts.

"Big or small . . ."

"Long and green, a green mamba, perhaps. The thing fell out of a tree right in front of me. Instead of slithering off, it headed straight towards me."

We decide not to investigate further. Some creatures are best left to their own devices.

"You'll never guess what," he greets Ali on her return to camp, soaking wet and having been bitten copiously by insects.

"No, *you'll* never guess what," she interrupts. "I nearly trod on a snake."

Having escaped the perils of eating the wrong kind of mushroom, both of them have now bizarrely had close encounters of the second kind with snakes. The first kind actually being bitten by one which, thankfully, neither of them was because, in Africa, there's the added complication of catching the snake, then taking it with you to hospital for identification. It's almost as dangerous to administer the wrong antidote as it is getting bitten in the first place. Besides, goodness knows where the nearest hospital is from here.

"So what happened?"

"It was right on the path in front of me about to eat a frog. I nearly stepped on it. The guide just called out in time."

"Was it big? Was it dangerous?"

"Not so big, but the guide reckoned it was dangerous."

Perish the thought! Africa may be a wonderful place; it's just such a pity about inherent dangers such as snakes, crocs, malaria, HIV AIDS and other scary, even deadly things.

"Do you think Africa's more dangerous than when we lived here before?" I muse. "Or am I just getting older?"

"Both," responds Bob discouragingly. "Certainly, places like here are as raw and untamed as ever, and definitely not for the faint hearted!"

Secretly I ponder whether in fact I'm not one of the latter and shouldn't really be here at all.

The joys of today are not yet over. Darkness is falling as Bob discovers he has lost the car keys.

"You haven't lost them, you just haven't found where they are," I say unhelpfully.

"Maybe I dropped them by the car when we came back from the house." Off he pootles in rapidly advancing darkness to root around by the car, even though the green mamba is still out there, the mozzies are already biting, while the croc may right now be out the water looking for . . .

"Aaaagh!" Screams pierce the gathering gloom. Ali and I race outside, wondering which deadly danger has robbed us of husband and father in one fell swoop.

"Hang on, I'll bring a torch!" The beam picks out Bob hopping from one foot to another, shaking himself all over. No sign of croc or green mamba.

"Ants!" he explodes. "All over me."

I flash the torch closer, examining the ground for evidence. "What sort, Matabele or red?"

"Does it matter? The blighters are eating me alive!"

There's nothing for it. For the second time today, Bob divests himself of every stitch of clothing, this time outside under the velvet cloak of darkness. He shakes everything thoroughly till every last ant is out of his particular pants. Just as well white wine spritzers are waiting by the brazier along with dinner of sausages, macaroni, baby aubergines and homemade pickles.

"There, there, better all ready!" I raise my glass. "Chin, chin! You'll live to face another day in Africa, but only just."

"Some trip down memory lane this is turning out to be!" he grunts.

My, haven't some people changed their tune!

CHAPTER SIX: A PEP TALK EN ROUTE TO CHRISTMAS
December 23rd - >26th, 2002

"We really must pick up a pair of red warning triangles today," announces Bob as we leave Shiwa Ngandu for the long drive south to spend Christmas on the shores of Lake Kariba. "Police could fine us for not carrying them."

Ali has already warned police will be out in force over the next few days trying to make a few pin in time for Christmas. They've already asked several times at police checkpoints to see her driving licence in the hope of catching her for driving under age. To be on the safe side, we buy a set of red warning triangles at the next garage.

"But what about the brake light that's not working?" Since I'm driving, I don't fancy getting caught.

"Just stop level with the police officer; they'll never notice what's around the back." *Famous last words!*

As we approach the Kabwe checkpoint, a policeman steps out into the road, hand raised. Unfortunately, just as he completes his inspection of the vehicle, I inadvertently press the foot brake. Like a shot he reappears round the front. "Your brake is light not working, for that there is a fine of K54 000."

"Ah, the hire company must have hired out the vehicle with the bulb not working."

He eyes us expectantly, perhaps hoping for something more than a feeble excuse. Yet offer money to the wrong policeman and we'd be in far more trouble than a mere fine. However, with a flick of one finger, he waves us on having spotted instead a battered and overloaded VW Kombi approaching and belching more black smoke than a chimney on fire, the driver of which can be done for more serious infringements than 'mzungus' with missing light bulbs. Nevertheless, we replace it at the first opportunity. Although this policeman didn't fine us, the next one might.

Continuing south we detour off into the bush to reach the little known Kundalila Falls, located down a rough dirt road pockmarked with large, loose stones making progress slow. Nevertheless, a man riding a bicycle peddles past like someone possessed, in haste to reach the car park first where he dismounts and panting greets us with, "I am the official guide to the waterfall. Please follow me."

We troop in single file along a rocky, boulder strewn path to reach a dizzying viewpoint. Victoria Falls it may not be, yet a diaphanous curtain of water tumbles diagonally across the rock face before cascading vertiginously into the depths far below. Photos taken, we retreat thankfully from the overhanging lip of rock. One slip could set us also tumbling far below.

Heading back to the car, Ali draws the zealous guide into conversation. She has been in Zambia a mere six months advising people with HIV AIDS and related illnesses, yet has already developed a forthrightness regarding matters of a sexual nature. "So, do you practise safe sex?" she demands.

"Ah for me, I am not married," he prevaricates. Does he for one moment imagine bachelorhood will let him off the hook?

"But you like a drink on a Friday night, and afterwards, what then?"

The man grins sheepishly, knowing very well what comes after a drink.

"You know, staying safe is as easy as A B C!" Ali falls into her stride. "A is for *abstinence*, B remember to *be* faithful and C always use a *condom*!"

"Ah me, I can't use those things!" He wrinkles his broad black nose in disgust.

Ali shakes her head, resisting the temptation to spell out that, should he persist in such foolishness, he risks becoming yet another statistic in the tragic toll of AIDS.

Next day is Christmas Eve and another travelling day. It may not feel much like Christmas with temperatures soaring into the nineties and so far no turkey or tinsel in sight. However, as we reach Cairo Road in Lusaka, the sound of sleigh bells is finally in the air. Christmas is a-coming to Zambia.

"We need to change some money," announces Bob.

My heart sinks. It's midday and we're crawling at five miles an hour through Lusaka's chaotic lunchtime traffic. Everyone seems determined to make it home in time for Christmas, many, like us, with long journeys ahead.

"There's an ATM at the Holiday Inn," I suggest, unwilling to face the dodgy Cairo Road exchange bureau again.

"In this traffic, it'll take an hour there and back," responds Bob.

Just then, amidst a swirling sea of black faces, I spot a familiar one. "Look, isn't that Alex?" Delighted to meet up with us or just glad of a lift, Alex leaps into the back seat. At least he can now accompany us to an exchange bureau, yet on Christmas Eve the exchange bureau has run out of kwachas.

"Look, there's a bank over the road." Ali points through the seething mass of black bodies and jam-packed traffic thronging Cairo Road.

"What, park on Cairo Road, leaving all our stuff in the car to dice with death crossing that lot?"

Yet nothing fazes our daughter who insists we carry all our cash and valuables with us. Thus, we thread our way through the seething sea of humanity and cars to reach a bank on the opposite side. Then, with over two million kwachas between us, we worm our way back, all the while watching out for muggers and pick-pockets and praying our baggage hasn't disappeared in the meantime. But where's Alex gone? Somewhere along the line, he's vanished or else been swallowed up by the swirling crowd, never to be seen again. At least not this side of Christmas!

Traffic along Cairo Road is now at a standstill. Horns are tooting. Drivers of blue and white Kombi taxis lean out their windows, shaking their fists at anyone who dares to squeeze in front, including us, as we crawl around the south end roundabout and escape onto the Kafue road.

Traffic doesn't thin until near the Zimbabwean border post at Chirundu, where roadside sellers are lined up shaking fistfuls of Zimbabwean dollars at passing vehicles, hoping anyone still heading there will swap kwachas or dollars for useless Zimbabwean currency, which we're not. Just short of the border post we turn right instead to Siavonga and Lake Kariba.

Entering Siavonga, not a breath of air stirs in the hot, sultry afternoon. Siavonga lies one thousand feet lower in altitude than Lusaka so, not surprisingly, both heat and humidity move up several notches. Yet to our relief Eagles Rest Lodge has hardly changed, other than the now modernised chalets of yesteryear and concrete pathways meandering here and there. And the view's as stunning as ever across Lake Kariba towards the mountains of distant Zimbabwe. "And it isn't even sunset yet!" I exclaim.

"Why, what happens then, apart from sundowners?" quips Ali.

"If it's a good one, God in all his glory opens his paint box and paints the sky orange, red, vermilion, in case the view alone isn't impressive enough."

Later we crack a bottle of champagne, before strolling over to the beach area for a braai under the stars. Far away across the water, lightning flashes and thunder rumbles incessantly. Management have laid out a magnificent spread of chicken, T-bones, pork chops, boerwurst sausages, salads of every description accompanied by a killer fruit punch concocted from vodka, cane and red wine, though noticeably short on fruit.

Cheers, here's to Christmas Eve, even if it is hotter than Hades!

An eclectic bunch has gathered for the Eagles Rest Christmas package: young Brits backpacking around Zambia, as well as New Zealand and British church workers, Finnish and Swedish missionaries on leave from the Congo and ex-Zimbabweans who've fled Mugabe's repressive regime for the good life in relatively peaceful Zambia.

Children mill around, though it's not always apparent to whom they belong, but any confusion could be due to the effects of the punch. The kids have found their own way around any language barriers and the big debate centres on which chalet Father Christmas will visit later tonight. Odds are on number thirteen. That settled, we retire for a peaceful night before Christmas.

Champagne combined with mulled wine is perhaps not wise. Add to the cocktail, noise emanating from 'white' Zambians celebrating into the early hours and shake vigorously. Don't be surprised if it explodes!

At 5am on Christmas morning a storm fit to lift the roof off heaven itself, never mind that of the chalet, banishes sleep as the inky darkness of the

African night is repeatedly rent apart by sheets of lightning. I lie there counting the seconds between flash and subsequent thunderclap, but the storm has melded into one vast melting pot of tropical dimensions.

Burrowing under the duvet becomes futile, so I climb into Bob's bed then recall, "Oh no, Ali's outside in the tent!" I leap out of bed and open the chalet door to find her drenched and shivering from over-exposure to cold and wet.

"The tent will just have to survive as best it can," she says through chattering teeth. "As for Father Christmas, if he's any sense, he'll have emigrated to a better climate than Zambia in the rainy season."

We sit huddled together drinking scalding cups of tea, waiting for the storm to abate. At half past eight we struggle into warm clothing and head for breakfast. The rain has eased and miraculously, the tent's still standing, though everywhere is awash with a distinctly un-Christmas like atmosphere.

Later, we go in search of a Christmas Day service, but the only choice is a New Apostolic service in Tonga or a Catholic Mass in English. Since our Tonga's non-existent, the Catholic Mass it is. The Eucharist has already begun and the air is heady with the scent of incense, though not a wise man in sight. Nevertheless, a couple of carols sung slowly to the incredible harmony of African voices, temporarily banishes the horrors of the night and even restores the festive mood.

Meanwhile, back at Eagles Rest, more members of Africa's 'lost white tribe' have begun arriving. Chased out of East Africa, shot, raped, burned or pillaged out of Zimbabwe and constantly under threat in South Africa, many now live in Zambia, attempting to recreate here the lifestyle previously enjoyed elsewhere. One after another massive 4x4 rolls up, discharging pot-bellied males humping beer crates, women in skimpy tops, shorts and glittery sandals and blond-haired, sun-bronzed kids.

"Don't they realise the political situation here's only held together by a piece of string?" remarks Bob. "One sharp tug in the wrong direction and it'll be a Mugabe set-up here, then where will they go?"

But who are we to judge, after all, we're all just here to enjoy Christmas!

Inevitably the same polyglot mix as last night gathers: Finnish, Swedish, missionaries from the Congo and bizarrely a party of Japanese also arrives. Christmas dinner is a gargantuan spread of turkey, beef, ham and vegetables followed by desserts, tea, coffee and Christmas cake though, mercifully, not a mince pie in sight. Towards the end of the meal, we join members of the 'lost white tribe' currently enlightening the backpacking Brits, enjoying their first taste of the real Africa, as to the 'true' state of affairs here.

"Man, the economy here is pure s***!" thunders one. "The guys in charge couldn't even manage fleas in a flea circus, let alone the country's economy." He pauses to swig from his beer bottle. Only softies drink beer from a glass, even on Christmas Day.

"As for AIDS, man, if they all stopped sh****** each other, that would soon get rid of their crisis!"

Once upon a time, I *might* have agreed, yet beside me, Alison bristles with righteous indignation that proves strangely infectious. Fearing an explosion to rival last night's storm, I suggest a walk along the beach, rather a grand name for the narrow swathe of sand lining the shore where the lodge's new owners plan to build a beach bar.

As long as they don't forget a notice warning people not to swim there!

However, there is no peace on earth for anyone, even down on the shoreline where waves invitingly lap the sand. One group of 'white' Zambians has upped the volume on their car radio, belting out tapes from yesteryear so loudly, the noise traverses the lake to resound amongst the purple hills of distant Zimbabwe.

Elsewhere blokes have sent their wives and kids out water-skiing, being tugged at high speed behind speedboats looping the loop out on the crocodile infested waters of the lake. Meanwhile the men stand on the shore, legs planted firmly apart like baobab tree trunks, beer bottles in hand and hollering such diabolical encouragement as, "Watch the crocs don't get you!" They cheer every time one of their wives or kids falls off into the water.

The potential for a bloodbath doubtless adds to the spectacle. Since the early days of the 'voortrekkers', the 'white' man or woman in Africa has learnt the hard way to live alongside its ever-present dangers. Moreover, when in doubt, to joke about them . . . *though, maybe they shouldn't tempt fate quite so blatantly as to water-ski on the crocodile infested waters of Lake Kariba!*

The second night is more peaceful, until Bob decides to capture dawn breaking over Lake Kariba. True, with black storm clouds looming ominously and silhouetted against the golden streaks of the dawn, the sight is stunning. But at 5.30am . . .

After breakfast, we set off along with the backpacking Brits for the dam wall which forms the no-man's land between Zambia and Zimbabwe. Hopefully there's safety in numbers, since this area is reputedly risky. But first we need a day pass from the customs post allowing us not only onto the dam wall but, more importantly, back into Zambia.

"You want to keep our passports?" I glare at the customs officer. This lady does not part easily with her British passport.

He is not easily deterred. "In fact, you may not proceed further unless you hand them over for safekeeping."

At this point I would happily renounce the expedition. However, while the others aren't happy about it, they agree to part with theirs leaving me to choose between remaining here alone with a hostile customs officer or . . . I handover my passport.

It is now mid-morning. The sky has cleared dramatically, causing the sun's scorching rays to bounce blisteringly back off the concrete surrounds of the dam wall. Not a creature stirs apart from a group of stragglers that suddenly materialises from nowhere. Bob eyes them suspiciously. "They don't exactly look as if they're visiting the dam wall, so what are they after?"

His camera perhaps, as it's the largest one around?

Sensing us watching them, the group saunters nonchalantly past, so we focus instead on the immense dam wall spanning the Zambezi Gorge hundreds of feet below which joins Zambia and Zimbabwe in an uneasy marriage of convenience, where electricity provides an ill-fitting wedding ring.

Historically, it's a miracle the dam was ever built. The Tonga, who lived in the valley before the lake filled up, believed a river god called Nyaminyami inhabited the gorge who would destroy any attempts to tamper with his river.

Certainly, construction of the dam wall was dogged with disaster. Several Italian engineers and members of the workforce lost their lives in a chapter of accidents. One group was buried beneath thousands of tons of concrete when a platform on which they were standing collapsed. Walls of the coffer dam flooded over several times following record rainfalls for the area. Even today the Tonga still believe that one day, Nyaminyami will exact his revenge.

Hopefully not today though, as we stroll across the dam wall, still dogged by our hangers-on. Down in the gorge below, an enormous croc lies prone sunning itself on the rocks. A second one swims idly in the water, perhaps hoping one of us might topple over the edge for his dinner, though one of our hangers-on might do just as well ...

Retrieving our passports and praying they haven't been photocopied or tampered with, we head into town in search of supplies, only to find Siavonga's one store has less on sale than an eastern bloc shop under a communist regime. The African market must do instead, though it's little more than a huddle of tightly packed stalls at a point where surrounding hills fold together into a small valley down which a filthy stream tumbles into the waters of the lake. There is no entrance or exit, just narrow, stony pathways winding between stalls packed higgledy-piggledy together.

Since no-one wants to remain alone in the car, all five of us dive into the market in search of fruit and vegetables which are either overripe or swarming with flies. One lady tries to sell us dried kapenta, small sardine-like fish caught in their millions each night by fishing boats in the waters of the lake. But the rank, sickly smell emanating from fly-ridden buckets turns our stomachs, so we stick to the scrappy fruit and vegetables in need of thorough washing.

Later that afternoon a sun-downer cruise comes as part of the Christmas package. At 5pm we wait impatiently on the boat for another couple to join us. "We could just go without them?" I suggest. "Otherwise, we'll be cruising by moonlight."

Just then the missing couple appear. As they approach the landing stage, their small terrier races straight into the water. Instantly the woman plunges in, scoops him out the water and onto dry land, scolding him for his stupid action, then introduces themselves as the new owners of Eagles Rest.

"Sorry, only this little mutt lost her companion last year to a croc in the same creek."

Anyone for water-skiing?

Conversation reveals not only was this couple in Zim in the seventies when we were, they also lived in the same road and their kids went to schools we taught in. It's a small world, though maybe not so small here, where anyone who's been around for a few years, shares at least some history.

Ah, the stuff memories are made of!

That and the incredible orange ball of the sun balancing on the rim of the horizon as if it can't bear to disappear for another night but might hang around allowing the splendours of an African sunset to dazzle a while longer. Meanwhile we try to forget that in one week we return to the grey skies of UK.

"I wonder if we will be back," Bob murmurs wistfully.

"Hopefully you will," pipes up Ali, "to see me!"

As yet, neither of us has given this much thought. Returning to Africa after twenty-six years absence has proved such an emotional roller-coaster, we haven't got our heads around a repeat performance.

"Surely it couldn't be as traumatic second time round?" suggests Ali.

But this question hovers unanswered between us, neither one or the other wanting to commit. In eighteen months Ali's contract here will end. In the meantime, what could possibly happen to bring us back a second time?

CHAPTER SEVEN: THE SMOKE THAT THUNDERS
December 27th & 28th, 2002

Christmas over, we leave Lake Kariba for another familiar destination: Victoria Falls. Or as locals call it: Mosi oa Tunya, the smoke that thunders.

Those in the know advise visiting the Falls in different seasons in order to appreciate their different guises. At the end of the dry season, when water levels are low, visitors can best appreciate their true width and depth. Rock formations are clearly visible and it's even possible to walk across the rim, even stopping for a while to relax in a pool called the Armchair.

However, it's at the end of the rainy season that visitors become truly awestruck at the immensity of the falls, as thousands of gallons of water plunge over the rim and fall thundering onto the rocks far below. What doesn't bounce back up as mist and spray, forms a raging torrent racing through the gorge in the suddenly narrowing river.

Right now, it's December and two months into the rainy season, so what to expect? Will we get a soaking, or will waters be low enough to chance a death-defying stroll across the rim? Perhaps not! The story is told of a mother and baby elephant who chanced this very crossing. Midway the baby was swept over the edge. The mother remained for twenty-four hours bemoaning its sad ending, only to be overcome by weakness and also fall to her death.

The journey from Siavonga to Vic Falls is over 550kms and will take an entire day. Nevertheless, Ali insists on stopping outside Siavonga at roadside basket sellers, where a lone boy clad in rags sits guarding his family's supply of baskets.

"How much are your laundry baskets?" Ali asks.

"Forty thousand pin." The boy eyes us cagily, wondering whether well-heeled 'mzungus' will pay the full asking price.

"That's a lot of money," I say, though actually it's less than six pounds. "Come on, what's your best price?"

The boy glances round uneasily. Should he reduce the price for a quick sale, or stick to his guns possibly losing his customers and maybe getting a beating into the bargain. "Forty thousand pin," he repeats stubbornly.

"We'll give you thirty-five thousand."

A 75p reduction, why are we even haggling at all?

"Okay, thirty-five thousand . . . but you can give me some food!"

I root around in the boot and unearth a packet of cheese and onion crisps. Perhaps not the wisest offering since, if his stomach is empty or he's not used to artificial flavourings, the crisps could make him sick instead of satisfied. Already in south-eastern Zambia, we've witnessed the heart-rending sight of children, hands outstretched at the roadside, begging for food. This was unheard of thirty years ago, yet now it's another sign of the breakdown of the extended family.

"You'll go a long way," I joke, handing over the crisps. "Maybe one day you'll even become a big businessman in Lusaka!"

A cheeky grin lights up the boy's face, only to vanish as quickly as the sun going behind a cloud. An older man has appeared out of bushes lining the roadside. He mutters something to him. Then a second man pushing a wheelbarrow along the road stops and joins in the conversation.

"Er, shall we go?" Doubtless these two are now informing the boy that people like us have more money than sense and *never* on any account to drop the price. He may even get a clout as a reward for doing a deal.

We resume the long journey to Livingstone, noting how new development is springing up all along the road. Towns like Monze and Mazabuka, centre of the Zambian sugar growing industry, are now bustling centres with shops, banks, even a sprinkling of 'mzungus' dusting the streets like icing sugar on a posh restaurant pudding.

From Choma, there's still 200kms to go. Ali is driving the last stretch, when she suddenly brakes to avoid a troupe of baboons crossing the road in front of the vehicle and treating us to a wonderful display of brightly coloured backsides.

I yawn sleepily. "Surely we're nearly there?"

However, just before Livingstone, the heavens open and the force of the rain causes a windscreen wiper to fly off never to be seen again.

"Now what?" Ali slows to a crawl, peering out through the streaming windscreen. "I can't see a thing."

A search in the boot unearths a spare wiper, yet how difficult can it be to replace a windscreen wiper? Quite difficult as it turns out, since without tools we fail abysmally, while the man at the next garage equally struggles. Firstly, he tries a piece of wire, then attacks it with a lethal looking kitchen knife. Unbelievably the knife does the trick. Bob gives him three pin, about 30p, hoping this is the going rate for fixing a windscreen wiper with a carving knife.

Finally, we reach Livingstone. Because of the Falls, Livingstone is one of the few places in Zambia boasting an array of places to stay. But which one to choose? Debating their pros and cons, we drive past almost every single hotel and lodge in town.

Ngolide looks nice but is in town with no pool, essential since the thermometer has moved up yet another notch. The Crocodile Park steams hotter than a sauna and besides, who wants to be so close such large crocs and other hostile reptiles. Maramba River Lodge looks nice, but chalets and campsite are adjacent and since the campsite contains leather-clad bikers on thunderous machines, it doesn't bode well for a quiet night.

As soon as we drive into The Waterfront, it's the place. The bar area, restaurant and decked pool area all but fall into the Zambezi River. Later, over sundowners on the terrace overlooking the river, a school of hippo obligingly disports themselves, snorting loudly, then sinking out of sight only to resurface with jaw-splitting yawns, revealing the pink insides of cavernous mouths filled with thick pronged teeth capable of demolishing a small boat or its occupants foolish enough to get in their way.

Downriver towards the Falls, a herd of elephant begins its nightly crossing of the river from Zambia to Zimbabwe. Large ones enter the water first with young ellies and nellies in the middle holding on with mini trunks to the tails of larger females in front. More adults make up the rearguard until every last elephant is safely on the other side.

"Don't they need passports to enter Zimbabwe?" jokes Ali.

"No, they just pack their trunks and off they go," Bob is quick to respond.

The first sight of Victoria Falls is never to be forgotten; it takes your breath away. 'Angels in all their glory must have feasted on sights such as these,' David Livingstone wrote after first seeing them. But then he'd trudged miles through endlessly monotonous Zambian bush in order to reach them.

What is amazing is that, since the escalation of troubles and the collapse of tourism in Zimbabwe, the Zambian side has benefited from more development. Also, although it's the height of the rainy season, water levels are as low as we've seen them, because the full volume of water has not yet travelled down rivers that join the Zambezi and feed the volume of water.

Nevertheless, it's still sufficient to drench visitors with spray powering up from the foot of the Falls, soaking anyone foolish enough to walk around minus cagoule or umbrella. The spray creates a perfect rainbow, though it's too dangerous by far to scramble down in search of the mythical pot of gold at its end. As for walking across the rim? Forget it!

Near the entrance to the Falls area sits the largest collection of curio sellers found anywhere in Zambia. Not all are Zambians, some come from the Congo, or as far away as East Africa, selling everything from wooden masks and soapstone carvings to batik prints and animal skins.

We stroll past the stalls, employing the age-old trick of spotting what we're interested in, then strolling nonchalantly past and feigning interest in something else. After considerable haggling over something we don't want, I idly pick up a soapstone figure. "How much are these?"

By this time the curio seller, convinced these 'mzungus' have no intention of buying anything, halves what he would have asked. Thus we end up with two carvings for half the original asking price.

"Clearly you two haven't lost your touch," admits Ali.

Nearby lies Livingstone Game Park, reputedly containing the largest concentration of small game in such a small area. By 10am the day is already seriously hot as we crawl around the main circular route in search of game that has wisely retreated to the shade. The steering wheel is searing hot between my sweaty palms.

"Why not try a smaller track?" suggests Bob.

Reluctantly I turn off, not at all happy about it.

"Just keep going," advise the other two. "It'll be fine."

Foolish advice, since before long I'm surveying a hollow filled with muddy water. It's impossible to gauge its true depth. "Don't like the look of that," I decide.

Not so father and daughter who are convinced a four wheel drive will easily get through a puddle that size.

I inch the vehicle into the muddy water which doesn't reveal its hidden depths until the car reaches the middle. By which time, emitting a whine of protest, its rear wheels whizz to a halt with ne'er a hope of making it to the other side. We leap out into the muddy water and survey the damage. The rear offside wheel lies buried up to the top of its hub-cab in thick red oozing mud.

"Great, now we're stuck down a track where no-one with any sense goes. Any ideas how to get out of this?"

Yet father and daughter like nothing better than a challenge. "We need to get something under the wheels." Metaphorically Bob rolls up his sleeves ready for action.

"This isn't the first time we've been in a mess like this," I remind him.

Years ago in Zimbabwe, we broke down one Sunday afternoon in a small game park near Harare. Bob left me alone in the car with two small children, while he walked back through the game park in search of help. After waiting for what seemed like hours, a lorry containing drunken locals, singing and chanting, bore down on the stranded car. Fearing my end had finally come, I suddenly spotted Bob atop the lorry with the drunken mob. Help had arrived!

Meanwhile Ali grabs handfuls of brush and dry leaf fronds from yards away, then carts armloads back to stuff under the wheels. My feeble offerings, grabbed in haste from close proximity to the vehicle, are dismissed as 'totally unsuitable.' Instead I stand aside contemplating our predicament. Dire to say the least.

"It's not exactly the West Midlands Safari Park," I say. "Where everyone who went in, is checked out before they close for the day. Would anyone here even bother to check, or would they simply abandon us to our fate?"

Not receiving any response, I change tack. "Isn't there supposedly an ill-tempered rhino in here somewhere which, according to the guidebook, is rather fond of charging both vehicles and passengers. Maybe I should keep an eye out for him."

So, while the other two work themselves into a sweat, I position myself on rhino watch. Suddenly I spot something. "Ha, look right there!"

"What? Where?" Feverish activity halts abruptly and they both dart back to the vehicle. One word from me and they'll be first inside.

"Look, right there!" Two pairs of eyes drop earthwards where a shiny black dung beetle no longer than five centimetres patiently rolls along a ball of dung several times its size and weight. "How do you suppose it manages that?" I am awestruck.

"I would've thought what was far more important is *whose* dung it's pushing along!" snaps Bob.

"Oh, don't worry, there's no sign of the rhino," I assure them.

After a solid hour of backbreaking effort piling dead scrub and brush under wheels and of patient manoeuvring forwards then backwards, finally, and with a silent prayer to the Almighty, the behemoth frees itself to ride once more.

And as we round the first bend, what do we come face to face with but the immense armour-tanked hulk of a white rhino standing stock-still staring at us.

"Do you suppose it had its eye on us all the time?"

Thereafter we stick to main roads in order to reach the entrance gate and avoid getting stranded inside the game park all night. Mainly because later that afternoon we're taking another sunset cruise, this time on the Zambezi River.

The sunset cruise on Lake Kariba was a rather informal affair. Here at Livingstone, it's clear from the start both staff and clients take this sunset cruise seriously. Consumption of snacks is only outstripped by consumption of alcohol. Hardly has the boat chugged out mid-stream heading towards the rim of the Falls than the first drinks are poured and served with sausage rolls, samosas, potato balls, cheese toasts, savoury potato skins, all washed down with white wine spritzers and Mosis.

"When in Rome . . ." Bob raises his beer in cheers.

"Better there than stuck in a game park!" I remind him.

Only one thing slightly mars the fun. We're currently chugging downstream towards the lip of the Falls.

Not wanting to spoil anyone's fun, nevertheless it's important to ask, "What happens should the boat's engine fail?"

However, everyone is too busy eating and drinking and making merry to care. If we should go over the edge, I can only assume we chorus in tongues more varied than those surrounding the Tower of Babel, "What a way to go!"

The hippo put on a magnificent display of spouting, yawning and frolicking about, as if booked to perform. Since it's evening time, smaller antelope and buck are down by the river drinking, yet hopefully keeping a wary eye out for crocs lurking in the shallows. A crocodile's favourite way of catching dinner is to drag its hapless victim into water then, rolling over and over, submerge it until it drowns. How's that for table manners!

As the sun sets and darkness spreads its cloak over the evening sky, the boat chugs back to base with all aboard safe and accounted for. But is anyone sober enough to care? The evening ends with a resounding, "Cheers!" in several different languages.

It's as much as we can do to stagger back up the path to our chalet, there to collapse into bed with the thought, 'Gosh, isn't Zambia exhausting!'

CHAPTER EIGHT: DEATH ON PARADISE ISLAND
December 29th 2002 - > January 1st 2003

Chikanka Island, the name alone has an exotic ring. Today we're heading back to Lake Kariba, this time to stay on an island in the middle of the lake. Kariba is dotted with islands, remnants of hilltops left exposed when the lake filled up. Some belong to Zambia, others to Zimbabwe. Chikanka Island belongs to Zambia, but is so far out in the middle of the lake as to seem lost in the middle of a vast inland sea.

As the tri-maran slips away from the tiny village of Sinazongwe on the one and a half hours trip out to the island, the glassy surface of the lake mirrors the sky. Soon we're passing through a fossilized forest of bleached white trunks created when the lake filled up. Out in the middle of the lake, the scene is reminiscent of Wordsworth's poetry. The steep hills of the Zambezi escarpment form a dramatic backdrop on one side, while on the far shore the purple hills of Zimbabwe loom large.

At this time of year, Chikanka Island is not one island but three separate knolls. However, when water levels drop in the dry season, they become one island again. Waiting on the shore is an impressive welcome committee consisting of three elephant and a crocodile.

The sun is just setting, blazing streaks of gold across the sky, in turn mirrored in the glassy surface of the water. Out on the lake a lone dugout canoe slides silently by, while kapenta fishing boats, their huge nets hoisted high out of the water, are setting off on their nightly trawl for millions of tiny fish that populate the waters of the lake.

Ah, paradise . . . but only if you ignore scorpions, snakes, lizards, hippos, crocodiles, mosquitoes and other creatures also stranded on the island when the waters rose. Two nights marooned on an island with all these, *I must be mad!*

Three members of staff who look after guests' needs also stay on the island: Niros the cook, who hopefully can work miracles with our meagre stock of provisions, Mike the game guide and Noah, the odd-job man.

"It's somewhat lonely out on an island in the middle of nowhere," I happen to say as we dine that evening. Just then a distinctly un-human scrunching and munching rather too close for comfort shatters the stillness.

Forks pause mid-air. "Well, something's out there," concedes Bob.

Just then Niros strolls in. "Elephant, three of them, I think and quite near," he says obliquely as if announcing the arrival of the number ten bus.

Standing on the dining room veranda, we beam torches out into the surrounding bush. Is that three massive elephant or just darkness?

"Exactly how do we reach our chalets with nothing but torches or Tilley lamps?" I whisper. "Not forgetting, the lamps stop at our chalet."

We tiptoe along the first stretch to reach our chalet, beaming the torches around for any sign of immense grey backsides, flapping ears or waving trunks. Ali's chalet lies fifty yards further along the path in pitch darkness.

"I'll come with you to your chalet," Bob offers magnanimously.

"But how will you get back?"

She has a point, yet he does it anyways. In spite of the heat, I wait outside alone, shivering and listening to unnerving rustlings, scratchings and cracklings of a thousand tiny and not so tiny creatures going about their nightly business.

"Whose bright idea was it to come here?" I demand when Bob returns.

"Actually, it was you found this place."

Hmmm, know what, he's absolutely right!

Daylight confirms last night's worst fears. The pathway from dining area to both chalets, as well as ground underneath our chalet window, is littered with immense droppings. Not only that, but huge elephant footprints have sunk into soft earth not eighteen inches from where my head lay on the pillow. To think, I went to sleep worrying about spiders the size of saucers *inside* the chalet, when elephant were right *outside* the windows!

Aieeh, definitely too close for comfort!

The morning passes pleasantly enough on the dining room veranda enjoying the view and watching lizards, skins mottled black and white and with bright orange or turquoise tails, darting in and out of cracks in the rocks. On the shore below a monitor lizard and a lone croc add further interest.

Around mid-morning Niros approaches Ali and murmurs, "Excuse me, madam, there is something you might like to see."

Not sure what to expect, Ali toddles off in his wake, but soon returns. "This one's for Dad," she mutters darkly, yet declines to elaborate.

Never one to miss a good shot, Bob pootles off down the sandy track to the kitchen area. Curiosity aroused, I follow at a discreet distance.

"Ah no madam, snake!" Niros leaps across barring my path.

Too late, I've already spotted the long, thin, brown snake with white stripes running along the sides of its body. It has caught a brown lizard with a bright orange tail and is in the process of squeezing out its life breath. As the lizard struggles in its death throes, the snake doubles back on its length and bites the hapless lizard, thus hastening the process. Within seconds the lizard hangs lifeless. The snake then swallows it whole, inch by inch, unhinging its jaws and engulfing an entire body almost as wide as its own. Finally, only the tip of the lizard's tail pokes out of the snake's mouth. With one last gulp, the lizard becomes simply a huge swelling working its way along inside the snake's gut.

"Ugh, gross!" Nevertheless, I watch the entire process, fascinated yet helpless to rescue the lizard.

"Fantastic shots!" Bob flicks through his camera screen, ensuring he's captured every single moment of the death of the lizard.

Meanwhile, sated to the point of engorgement, the snake slithers away to digest its meal. It attempts to slide up into the lower branches of a nearby tree, but is weighed down by the lizard bulging inside its body and promptly falls out again. For a brief moment, the snake heads our way, but suddenly changes its mind and veers away.

"Wow, that was something!" exclaims Bob.

Wasn't it just, almost but not quite enough to put us off lunch!

In the afternoon a storm brews over the lake, turning the water steely grey and whipping the surface into choppy white crested waves. Although the storm blows itself out, the lake remains too turbulent for boating. Instead the guide accompanies us on a short walk over to the far side of the island.

"The elephant are still around?" It's always as well to know these things.

"Maybe they swam to another island. But look, some kudu and a waterbuck have come down to drink from the lake, also a *tiger*."

Surely not? The last I heard, *tigers* were not native to Africa. Then it dawns, "Do you by any chance mean duiker?"

"Yes, *tiger, tiger!*" he responds eagerly.

Tiger it is then, even though duiker more accurately describes the gentle, wet-nosed antelope currently nosing its way along the shore. But watch out, *tiger*! The croc once more lies motionless on the shore waiting for supper to chance along. Let's hope the *tiger* is sufficiently aware to stay clear of its jaws.

Darkness is falling as we head back for supper. Tonight there are no elephant munching and chomping. However, halfway through supper a creature resembling a monster motor-scooter zooms in and begins frantically careering around the room. Uncertain what it is, we leap out of its way. Getting stung so far from civilisation would not be wise. Eventually, it settles and we approach with caution.

"There's no curved tail so it's not a scorpion."

"More like some sort of gigantic double-bodied spider . . ."

"Just look at those huge pincers at both ends!"

"I *definitely* don't like the look of it!" And that from the male of the species, who agrees this is not a creature to dabble with. Eventually it resumes its frenzied zooming before departing in search of other distractions. The excitement of its arrival even put the appearance of several immense cockroaches completely in the shade.

Aren't we the lucky ones spending an extra night here!

Next day disaster strikes, and I'm not even the one struggling to digest an entire lizard, although my protesting gut feels as if it might be. And a boat trip around the three islands is booked for later this morning, rather unfortunate timing since both gut problems and heat are intensifying by the minute. Nevertheless, we plaster up with sun cream and set off in the company of Mike and Noah who will paddle the boat.

But where is the engine? The boat that will navigate the remote reaches of the island is little more than a large dugout canoe. Paddles it is then.

Today there's no sign of elephant, or indeed any other animals. Doubtless they've more sense than to be out in scorching heat and have retired to the shade. There are however plenty of birds: plover, egrets, pied and malachite kingfishers, fish eagles soaring high into the sky emitting plaintive cries. Cormorants balance out on rocks, hanging out their wings to dry like wet washing in the sun.

Round the far side of the third island lies the harbour where kapenta boats moor up during daylight hours. Most of the fishermen sleep in temporary huts on the island, but one man always stays on board to guard the boat. Up close the boats are huge, yet at night they're mere specks of light out on the lake. Spotting a sleeping guard, Mike and Noah are unable to resist the temptation.

"Iwe!" they holler, like kids enjoying a joke, then laugh because they've woken up the sleeping guard. They wave cheerily and paddle on by.

It takes two hours to circumnavigate the islands. As the boat pulls back into shore, the tri-maran is crossing from the mainland bringing over a second group of guests who will share our last night on the island.

It's New Year's Eve, our last day here, and the last day of the trip. Tomorrow we head back to Lusaka before catching the plane back to the UK.

"Actually, it'll be hard going back to the UK." I lie, cool drink to hand, submerged up to my neck in a splash pool dug out of the bare rock.

"Hmmm, perhaps we've slotted rather too easily back into Africa," agrees Bob.

"So, you'll be coming back then?" laughs Ali. "Even though nowadays it's not quite the life you enjoyed before?"

"Possibly," we concede. "After all, you've adapted so well to the new Zambia, why shouldn't we?" *Why indeed!*

It's one of the quietest New Year's Eves ever. Even the elephant have packed their trunks and gone elsewhere. On New Year's Day, we rise at 6am ready to take the tri-maran back to the mainland. Noah, Mike and Niros jump up and down on the shore, waving goodbye and shouting, "Happy New Year!"

Today the lake is choppy and the wind against us. The crossing takes longer than expected. As we near the mainland, one guy positions himself at the front of the boat to watch out for submerged tree trunks. Suddenly he yells out, "Snake, ahead!"

Head raised high out the water like a lady doing breaststroke and trying not to get her hair wet, the snake swims determinedly towards the boat. It's a seven to eight foot long greenish-brown snake with a cream underbelly.

"Could be a boomslang or a mamba," I say. Not that it matters since they're both deadly.

"How on earth did it get so far out from land?" exclaims Bob.

"Never mind that, it looks pretty determined to hitch a ride back to shore . . . *on our boat*!"

So what does the guy driving the boat do, but slow the engine all the more to enjoy the spectacle, even take a picture of it. Meanwhile the snake swims ever nearer . . .

"Can we go?" I protest feebly.

But no, the guy guns the boat round in a complete circle. "So you can have a better view," he grins.

The snake grows ever more bemused, uncertain which direction to swim. Fear not, the guys on the boat have armed themselves with oars and paddles. Should it come any nearer, they doubtless intend braining it. There is only one sort of snake Africans delight in, and that is a dead one.

"Can we *please* just get out of here?"

Mercifully we reach land minus an extra passenger, hoping to find the Hilux where we left it, still caked in mud and dust and still with a cracked windscreen, legacy of the sickening thud when someone bounced over the speed hump at Shiwa Ngandu.

Back in Lusaka everything seems noisy and chaotic after the places we've been. Yet nowhere is more chaotic than Ali's flat. Two street kids, Alex and Kay, are still in residence along with her maid who is currently homeless and has moved in with her entire family. To make matters worse, the two camps have fallen out with each other and have divided the flat into two clearly demarcated camps.

Leaving Ali to sort out a crisis on a scale worthy of employing the services of the United Nations peace keeping corps, we decamp to the Holiday Inn. First out of my suitcase is a giant spider, closely followed by a cockroach. All suitcases and bags must be emptied, shaken out and repacked into one case and one handgrip each ready for the plane tomorrow, hopefully minus any unwanted hitch-hikers.

Later Bob muses, "So, from what you said earlier, you really think we will come back?"

"Possibly," I respond cagily. "Though I'm not really sure how we'd fill a second trip, since we've probably pretty much exhausted Zambia's possibilities this time round. And besides, Zambia never was my favourite place." My mind drifts instead to the many delights Zimbabwe had to offer . . .

"So apart from visiting Ali," Bob pushes the point, "what else *could* bring us back here?"

"Stop, don't even go there!" I retort. "You're tempting fate and that's a dangerous thing to do!" I turn over to sleep with my last waking thought . . . what could possibly tempt us to return? *What indeed!*

End of part one/part two follows

Lake Bangwuelo ant hills

Lake Kariba - kapenta fishing boats

Shiwa Ngandu

Vic Falls

ZAMBIA UP CLOSE AND PERSONAL

PART TWO: JULY 2003 - > JUNE 2011

WHAT ACTUALLY HAPPENED . . .

CHAPTER NINE: THE ELUSIVE STATE OF INNER THANKFULNESS
July 17th - > 20th, 2003

So, there we were imagining there wasn't anything to keep bringing us back to Zambia yet, between saying goodbye in January and returning in July this year, a great deal has happened to bring about a second visit.

One totally unforeseen event is the prospect of acquiring a Zambian son-in-law. We certainly didn't see that one coming! Thus, as we descend the plane steps, we spot Ali and her fiancé waving furiously from the viewing platform. What will he be like? Only time and further acquaintance will tell. For the moment, after a night cramped in economy, all we want is a bath and bed.

That afternoon, in a bid to become better acquainted, our prospective son-in-law accompanies us to the same currency exchange bureau as last visit, then on to the same safari company as before to collect a hired vehicle.

"Unfortunately, the car you hired last time is not available until Sunday evening." Steepling his fingers in front of him, the Zambian behind the desk adopts an impassive expression. "However, in the meantime, we can offer you an identical vehicle."

Is there something he's not telling us?

"At least it's another Hilux Surf." Bob unlocks the door of the replacement vehicle, which is wine red in colour, not navy.

I clamber in the other side. "And it reeks of furniture polish. What have they been doing to it?"

"Hang on, it's *not* an automatic."

"Don't tell me you're disappointed, after all your battles last time with the automatic?" I joke. "Anyway, gears are easier to communicate with. And there's even a crack in the windscreen. Perhaps the last driver also had a habit of thundering over speed humps."

"Well, at fifteen dollars a day less," Bob resigns himself to his fate, "we'll save two hundred pounds in rental costs." Not that economy is everything, but since this expense comes out of our own pockets and not from the coffers of the newly formed charity, that's maybe no bad thing. Oh, did we forget to mention, we've now set up a charity to help victims of the Aids crisis in Zambia!

Next day, as we load up the car in preparation for a weekend away, Ali's fiancé, who knows a thing or two about cars, casts a knowing eye over the vehicle and announces, "This is a crash vehicle."

To us, one Hilux Surf looks much the same as another, apart from its colour or the smell of furniture polish. "How can you tell?"

He points along the side of the vehicle. "Look, this side is out of alignment. Clearly the front and back were welded together at some point possibly using two different vehicles."

"Right, this vehicle is going straight back where it came from!" Bob clambers in and turns the key in the ignition. Nothing happens.

"Maybe if I jumpstart it?" offers our prospective son-in-law and then proceeds to do so using a pair of pliers which merely produces the wheezy splutters of a none too healthy engine coughing into action.

Bob lifts the bonnet to find fluid oozing from the battery. "That's it, it's definitely going back now."

Excuse me, but was there ever any doubt!

Even though we're already late setting off for the weekend away, we head back into town to swap this death trap for a vehicle which might get us to our destination alive, rather than leaving us all dead by the roadside en route.

Back at the safari company and still wearing his impassive expression, the desk clerk informs us only a saloon car is available. Not good news, since no-one seems certain about the state of the road leading from the tarmac to Gwabi Lodge, our destination on the confluence of the Kafue and Zambezi rivers.

"Let's risk it anyway," proposes Bob.

"Except we'll be lucky now to reach Gwabi before dark," I remind him. All thoughts of a relaxing swim in the pool have long vanished, along with any confidence in the safari company.

But that's supposing we can find the road to Gwabi. As the late afternoon sun begins its rapid descent, we reach Chirundu to find the longest logjam of lorries ever, tailing back along the roadside for over three miles from the Chirundu border post between Zambia and Zimbabwe. Since no-one is allowed to cross from one country to the other without the correct papers, the queue increases daily. Somewhere, buried in there, lies the road to Gwabi.

"How do they ever know who's first or last?" In places lorries are all but piled one on top of another. Women, clad in brightly coloured 'chitenges' and balancing bowls and baskets on their heads heaped high with bananas and toasted mealies, ply their trade to drivers trapped inside stationary vehicles. It is complete chaos.

"Drivers can wait three days here to get their papers cleared," Ali tells us. "Which is why Chirundu has one of the highest incidences of HIV AIDS in the country."

"Er, am I missing something here?"

"Women here sell more than bananas to the drivers." Ali treats me to that *duh* look.

"You mean they're prostitutes?"

"Casual sex workers, please!" Ali adopts a more politically correct term for what may well be the oldest profession, but is also possibly the best paid job around here.

"It's still prostitution where I come from!" I say tartly.

"For heaven sake Mum, these women are desperate. How else are they supposed to feed their children? What would you do if your own kids were starving?"

"But they're not . . ."

"So maybe you should be thankful!"

The state of thankfulness doesn't come as readily as it might. What if I *was* in that situation and desperate to feed my own children, would I sell my body? But that's one of those questions you never know the answer to, unless you're in that situation. And, God willing, I never have to make that choice.

"Actually, incidences of HIV here are as high as one in three people."

I shudder. Later on this trip the plan is to return to Kitwe, to hand over school materials bought with money donated by people in the UK. So far so good. Why then am I struggling to reconcile my newly acquired charitable conscience with the plight of desperate women openly plying their trade along a line of lorry drivers simply to feed their starving children? I don't come up with any answer.

Leaving Chirundu, we turn off onto a dirt road.

"Did anyone actually see a sign saying this road goes to Gwabi?"

There's no response.

"So, since we're still passing lined up lorries, we could simply be burying ourselves deeper in the mire of Chirundu."

"It was the only dirt road turning left before the border post, so it must be the correct one." Bob employs some strange logic to which I'm not party.

The road is deeply ridged and potholed and probably hasn't been graded since Independence Day. "Pity we're in a saloon car," I grumble from the back seat. "A 4x4 would ride these ridges and potholes with never a murmur of protest."

"Except we'd have come to grief in the one they gave us," Bob reminds me. "With jarring and juddering, the front of a shunt job could at any moment part company from the back end."

Enough said. For the rest of the journey I suffer in silence, still striving to achieve that elusive inner state of thankfulness which continues to evade me.

We reach Gwabi as the sun sinks below the horizon. Bob and I are staying in a chalet perched high on a ridge overlooking the Kafue River. At this point on its long journey, the river becomes a swiftly flowing torrent. Barely one mile away, it joins forces with the mighty Zambezi. At least I'm thankful for our high up perch. The other two are down on the riverside campsite where nightly visitors include rampaging elephant and hippo.

As we relax over sundowners, the owners of the lodge join us on the terrace, faces tense and drawn. The expression 'at the end of their tether' springs to mind.

"Man, I don't know how much longer we can survive here." And that from white Zambians who've spent their whole lives here. "There's no place here for whites any longer."

Actually, that statement is arguable, since people like our philanthropic daughter seem to blend in seamlessly. We keep such thoughts to ourselves, since a flood of criticism against modern day Zambia is currently flowing faster in the gathering darkness than the swiftly flowing river far below.

"If it's not the taxman, then it's the man from the VAT breathing down our necks, demanding forms we've already sent them." The owner pauses to swig from his beer. "Back they come, until eventually we've no alternative but to pay them again just to get the b****** off our backs."

The owner's wife is a frazzled blond, who could be forty going on sixty, or equally sixty going on forty. Looking at the ridged veins on the back of her hands, maybe it's the latter. "They want to know have we contributed to our workers' pension rights," she chips in. "As if blacks working for us will ever see one penny of what we pay in for them!"

Maybe it's as well our daughter and partner are down on the campsite where elephant and hippo may prove more congenial companions than this ungrateful pair who not only have failed to adapt to the new Zambia, but also are not in the least thankful for the stunningly beautiful location they enjoy here.

Next day the lack of a 4x4 vehicle impedes the choice of activities. A saloon car would never stand up to the rigours of dirt road driving inside Lower Zambezi Game Park. Instead we hire a boat for a fishing trip downriver to where the Kafue River joins the Zambezi.

"This boat does have an engine?" asks Ali.

"You don't usually bother about such minor details as an engine?" I quip.

"Someone I know went canoeing down this stretch of river with her boyfriend," Ali starts to say . . .

Oh dear, maybe I don't need to hear the rest!

"A rogue hippo appeared from nowhere and turned the boat over. She and her boyfriend had to swim for the bank where they spent the entire night stranded on a tiny island shouting and singing to keep the crocs away. They weren't rescued till the next day when they flagged down a passing boat. Lucky for them, since some days nothing passes down this stretch."

Hmmm, bet they were thankful that particular boat passed by!

We set off at high speed down the Kafue River, thankfully faster than a charging hippo could hope to keep pace with. At the point where the two rivers join, the water widens to become almost an inland lake. As the passing wind whips through my hair, I reflect: it's Saturday morning, we're out on a motorboat in the middle of the Zambezi River under a cloudless blue heaven. Surely this is one of those pinch me and tell me it's true experiences. All thoughts of hippo, rogue or otherwise, vanish in the sheer exhilaration of the moment.

We moor up in reeds along the shore of an island, so far out midstream, it's beyond range of calling for help. I silently pray nothing untoward suddenly appears to mar the moment.

We're here to fish, or rather, the men are. Ali objects to harming God's creatures, be they worm or fish, while I can't stomach picking up a wriggling worm, then impaling its squirming body onto a hook.

Bob has borrowed a fancy rod and line from the lodge owners, while Ali's young man uses a pole snatched from a tree with a bit of string dangling from the end and has scrounged some fishhooks from Bob. Technology versus tradition, which will win the day?

Yet it's not long before a tiddler is nibbling on the primitive line. Bob watches enviously. So far nothing has fancied his expensive tackle.

Suddenly it happens. "Help, I've got a bite!" Sure enough, the primitive pole bends and twitches under the tug of what can only be . . .

"A tiger fish!" Bob is outraged. "You caught a ruddy tiger fish with a stick and bit of string!"

Ali's fiancé grins from ear to ear as he holds aloft a tiger fish about two and a half kilos in weight, silvery scales sparkling in the sun as it bravely struggles to return to its watery home. To no avail, this one is destined for the cooking fire.

We leap out the boat and onto the island. Ignoring footprints the size of dinner plates that can only belong to hippo and huge gouges made by the primordial claws of some immense crocodile that passed this way earlier, we set to, rediscovering the art of making fire. Fortunately, we had the foresight to bring along the makings of a simple meal: bread and butter, crisps, beer and bottled water. What more could we want?

By 3pm no further fish have succumbed to the bait. It's too cold in July in Zambia and the fish aren't biting. It does however feel marginally warmer than last night. Warm enough for a quick swim, before a barbecue at the campsite. Late this afternoon the other two drove back up to Chirundu and bought four large bream, surely a far more civilised method of obtaining fish than spending hours out in a boat waiting for the fish to bite. We barbecue these along with mealies and sweet potatoes, washed down with beer and white wine spritzers, only retiring to the comfort of the chalet when the candles have burned down and the last log has burnt out on the campfire.

The stars are sprinkling the heavens with stardust as Bob and I pick our way gingerly back up the pathway to the chalet, sharing what each of us thinks of our prospective son-in-law. This weekend away was intended as an opportunity to get to know each other. Pleasant enough, but too soon to tell is the general consensus. As to when they intend getting married, so far they haven't imparted that information.

But then we haven't asked, so maybe we just wait and see. So we do just that. After all we're in Zambia for three weeks and the subject of when they're likely to get married is *bound* to arise sometime. For the moment, there are other things to contend with. The return journey to Lusaka in a vehicle not designed for the purpose, then exchanging it for one better fitted for travelling over dirt roads.

True, the spirit of thankfulness finally flickered into existence earlier today. Yet returning next week to the harsh realities Kitwe threw at us last time, might render that somewhat short-lived. As yet, we've no idea what will come of it. And if we had known, might we not have caught the next plane back to the UK instead of hanging around long enough to find out!

CHAPTER TEN: THE RIGHT GIFT
July 26th – 27th, 2003

Invitations to dinner invariably create one major dilemma . . . what to give the hostess by way of a thank you gift. A bottle of supermarket plonk, its label betraying its humble origins, a bunch of faded flowers grabbed in haste from the nearest garage forecourt or, when all else fails, a box of last Christmas's chocolates, rapidly approaching their sell by date!

Today, not one of the above is appropriate, because tonight's hostess lives in a mud hut in a rural area a hundred and fifty miles due west of Lusaka. 'Meet the Fockers' could well pale into insignificance . . . the time has arrived to meet our prospective in-laws.

But first, we must get there.

Roads in Zambia leave a lot to be desired, even for some to qualify as roads in the first place. However, the main road west from Lusaka has, up till the present time, defied all ministerial or public efforts at improvement and has justifiably earned the reputation of being the worst road in Zambia. Today's journey over potholed and broken roads, instead of taking an easy one and a half hours, becomes an endurance marathon lasting six long hours.

Despite a desire to demonstrate his dirt road driving skills, particularly in regard to the negotiation of potholes, Bob concedes our future son-in-law is more likely to get us there in one piece. We are off to his village to meet his family. The plan is to spend the night in a mud hut there, which prospect has generated some anxiety.

"I don't suppose this mud hut is anything like ones tourists stay in?" I ask.

"You mean equipped with all mod cons and a shower under the stars like in pricier safari camps?" responds Bob. "Frankly, if it's got any washing facilities at all, I'll eat my hat."

This may perhaps be rather an extreme length to go to, simply because of a lack of washing facilities. Our daughter, who has already stayed there, attempts to encourage us with, "Think of it as an opportunity to experience the real Africa."

Ah, the real Africa . . . no electricity, running water or sanitation! Where water is available, it invariably comes from a shared village pump and borehole, or else is ferried in buckets from the local stream. And that's without the thorny issue as to what might be on the menu for supper!

"Far be it from us to balk at the prospect of what could be called 'a once in a lifetime experience!'" Bob says stoically. "If people with so little are prepared to offer hospitality to people like us who have so much, then somehow we'll survive. It is only one night after all."

If only I was half as convinced as he is, even half as optimistic would do.

In the mid-afternoon lull of drowsy villagers and unwary animals, and having survived a six hour marathon to get here, the Toyota Hi-Lux erupts onto the peaceful village scene in a shower of red dust, scattering chickens and guinea fowl alarmed at the unexpected arrival of a motorised vehicle so far off the beaten track.

"Welcome, welcome to our village!" Mother-in-law to be throws her arms wide and enfolds us tightly to her ample bosom. Then she lapses into profound silence, clearly induced by a lack of any further command of English.

We eye each other up. I'm no skinny rabbit, yet my opposite number would easily make two of me. And if we never imagined our daughter marrying the grandson of a Zulu chief with reputedly seventeen wives, then even less did this immense African momma anticipate her son turning up with a 'mzungu' as a prospective daughter-in-law and accompanied by parents driving a shiny Toyota Hi-Lux. Mercifully by this stage of the journey, the saloon has been replaced by the original Hi-Lux for the remainder of the trip.

"Er, what do we call your mother?" I ask.

Both her first-born and his younger brother appear uncertain. Indeed, the question creates so much head-shaking and casting of eyes askance, that eventually they resort to asking their mother what her name is.

"My name is *Sara," she responds, keeping her head lowered as if unaccustomed to the sound of her own name. We repeat the name after her, since neither son seems willing to use it.

Later we learn that in rural areas it's still common that, on marriage, a Zambian woman becomes simply 'the wife of . . .' Then when her first son is born she becomes 'the mother of . . .' And finally, with the birth of a first grandson, 'the grandmother of . . .' Yet Sara is so large, that maybe she didn't lose quite so much personality along with the loss of her Christian name after all.

Sara is originally from Zimbabwe. Since the death of her husband, she has become matriarch of this small village settlement. While many rural Zambians migrate towards the cities, either in search of work or in the wake of other family members, Sara prefers the rural life. And she certainly knows how to live it.

On the surface Sara appears to want for little. A circle of some six or seven huts surrounds a communal area. This circle is dominated by one large living hut spacious enough to stand up in. Inside is a welsh dresser lining one wall, complete with rose patterned china tea-set. The dresser is made from dried, sun-hardened mud. There is also a settee, two armchairs and two battery operated portable TV sets.

The circle of dwellings is completed with three sleeping huts and a smoke-filled kitchen hut. A small hut housing a pit toilet stands a discreet distance apart from the other huts. There are also assorted animal pens and shelters. Yes, Sara enjoys village life to the full.

We gaze round nervously, unsure of what comes next in the etiquette of life here. Which of the unprepossessing huts is to be our abode for the night? Should we hand over the gifts we've brought with us now, or wait for a more auspicious moment?

At that moment, the wife of the younger son emerges from the kitchen hut where she has been busy preparing food. Head hung low, she sidles across to greet us. As she moves, the small child tied on her back slips around to the front and begins nuzzling her flaccid breast, only to stop suckling and gaze bleary eyed at us. The young woman leaves one breast poking incongruously out from under her tattered T-shirt as she bobs a curtsy and offers a limp handshake. Yet despite considerable persistence, we cannot discover a name for her. She is simply 'the wife of *[2]Duane', Sara's younger son.

Duane is a small-time farmer doing well in cotton, which he sells to the local ginnery. Yet hardship is never far away. In Zambia, the rains frequently arrive too early or too late, or else they fail entirely resulting in crop failure and starvation. Then, even in rural areas where superstition is rife, there is still the ever-present threat of HIV AIDS.

Conversation threatens to dry up quicker than an unpromising rainy season. We have no knowledge of the local language, while Sara's English is unequal to the task. She waves her hand around her settlement, which we take to mean, 'Would we like a tour of the village?'

Yes indeed, except that, after six hours on the road, seeking relief for bursting bladders takes precedence. There is however only a pit toilet. Memories of stinking campsite latrines and overflowing portaloos at arts festivals have done little to dispel our anxieties. A village pit toilet may yet prove one experience too far.

The hut housing the pit toilet is located away from sleeping and living huts and is reached down a winding path leading between the spiked stubbles of last year's maize crop. Curious eyes follow our every step, knowing exactly where the 'mzungus' are headed. Ali has warned us what to expect. Nevertheless, now the moment has finally arrived to brave the pit toilet, anxiety is rapidly winning the day.

"What if the hole's so large that one of us stumbles and falls in, lost for ever in a mire of you-know-what?" I mutter to Bob.

"Or else so small, we miss it entirely and end up using our feet to deal with the consequences."

"Worse, if the whole thing caves in while we're inside! Surely this must happen sometimes?"[3]

---

[2] Duane and Sara are not real names for obvious reasons
[3] We read later of someone who was inside a pit toilet as it began to collapse. She escaped shaken, mercifully, from a fate surely worse than death!

Thus, wallowing in a mire of insurmountable fears, Bob stands guard outside while I brave the pit, then I do the same for him. Though, should the worst-case scenario occur, what possible assistance would one be to the other without a rope or a lifebelt at the very least?

"What *are* the pair of you worrying about?" Ali finds these insecurities highly amusing, but then she's been here before and survived. "You may like to know Landrover Chassis make the strongest supports and one is concreted in the base of this pit toilet."

And if she'd told us this before, would it have helped? I doubt it!

Back at the huts, it's time to view the animals. Chickens, pigeons, goats, guinea fowl, each group has an allotted house or pen skilfully constructed from poles and thatch. These have been raised where necessary on stilts away from predators prowling on the ground.

The flock of goats is delightful. As I reach over to pat a particularly cute little one, Sara indicates a timid black female cowering and bleating in the corner. "That one is your goat," she announces delightedly.

It's not long since we ate a late lunch consisting of tough, stringy village chicken accompanied by 'nshima' and greens cooked in oil with ground peanuts. The sun is already dropping in the late afternoon sky and night-time is rapidly approaching. With their limited cooking facilities, there is hardly time tonight to set about the elaborate process of killing and cooking a live goat. Tomorrow we'll be gone before anyone can say . . . *goat stew perhaps!*

Lulled by a false sense of security, relaxed and wondering what might constitute evening entertainment in a village in the heart of the African bush, battery operated TV perhaps, we are unprepared for what happens next. . . .

"Mum, Dad, come outside quickly!" Clearly this means another photo opportunity, of which there have been many already.

We rush outside to find the delightful black goat, which not five minutes previously we'd petted and admired, now gasping out its last breath. Blood gushes from its slit throat, pumping out and staining the dusty earth scarlet.

"Who mentioned seeing the real Africa?" Bile rises in my throat. "This is one image we could well have done without."

"Well, you'll be pleased to know, I'm not even going to photograph it!" declares Bob.

"What, no photo for the album?" This has got to be a first for the man who, so far, has photographed everything, merely to prove we did indeed spend the night in an African village.

By 6pm darkness has fallen. Sara lights a log fire in the open space between the encircling huts. Each time the flames die, she replenishes them by pushing an entire tree trunk into the centre of the fire. The sacrifice of a goat momentarily forgotten, these are magical moments indeed, seated around an open fire beneath the immensity of the star-filled African heavens.

Is it true there are more stars in the southern hemisphere than in the north? It certainly seems so tonight. And how many people get to experience this?

Silently we thank God for good fortune, along with narrowly escaping having to eat the goat slaughtered in our honour.

"Maybe it was just a symbolic slaughtering and the unfortunate beast will be shared out amongst the villagers after our departure tomorrow," I say as we prepare for bed. Sara has given up her own hut in our honour. The hut contains two small rooms, one for storing food, grain and implements, while the other contains her most prized possession, a large double bed. Despite this great honour, it's difficult to settle.

"Just check there's nothing under the bed," I ask Bob.

"What do you imagine is under there?" He remains impassive.

"Things with or without legs, lurking in the darkness." There is no electric light, so he's forced to scrabble around on hands and knees in the semi-darkness with only a flickering torch to guide him.

"There's nothing under there, okay!"

He switches off the torch and climbs into bed. I lie in pitch darkness listening to creaks and rustles as Sara's thatched hut settles for the night . . .

"What's that?"

On goes the torch again. Was it a mouse sneaking a nibble at the grain store, or something larger, a rat perhaps? And was that the surreptitious slither of a snake hidden in the thatch, contemplating our unwelcome presence down below? But there's nothing to see. Or, if anything was there, it's been scared away by the light anyways.

"What about needing the loo in the night?" The anxieties are back, not that they ever entirely went away.

"The pit toilet, I guess." Bob doesn't sound convincing. "After all, we do have a torch."

"Torch or no torch, I'm not going down that track in pitch darkness. It's even darker in the middle of nowhere than I expected," I declare.

"Even if I'm with you?" he offers.

"Whether you come or stay, it makes no difference. We've only one torch between us. At some point one of us will be left alone with no light." I pause, before saying longingly, "A potty-goes-under would've been welcome!"

But there is no potty-goes-under. Sara later confesses she was too embarrassed to offer it. A pity, because it would have saved our blushes next day on discovering a telltale ring of damp patches encircling the hut and still drying out in the chilly dawn air.

Next morning early sunshine, poking its way through the slats in the thatch, rouses us from fitful slumber, banishing night-time fears with its reassuring gleam. A dog barks outside and a goat bleats pitifully, perhaps lamenting the demise of its late sister or brother. Our stay in the village is almost over. A quick breakfast and we'll be on our way.

Washing facilities are basic. A quick splash in an enamel bowl containing lukewarm water, heated over the kitchen fire that has sprung to new life, is all that is on offer. Later in the day, a hut with all mod cons including running hot water does indeed await us in a safari camp. Yesterday we brought fresh bread with us so breakfast should be adequate if simple.

But what is this? Sara emerges triumphant from the kitchen hut, a wide grin dimpling her plump cheeks. In her hands, she bears the supreme reward for getting gifts to our hostess exactly right: bags of salt and sugar plus a bottle of cooking oil, all in sufficiently large quantities to last her for months, even if they don't do much for her diabetes and high blood pressure.

Sara was so delighted with her gifts, in return she is overjoyed to repay our kindness with the ultimate reward . . . *goat stew for breakfast!* Washed down with tea made with . . .

"Ah, even we have our own river water close by. But don't worry, it has been freshly boiled."

Feeling suddenly faint, I toss a quick prayer heavenwards for protection against all things visible and invisible, before tucking in with feigned gusto to goat stew, washed down with tea made from freshly boiled river water, all the while telling myself, a few mouthfuls will suffice if only to see duty done.

"Let's hope we're not in one of those African regions where eyeballs and testicles are considered the ultimate delicacy," Bob mutters under his breath.

I gag on a glob of goat stew, hair still attached to the larger lumps. "You are joking?"

"Only for the most honoured guests, naturally!" he sniggers.

"I don't think I saw any . . ." But what about when I gagged on that gristly lump, did I perhaps inadvertently swallow one these so-called delicacies?

This particular bush tucker trial has turned out to be for real, except I'm *not* a celebrity. There is however both a husband and a Hi-Lux Surf on hand to get me out of here *fast!* "Help . . ."

CHAPTER ELEVEN: MORE THAN ONE KIND OF ROGUE!
July 27th -> 31st 2003

With remnants of the *'real Africa'* still digesting in our guts, we head for what most overseas tourists imagine *is* the real Africa: ethnic chalets with showers, flush toilets, hot and cold running water and three meals a day prepared by smiling staff eager to please because tourists' tips feed families stretched to bursting point by orphans and sick or dying relatives.

If only overseas visitors knew what it's really like out there!

Sadly, any prospects of luxury vanish quicker than early morning mist as we arrive at Chunga Camp in the Kafue National Park. Although we have a confirmed reservation, the camp is so rundown it can't have seen any life in a long time. After much pacing around calling at the tops of our voices, eventually a lone figure rows across from the opposite shore.

"Ah, there is not now any Chunga Camp." The man shakes his head as he scrutinises the paper. "Your reservation is not for here but for the camp on the island in the middle of the river."

I observe his small boat and the swollen Kafue River. "So how exactly do we get ourselves and all our stuff across there?"

"Ah, no problem," he responds. "However, we are not expecting you."

Anything else we should know? *Quite a lot actually!*

The boat sinks visibly under the weight of four passengers plus an incredible amount of stuff for four nights self-catering. As we reach midstream, the man points to an abandoned boat partially concealed amongst overhanging trees lining the bank of the island. One end has a gaping cavity, as if an incompetent dentist botched an extraction.

"There is a rogue hippo in this stretch of water," he informs us. "It attacked this boat, also the guide who was in it, biting him in the leg. Now he can no longer walk."

Hippos are amongst the most dangerous animals in Africa, reputedly killing more people than lion or elephant. Most dangerous of all is a rogue hippo, generally a lone male, driven out of the pod in a territorial squabble. Left to fend for itself, it will attack anything. Yet this is not all . . .

Safely ashore, our daughter asks where they should pitch their tent.

The man gasps, "Aieeh, you cannot camp here!"

"Why ever not?" Ali has inherited a determined spirit from at least one parent.

"There are many lions here, also elephant cross to this island. Even hippo come out the water here."

This creates a dilemma. Being of advanced years, we've booked a chalet while the other two prefer camping. Must we all now squeeze into one chalet? But no, our man will go to any lengths for us not to get trampled upon by elephant or eaten by lion. Though there is still the matter of a tip!

"You may use two chalets, but I will only charge the campsite fee for the second one."

On the island stand five beautiful lodges, tastefully decorated and with balconies overhanging the river. To the rear is a watering hole where lion, elephant, buck and antelope come to drink in the early morning or late evening. Except where are the other guests?

"Ah, they don't come now," reveals Moses, the boat driver who doubles as general help lighting fires and lamps.

Sparrow, the resident cook who will knock up meals from our limited supplies, has also now arrived from whatever he does when there are no guests here. "In fact, the owner fled to South Africa because of issues over fraud," he says.

Are we right in wondering should we even be here? Officially the place no longer operates. No-one knows we're here, apart from Moses and Sparrow plus any baboon, elephant, zebra, impala, waterbuck or sable antelope that witnessed our arrival. Oh, and a rogue hippo that doubtless is around somewhere.

"In fact, we have not been paid for two months," Moses informs us.

"But we are willing to work for you!" Sparrow's swift interjection leaves no doubt about his expectations.

We reserve judgement till we see what Sparrow creates for supper tonight. He doesn't disappoint: minestrone soup followed by shepherd's pie made with tinned corned beef.

Meanwhile Moses gathers firewood and lights Tilley lamps. However, their feeble light reaches no further than a small circle around each lamp. Sitting around the dying embers of the fire, we reflect yet again how far the *'real Africa'* is removed from what foreign tourists see on neatly packaged and sanitised safaris. This *surely* is Africa in the raw!

"What was that?" I peer into impenetrable darkness beyond the lamps.

Suddenly Moses and Sparrow appear from the kitchen area. "You must return to your chalets."

True we're bushed, yet something more than our tiredness concerns them.

"Maybe a lion is out there, so we will escort you to your rooms where you must remain for the night."

"Do you also sleep here?"

Moses and Sparrow glance nervously at each other. "Ah no, we sleep in our village which is maybe not so near. Even we walk there, but making much noise so that the lion thinks we are many and will not attack."

Sticking close together, singing and shouting, we set off for the first chalet to drop off the two younger ones. Then on to our chalet which we enter with a sigh of relief. Any relief is short-lived.

"How can I possibly sleep with what's going on here?" I rant. "We're in the middle of nowhere, not a single person in the whole wide world knows we're here."

In the distance, the voices of Sparrow and Moses gradually fade as they traipse ever further away. I pray they return in the morning.

During the night the unmistakeable roaring of lion, howling of hyena, crashing through the camp of elephant, then finally hippo taking a bath underneath the balcony, merely confirm how much danger is out there. Compared with this racket, the dawn chorus is a welcome but subdued affair.

The return of Moses and Sparrow is greeted with relief. They are however bemused by our lack of fresh meat. Maybe we should've brought along the dead goat! I'm not naïve enough to expect a Shoprite in the heart of the bush, however a villager with the odd chicken or some eggs to sell might be a bonus.

"There is a fishing camp close by," they reveal. "However, these people are on the island illegally. If the owner catches them, he beats them."

Without stopping to weigh up the risk factor, the four of us set off downstream in the boat in search of fish. As they push the boat out midstream, Moses and Sparrow assure us we'll easily find them.

Strange then, that neither of them offers to accompany us!

At the fishing camp, eight or nine malevolent looking men bunched together on the shore silently observe our arrival. Just as well there's a Zambian with us, since they don't or else won't speak English. One, clearly the leader, feet apart in a hostile stance, brandishes a large knife, which he sharpens menacingly while listening to our request for fish. Nearby on the ground lie more knives, any one capable of slitting intruders' throats. What chance would we have if these guys turned against us?

Even worse, these rogues now know we're upstream, unarmed, unguarded, complete with cash, cameras and other valuables. Let's hope there's nothing more bloodthirsty than lion on the prowl tonight!

Nevertheless, they sell us a bucketful of fresh bream and other small fish for about £1.50. Whoopee, a treat in store for lunch!

In fact, lunch produces more than one surprise. Apparently, we're not only planning a wedding, but also for the birth of our first grandchild, which unexpected news temporarily diverts our minds from the threat of nocturnal attacks from rogues downriver.

Later, we set off on a first game drive into the Kafue National Park. Kafue is one of Zambia's largest parks thus expectation is high of seeing the big five: lion, leopard, elephant, buffalo and rhino. Hopefully, not all at once *and* without any accompanying danger.

With us is a ranger carrying a loaded gun, yet he's not a happy person. Apparently, the ranger who should have accompanied us ran away. His replacement doesn't offer his name and later, when we about-turn the vehicle in deep sand, becomes extremely agitated at the sight of elephant dung, so fresh the steam is still rising from it.

Is there something this highly nervous ranger isn't revealing? Rogue elephant as well as rogue hippo? He gives nothing away.

The game drive is exciting with sightings of impala, puku, bushbuck, waterbuck, elephant, crocodile, buffalo, storks, warthog, turtle, bush harpies and spring hares. The last two are picked out by searchlight reflecting the red of their eyes, as we drive back in darkness sweeping the bush with the lamp. One moment their eyes flare red in the darkness and the next they've gone, like mini lights winking off and on in the darkness.

It's pitch black as we near Chunga Camp. Suddenly the morose guide springs to life. "I am asking for a lift to where I stay which is not far." In Africa not far can mean anything. It turns out to be three kilometres.

"You are not wanting to walk back, even with a gun?" I ask. Zambians walk everywhere, so three kilometres should be nothing.

"Even this gun is no good. If something attacked, it might wound them, but kill them, no. And a wounded animal is even more dangerous."

"You seem very nervous for a game ranger?"

He shakes his head solemnly. "So many of my friends have been killed or injured doing this job that I no longer want to do it. Elephant, hippo, crocodile, they all kill. Myself, I will leave as soon as I find another job."

The guide stays at a nearby boarding school, one of two in Zambia catering only for primary children who come mainly from Lusaka, sent there by parents who can no longer control them. The one thing these children dare not do in the middle of a game reserve is run away, since they'd almost certainly get eaten by lion or trampled by elephant. It's certainly a novel take on boot camp!

Only one problem remains, crossing the river in total darkness to reach the camp.

"Just look at all those stars in the sky," Bob waxes lyrical as the boat put-puts over the water towards the light of the campfire glowing on the island.

"I'm more concerned whether the hippo's hanging around waiting to tip the boat over."

"Ah no, by this time the hippo will be out the water feeding on the land," Moses says. "Indeed, we must be extra careful walking from the boat to camp."

We recall what Clifford said at Kasanka: the most dangerous thing is getting between a hippo and water. Hippo don't wait around, they just charge. Who said herbivores were placid animals? Moses lands the boat and we follow him in single file, shining torches around and praying their beams do not pick out the bulk of a charging hippo.

"Even these hippo, they can run *very* fast," whispers Moses.
Please, enough is enough!

Next morning the lack of fresh meat again arises. Bob and I agree to cross the river and drive to the school where we dropped off the ranger. "Even they have live chickens there," Moses promises.

Last night, with children of all ages milling around in the darkness, the place seemed chaotic. Maybe by the light of day, it will seem more normal.

"Yes, we have chickens for sale." The teacher in charge is perfectly happy to leave off teaching troublesome kids in order to sell a chicken, even to show us cramped dormitories where ten or more children sleep cooped up with chicken sheds right by them. But then perhaps hygiene is the least of their worries here. As he opens the shed door, the overpowering smell of ammonia combined chicken shit rises to greet us, transporting us back to early days in Zambia, when we reared chickens in the garage at the rear of the house. Mature birds were sold en masse to sellers in the African market.

"Four to four and half pounds," declares Bob, eyeing the bird we're given with the practised eye of a man who recognises a good bird when he sees one. Yet supermarket ones wrapped in polythene are easier to transport than this one. Legs tied neatly together, it sits in the back of the car contentedly pooing during the three kilometres back to the boat.

"You must hold the chicken tightly," advises Moses as we clamber into the boat. "If baboons do not come after it on land, then a crocodile might grab it while we are on the water."

Bob hugs the chicken tightly, yet the tighter he hugs it, the more scared it becomes and the more scared it becomes, the more it poos, all over him, the seat and the floor of the boat.

"Just look at my clean trousers!" he exclaims, handing the chicken over to Sparrow to clean and cook for this evening.

That afternoon the men decide to go fishing, this time with proper rods.

"Sorry, that is not possible," declares Moses.

"But I've always fished in Africa!" declares Bob. Always being, apart from recently at Gwabi, twenty-seven years ago.

"You cannot fish from a silent boat on this river," responds Moses. "Either the hippo will turn the boat over, or else take a bite out of it. Even from the shore crocs will come clean out the water to catch their prey."

"But that's small animals, surely?"

"Ah no, many local people have been attacked on the banks of the river while they are washing or fishing. The crocodile catches them by whatever part of the body it can take hold of. Even you can be standing watching your arm or your leg sail off down the river in the jaws of a crocodile."

This might sound funny, if it weren't true. Large numbers of Africans every year, especially young children, are attacked and killed on the water's edge by crocodiles. Thus convinced, we spend the afternoon instead watching four elephants feeding in trees beyond the water pan, before wandering across the camp not one hundred yards from where we're sitting.

Later we take a boat trip upstream keeping the engine running all the time. Immense, ugly crocs lie prone on sandbanks observing our approach, then slip silently into the water to hang menacingly suspended until we pass. The numerous hippo clearly resent our presence. One moment they're lazily spouting water and the next they disappear only to resurface threateningly right in front of the boat.

Heading back to camp, Moses indicates a lone hippo following the boat. "See, the rogue hippo has found us at last!"

And he's out to get us, one minute on one side of the boat, then on the other, resurfacing with a sudden spurt of water accompanied by an angry snort. Moses guns the engine, sweeping the boat from side to side to confuse the brute, yet possibly this only angers him more and he bides his time before attacking again.

For the moment, the chicken bought earlier is now hissing and spitting in a barbecue basket over the open fire. Peace descends, but not for long . . .

Tonight, something is *definitely* out there. Unfortunately, Moses and Sparrow have already left, leaving us to reach the safety of the chalets alone. We set off for the first chanting, "La, la, la, la!" at the tops of our voices, then stand outside shouting, "Rhubarb, rhubarb, rhubarb!" while the other two cover the next fifty yards alone. Goodness knows what's listening. Later a loud trumpet sounds, a bit too close for comfort.

Ah Africa, do we ever think we are mad? *Frequently!*

CHAPTER TWELVE: THOROUGHLY SPOOKED...
AND NOT JUST THE ANIMALS!
July 31st - > August 4th 2003

"Aieeh, did you hear those lions in the night?" ask Moses and Sparrow next morning. "Even they were roaring right by the camp." And we never heard a thing, though thankfully we're alive to tell the tale.

Today we're heading to Itezhi-tezhi in another part of the Kafue National Park. However, one problem about staying miles from anywhere is carrying sufficient fuel so it doesn't run out. We didn't and ours just has.

"No problem," Moses assures us. Reuben, the nervous game ranger, apparently runs a lucrative side-line selling drums of diesel to clients with empty tanks. His way, perhaps, of raising funds to escape the perils of being a game ranger.

But how to get the petrol into the tank? Firstly, Reuben inserts one end of rubber tubing into the tank inlet and the other into the neck of the drum containing diesel.

"That is diesel, isn't it?" asks Bob. "Because if not, it'll wreck the vehicle *and* cost us a fortune!"

"For sure, baas!" Reuben looks crestfallen. *What else would it be!*

In order to start the diesel flowing, Reuben sucks for all he's worth on one end of the pipe till inevitably he gets a mouthful of diesel. Spitting this out, he quickly inserts the end into the fuel tank using a funnel made from the neck of a plastic bottle. Clearly, he's performed this tricky manoeuvre before.

This morning it's my turn to drive. "Just keep the speed down," advises Bob as I turn onto the tarmac. "And watch out for elephant crossing."

Moses and Sparrow have warned that elephant here don't know where the game park starts and ends. But then, surely an elephant wandering in front of the car should be easy to spot.

Currently we're tailing a Land Cruiser, in turn following a truckload of Africans. Both drivers in front spot the lone elephant first and pull onto the verge, waiting to see whether the elephant crosses or not. I pull over behind and also await developments. Yet the elephant is more interested in finishing breakfast than in three vehicles parked on the roadside.

The truckload of Africans inches out and crawls safely past, then the Land Cruiser follows. Seeing both vehicles pass without incident, I also pull out. Are two vehicles interrupting an elephant's breakfast enough, or is he simply another Kafue rogue making a stance? Head raised, ears flapping like giant tent flaps and trunk waving wildly from side to side, the elephant charges from barely twenty feet away.

My foot hits the accelerator. Sluggish at the best of times, the Hilux is slow to respond. Heart thudding, I've only one thought, to get the four, or should that be five of us, out of here fast!

"But I didn't get a shot of him," wails Bob.

In the rear view mirror, the elephant stands stock still in the middle of the road, tossing its trunk angrily at the disappearing vehicle.

Let's hope there are no more frights like that one!

The rest of the journey to Musungwa Lodge is uneventful. Like Chungwa, Musungwa lies in a stunning setting on a slight rise overlooking a small lake. But yet again, where are the other guests? Does Kafue National Park have yet more rogues in store to scare visitors away?

"There is no need for you to camp here," the manager informs our daughter magnanimously. "You may use our self-catering lodge for free. I am always happy to offer guests small kindnesses."

Or does such generosity have more to do with rogue elephants rampaging through the campsite en route to the lake? Clearly an elephant's concept of campsite etiquette is as vague as it is of highway etiquette.

Next day a young white girl appears beside the pool. She reveals her folks farm near Monze. She cocks one eyebrow speculatively and asks, "Have you ventured into the game park yet?"

Instantly the word 'ventured' sets alarm bells start ringing. "Is there perhaps something . . ."

"Only my Dad refuses to go in there any more. Because of poachers after elephant tusks, the animals are completely spooked. If you're lucky they simply run away, if not, they attack without warning." She pauses, perhaps considering how much to reveal. After all, she wouldn't want to spook us as well as the animals. She makes up her mind, "Look, if I was you, I'd forget game viewing here."

This is not encouraging. Our first game drive is already booked for 3pm. We set off in our vehicle accompanied by a ranger called Bydon. Since he's also the barman, his knowledge of game may be challenged. Nevertheless, we spot impala leaping and jumping away from the vehicle, as well as kudu, waterbuck, guinea fowl, puku, oribi and gemsbok, also hippo piled one on top of another on their favourite sandbank out in the middle of the river.

The first elephants are far enough away to present little danger. Yesterday's narrow escape is still as fresh in everyone's mind as newly dropped dung. The elephant treats us to some ear flapping, but nothing too unnerving.

However, on the return, these elephants along with their young have moved on. Without warning we encounter them where the bush is so dense it almost grows over the dirt road. Bob is driving, while I have the camera.

"Look out, elephant!" I call out as an enormous bull, ears flapping, trunk waving and trumpeting loudly stampedes out from the surrounding bush.

"Go, go, go!" Ali and I chorus together.

With seconds to spare before the elephant reaches us, Bob's foot hits the accelerator. Leaving behind a cloud of dust, the vehicle zooms out of harm's way. In the wing mirror, I watch the entire herd emerge from surrounding bush in full charge stampeding down the road behind us.

"Did you get a picture?" Bob has the gall to ask.

No, I did not!

All is not over. Near the exit gate, we surprise another family group. The expression between a rock and a hard place springs to mind. We sit motionless inside the vehicle, hearts hammering, waiting for the herd to cross the road, all the while praying the ones behind are not still on the rampage.

Within seconds, the immense grey bulk of every last one is swallowed up by the bush. One minute they're there, the next they've vanished. Incredible, how something so large can disappear so swiftly and silently. Or have they?

Bob inches the vehicle forward. One herd of elephant is behind us, while another group is somewhere beside us. As to what's in front . . .

"Why don't you reverse, or turn around?" I whisper hoarsely.

Bob shakes his head. "Neither, there's no way we'd be out of harm's way before they're upon us."

"Bydon?" I turn for the game ranger's advice, but he's fast asleep. Still, would a barman have any more idea than us what to do?

Suddenly Bob spots more elephant ahead. "Enough of this!" Not waiting to see what happens, he revs the engine, foot flat on the floor and shoots past in a cloud of dust before the elephant realise what's happening.

"Is everything okay?" Bydon finally stirs as the exit gate comes into sight.

However, our troubles are far from over. At 6.20pm the warden has locked the barrier and gone home, effectively locking us inside the game park for the night along with goodness knows how many rampaging elephants.

"Maybe if you sound the horn," suggests Bydon.

Bob gives several loud blasts to no avail.

"Maybe I will seek the warden," Bydon offers half-heartedly. Doubtless he's also spotted lion spoor along the sandy track leading to the warden's house.

Not one of us offers to accompany him. Instead we sit in gathering darkness pondering our predicament. Father and daughter for once are remarkably silent.

I break the silence. "How long do you reckon he'll take to fetch the warden?"

"We don't even know whether she *(yes, the warden is indeed a she)* will agree to come back with him," says Bob.

"Even whether they'll make it back alive."

Silence reigns for several long moments. "If we're forced to spend the night shut inside the vehicle, what do we do for the loo, because I am *not* getting outside this vehicle in this game park!"

Eventually the warden appears, but only after she's fed the baby and cooked the 'nshima'. By which time it's dark, though not so dark her less that pleased expression at being called out at this hour is not clearly visible.

"Where did she suppose we'd gone?" I ask as we drive out through the gate. "She signed us into the park, wasn't she worried when we failed to reappear by lock-up time?"

Bydon has fallen silent again.

"Maybe she simply wrote us off?" suggests Bob.

Somehow, I don't think he's joking.

Finally, we reach the camp, where the third immense meal of the day awaits. Yet everything here from cakes to bread to pastries manages to taste of diesel fumes. Our guts are currently in revolt, caused by food tasting of diesel combined with the inevitable revenge of the village goat.

"Sometimes I think the only creature on this continent with any sense is the 'Go-way' bird!" Back safely in our chalet, I sniff into a tissue. "It sits up in a tree all day long shouting, 'Go-way, go-way!' Maybe we should go away and leave Africa to its own devices."

"There, there, it's been a difficult day!" Bob intends to inspire comfort but fails abysmally. "Just wait, tomorrow you'll be raring for more."

"But that's what I'm worrying about . . . *tomorrow!*" I fight back tears. Africa has been too much in our faces all day today. Yet he's right; tomorrow is always another day.

Unfortunately, the next twenty-four hours pass in a haze of Immodium and Lomotil as Bob and I struggle with upset tummies. Since there's no worse place with an upset stomach than out on a game drive, all activity temporarily ceases. It's Sunday afternoon before we tackle the game reserve again.

"But definitely no more elephant!" we inform Bydon before setting off. "Though lion would be good," we add wistfully. So far there's been no sign of them, but what a way to finish a sighting of lion would be!

Bydon follows a road skirting the lake. In the late afternoon, waterbuck, impala, puku, a lone duiker, black-faced vervet monkeys and the inevitable elephant are by the water's edge drinking their fill. Mercifully the elephant keep their distance. Maybe word has got around: *Beware, a rogue Toyota Hilux on the loose!*

First highlight is a flock of vultures feeding off a two days old buffalo carcass. If ever a bird is unsuited to being on the ground, it's the vulture. They hop and flop about, vying with each other to tear off morsels of stinking meat.

"Maybe this buffalo was killed by lion," announces Bydon. "When they have eaten their fill, the lion slink off to digest their meal."

I peer around anxiously. "So they could still be round here?"

Was that the sound of a lion burping? Indeed it was! Suddenly, four or five young lion race across the road right in front of the vehicle and are gone as suddenly as they appeared. No words can describe the heart-stopping moment of spotting lion in the wild.

"Lion!" All four of us are out our seats shouting as one. Yet unbelievably at that very moment not one of us had a camera to hand. Not a single photo exists to prove we saw them. Still, we do reach the exit gate without getting locked in *and* without getting charged by any more elephant.

Unfortunately, today is the end of our time at Kafue National Park. Despite elephant spooked by poachers and animals unused to the presence of humans, Kafue has a revealed a wildness all of its own, though maybe a bit too wild, which is probably why safari companies currently give this stretch of the park a wide berth.

In honour of our departure, the chef lays on a buffet meal. The table groans under the weight of food which our still sensitive guts struggle to eat, though we cannot deny his pièce de résistance, marmalade Swiss roll, certainly beats dead goat any day.

In a couple of days, we fly back to the UK to begin preparing for a big as well as a little event, a wedding and a birth, hoping the two events happen in the 'right' order. If not, things may become a little tricky.

Yet it couldn't possibly be any trickier than coping with the unexpected offering of goat for breakfast, or becoming more spooked than the elephants in Kafue, or could it? No, it'll be like taking in a walk in the park . . . though not in a game park, that's for sure!

CHAPTER THIRTEEN: ESTABLISHING ANOTHER LIFE SIX THOUSAND MILES AWAY!
April 2004

By the time we return to Zambia in April 2004, we have both a Zambian son-in-law and a first granddaughter. Not only that, but we're also committed to building a school here for more than two hundred orphans and vulnerable children. Our Zambian family has begun growing.

So much for wondering what could possibly keep bringing us back here!

From the aeroplane, we watch the roseate sun peep over the horizon, turning the early morning sky orange, vermilion and rose. Since it now seems likely we'll keep returning for some time into the future, maybe it's also time to get to grips with the country.

This is easier said than done. No sooner have we landed, than we're struggling with the interminable queue at immigration.

"I swear this queue gets longer every visit," moans Bob.

"What I don't understand, is why the queue for tourist visas is always longer than any of the others!" Drained and exhausted after a night sitting bolt upright in the cramped confines of economy, I glare enviously at shorter queues where VIPs, diplomats, returning residents and permit holders all sail through, while all we do is inch forward, inch by infuriating inch.

"We could sneak into one of those queues," suggests Bob.

"Except we're neither VIPs nor diplomats, nor as yet returning residents or permit holders."

So we continue shuffling forwards, feet shifting our hand baggage because we're too weary to pick the bags up. Entry visa duly stamped in passports, there's another interminable wait in the baggage hall while the creaky conveyor belt grinds into motion. Round and round it goes on a never-ending journey to nowhere. We stare fixedly at the same suitcases coming round again and again, willing our own to appear.

Even getting the suitcases still doesn't guarantee a swift exit. The queue for the green channel stretches halfway round the baggage hall, while there's not a soul in the red one. Customs officers have picked on Zambian women returning alone from the UK, trolleys piled high with three and four bulging suitcases. Clearly they suspect undeclared goods and are stopping and questioning every single woman travelling alone.

Eventually we're outside in the steamy heat of a late rainy season morning, where, a wriggling, squirming café au lait bundle, now sporting a mop of fuzzy black hair, is desperate to be back in grandma's arms. Once there, she gazes serenely up at me with eyes of molten chocolate, as if to say, *'Where have you been the past four months?'* Where indeed!

And so, another trip to Zambia begins...

What a difference twenty-four hours makes! Next morning we're sufficiently restored to cope with the practicalities of being back in Zambia, the first being to collect the same hired vehicle as last time, and the second to change some money.

"Your car is ready, though not any registration or insurance documents," announces the man in the safari company. "But that will be okay."

"But we haven't yet paid?"

"That also is okay," he assures us. "The boss trusts you."

"Just wish we trusted them as much!" I mutter as we head out to the car.

"More importantly, that police trust us," Bob responds. "Since we're driving a vehicle without registration, insurance and no proof we've paid for it."

Today is Good Friday and the usual dubious moneychangers along Cairo Road are closed. However, our new son-in-law knows someone in the back streets behind Cairo Road. We park in a side street in the second class trading area. Immediately a guy with bulging pockets and pock-marked features leaps into the back seat. "How much do you want?"

Not sure how to handle this gangster-style set-up, when the next thing to appear may be a knife or gun, we mutter, "A couple of hundred dollars maybe?"

From his back pocket, the man extracts several rolls of crumpled Zambian banknotes fastened with rubber bands which he flips through like a card sharp about to deal a dodgy hand to players unaware of the con he's pulling. "I can do five hundred," he rasps.

"Actually, three hundred and fifty would be okay," squeaks Bob.

The man produces an ancient calculator and punches in numbers, then passes it over for us to read the screen. What is the correct exchange rate for currency deals in the back seat of a car down a side street in Lusaka on Good Friday? We hand over seven genuine US fifty dollar bills, praying the filthy, much thumbed notes he gives in exchange are worth what it says on the screen. Kwachas millionaires we may now be, but there are no money back guarantees here. As for a receipt, forget it!

With a curt nod and a quick glance out the window to check whether any police are around, the man slides out the car. In seconds he melts into the Good Friday crowds and disappears.

Most places are closed today, so a trip out of town is planned. About twenty kilometres from Lusaka along a dirt road lies Kalimba Reptile Park. Apart from offering barbecue, fishing and picnic sites, management here goes to great lengths to remind visitors this is still Africa. Enclosed in glass cages near the entrance is a selection of Zambia's deadlier snakes: green and black mambas, puff adders, gaboon vipers and cobras. Nearby, two immense pythons lie comatose at the bottom of a pit.

'It is interesting to note,' we read on printed information, *'that poisonous snakes can be divided into two groups, neurotoxic and haemotoxic. The main difference being in the way the poison affects people who get bitten. In the former the poison acts on the neurological system and in the latter on the blood system, which then carries the poison to vital organs. A few of the deadlier snakes inject poisons which affect both systems.'*

"So, if you're lucky," I say, "it's a quick death. But if you're not, it's a long lingering death, your body struggling against poison which causes virtually every symptom there is."

"Not forgetting," adds Bob, "you must also catch the snake that bites you, then take it with you to hospital, since being given the wrong antidote is almost as bad as getting bitten in the first place."

"I'll try to remember that if ever I get bitten!" My tone is caustic.

Dotted around are also enclosures and dams containing crocodiles farmed for both skin and meat. Smaller pens contain crocs about one foot long, lying motionless waiting for their next feed to drop over the wall. Elsewhere, immense and ancient reptilian monsters, some up to fifteen feet long, lie sunning themselves beside the two main dams. All that separates visitors from these giants is a flimsy wire-netting fence. Clutching Thandi tightly, I slip swiftly past lest one of these brutes is tempted by a bite-sized snack and hurls its massive bulk against the fence. Then where would I and this new-found joy in my life be?

Later, heading back to Lusaka, the big orange ball of the sun balances on the horizon, before slipping away for another day, a familiar sight many times in Rhodesia, heading back to Salisbury after a day out at Lake MacIlwaine. Suddenly a lump chokes my throat. Coming here has suddenly become a home-coming. Things have gone full circle and, thirty years later, we're heading back to town again after a day out in the bush.

There is however one difference, one small but noisy granddaughter in the back who, like everyone else, simply wants to get back home for a bath, supper and bed.

Though we're not aware of it, this Easter weekend marks the first of many periods of calm between storms. Times spent with family or taking short breaks elsewhere which provide a much-needed respite from the trials and tribulations of charity work amongst impoverished communities. If nothing else, this book lets you in on some of the secrets as to how we coped.

But for the moment there are family barbecues in the back garden, then shopping for fishing rods.

"If we're going to keep coming back," argues Bob, "I may as well keep a proper fishing rod here."

"You have proper rods back in the UK," I remind him, since choosing one is taking forever. In fact, a Hardy's original split cane one, just about the best there is. My father used to work for Hardy's and made the rods himself.

"Ah but they're back in the UK!" An argument that leads to yet more time wasting before finally he purchases a vastly inferior fibre glass rod.

That evening we watch the video of 'Out of Africa'. I retire to bed still hearing Meryl Streep's voice droning the opening lines, "I had a farm in Africa, at the foot of the Ngong Hills . . ."

Maybe one day I should write a book about Africa and what happens here. Though actually maybe something needs to happen first and besides, what adventures will a couple of old fogies have in Zambia? This is hardly Kenya and the Ngong Hills.

"Besides, Karen Blixen never returned to Africa," Bob reminds me.

"Ah but we *have* returned, and what with family and charity work, maybe our fate is now so inextricably bound up with this continent, that's a good enough reason to write a book about it." I rest my case.

On Easter Monday, Bob and I head for a short break at Eagles Rest on the shores of Lake Kariba. There is that fishing rod to try out, plus the view to die for from the chalet veranda looking out over the lake towards distant Zimbabwe. Maybe my book should start, *'There was a place on the shores of Lake Kariba . . .'* Somehow this doesn't quite have the ring of Karen Blixen.

It's two years since our last trip here when the owner's wife snatched her small dog out the water before it fell into a crocodile's jaws. Yet by dinner on the first evening, it's apparent things have changed. Kapenta masquerading as deep-fried whitebait, cold, congealing fish followed by rubbery crème brûlée, accompanied by the last glasses of house white wine that also *taste* like the last glasses of house wine. All this does not bode well.

Nevertheless, anxious to test out his new rod, Bob is down first thing in the morning fishing from the rocks.

Watch out for crocs, they also might be biting!

Meanwhile, my thoughts turn to writing out the Starfish story that inspired the setting up of Starfish Fund, though I'm not entirely sure copyright allows this. Instead I begin sorting emails between ourselves and the organisation in Kitwe that we visited in December 2002. Yet neither of these produces quite the same ring as Karen Blixen achieved in 'Out of Africa'.

Maybe I'll go for a swim instead . . .

Meanwhile Bob has limited success with his new fishing rod, returning with a tiger fish so small it provides an excuse to fish all afternoon. Yet bigger fish most definitely are not biting.

Mosquitoes however are. We light up the braai in the evening, having decided against another restaurant fiasco. The foil wrapped potatoes get lost in the fire and the meat becomes charred and positively carcinogenic, yet who cares! On the shores of Lake Kariba, the only sounds are those made by God's creatures: the plaintiff cry of a fish eagle or the grunt of hippo disporting themselves in the bay.

The nostalgic lump rises once more as we share how natural it is to be here, completely detached from life in the UK. But are we meant to be here or there? Only one person knows the answer to that, though fate may yet tempt us to look for a plot of land. And if fate doesn't, God might nudge us in that direction. Though that could be pushing considerably more than just luck!

Next day kapenta served on the first night seek their revenge and I didn't even eat their eyeballs, while Bob blames dodgy crème caramel. Even fishing becomes a no-no, whereas return visits to this lodge seem highly unlikely.

During the ensuing night, our condition worsens. Bob spends more time out of bed, than lying in it. By which point, realising we have a bug restricts activities to enjoying the glorious view from the veranda. John Bell of the Iona Community talks of thin places where heaven meets earth and where God's presence is all pervading. One such place is surely right here.

In spite of prolonged inactivity, the creative muse finally kicks in. Bob settles to drawing his first pictures and I finally put pen to paper telling a story that hopefully will write itself. This sufficiently restores ailing appetites to seek dinner.

"Something simple, a grilled steak perhaps?" I say to the waiter.

Steak *is* on offer, though not the skill to cook it properly. It arrives blood raw, floating in an indescribable white sauce masquerading as pepper sauce. The potatoes have what my mother called 'a bone in them', while vegetables are more 'dente' than 'al.' Just as well we're leaving tomorrow. Not even eagles, partial as they are to bloody meat, could survive long here!

Yet the morrow has its own problems. We climb into the car, with one last glance at the view to die for, though still feeling we might well die for it, to find the car won't start and there isn't a garage for miles that might help.

However, Zambians delight in opportunities like this. In no time the gardener, who has probably never driven a car in his life, appears with a set of jump leads, which he connects to the battery. Instantly, it springs back into life, albeit emitting an alarming rattle.

Bob peers under the bonnet to discover there's absolutely nothing holding the battery in place. With the engine running, the battery wobbles like a jelly on a plate, threatening to spray battery acid all over the engine. More time is wasted searching for something to hold the battery in position for the four hours journey back to Lusaka.

"This," thunders Bob, "is the last straw with that safari company!"

After the traumas of the past week, it's tempting to remain in Lusaka and forget about Kitwe, except we're committed to building a community school there. A promise is a promise, even though we've no idea whether they're expecting us *or* whether it's actually going to happen. Oh well, if nothing's happening up there, we still have family down here. This thought merely confirms Lusaka's role as a bolthole for when the going gets tough up north.

With this in mind, we head for Kitwe, but only after changing the car. We can't risk a breakdown in a country with no roadside assistance nor, at this stage, reliable cell-phone coverage. Though, come to think of it, we don't as yet possess a Zambian cell-phone and here we are setting off alone on a two hundred and fifty miles journey north to Kitwe.

Suffice it to say, if we had any doubts about what we're doing here before going up there, then the whys and wherefores become more apparent by the time we return to Lusaka.

"So, you are actually building a school up there?" asks our daughter.

"Well, yes," we concede, "and the good thing is we'll see more of you here in Zambia than back in UK."

Ali looks puzzled. "But surely, if you're two hundred and fifty miles away in Kitwe while we're down here in Lusaka, it's not *us* you'll see more of, only the smoke and grime of Kitwe?"

This sobering thought gives rise to increased mental turmoil until the time comes for goodbyes. Again I'm holding that wriggling, squirming bundle at the airport, drinking in enough of those molten chocolate eyes to last me for the next few months back in the UK.

"Well, goodbye then!" Ali holds out her arms and, after one last, lingering hug, I hand over Thandi. Though maybe it's more au revoir, since family and building projects look set to bring us back here for quite some time yet.

In the meantime, there are other distractions, like writing that book, not to mention raising enough money to make building a school here viable. All the same, keeping two separate lives going six thousand miles apart seems set to create more than a few challenges.

CHAPTER FOURTEEN: SEARCHING FOR GOD IN KITWE
July & August 2004

Since we're making two trips here this year, you'd think we'd at least choose the most direct route to Zambia. But no, because this trip is lasting six weeks, we save on parking charges at Heathrow by flying from Birmingham instead, travelling the long way round via Amsterdam and Nairobi.

However, there is joy at the end of the long journey, watching Thandi's eyes light up as Grandma and Granddad step back into her life. Yet barely have our feet touched Zambian soil, than we're off up to Kitwe to argue the budget for Kaputula School. And, since smoke-filled Kitwe will be home for most of the next six weeks, there's a need to find distractions of some sort, especially as we're already running into the weekend.

Like other Copperbelt towns, Kitwe is rich in copper and its by-products cobalt and malachite, yet not quite so blessed with places for pleasant days out. However, en route to and from Kaputula, the dirt road passes Chembe Bird Sanctuary. The Lonely Planet Guide mentions its abundant bird life. What better place to explore on our first free Saturday. Besides, the fishing rod bought last trip has also been brought to Kitwe in anticipation of good fishing.

It's late morning as we turn onto the dirt track leading into the bird sanctuary. Nothing stirs, not a sign of human life and not a bird in sight. The lake, bordered by waving swathes of dense green reeds, shimmers invitingly in the midday sun.

"Mulishane!" A Zambian dressed in the ragged remnants of a warden's uniform materialises from the surrounding scrub.

"Bwino mulishane! We were hoping to picnic here, maybe hire a boat this afternoon for some fishing?"

"We have boats . . ." the man hesitates. "But unfortunately, there are holes in them . . . also there are crocodiles in the dam, even some of them sixteen feet long."

Heavens, Zambian crocs get bigger every time we encounter them!

"However, there is a circular drive around the lake where you will see many birds, maybe even animals."

This trip we've rented a single cab pickup privately from a Lusaka based NGO. The vehicle has high clearance, but not four-wheel drive, so is possibly not suited to the terrain. Nevertheless, we set off in search of animals large and small and birds feathered or otherwise.

At first the track meanders pleasantly through scrubby trees and shoulder high dried grass. Already the landscape is gasping from three months without rain. Above the throb of the engine, comes the first faint hiss, spit and angry crackle of flames catching hold of dry grass accompanied by an unmistakeable whiff of smoke.

"Not to worry," declares Bob. "In the dry season, there are bush fires all over Zambia. Besides, we're going around in a circle away from any danger."

No sooner has he spoken, than the track veers down towards the water's edge, becoming gradually more rutted, then muddier, until finally the vehicle comes to an ignominious halt in yes, yet another muddy hollow.

"Don't worry, we'll get through it, or round it." Such confidence is sadly misplaced. Without four-wheel drive, the pickup refuses to go through it or round it, but simply embeds itself deeper in the mire.

"Surely the warden realised this vehicle wouldn't make it around here," I say.

"If he even is the warden," responds Bob.

"Meaning what, he could be an axe-murderer?"

Bob presses the accelerator and the wheels spin ever deeper in thick black mud. How many times have we been stuck like this in Africa? Though, to be fair, never to date in a deserted, off the beaten track bird sanctuary with not a single sign of twitching, tweeting or twittering life.

"We'll have to walk back along the track," decides Bob.

"What, abandon the vehicle? What if it gets pinched? What about the bush fire?" The frontline of the fire, instead of creeping towards us, is now racing ahead devouring grass, trees and anything else in its path as it attempts to feed its insatiable appetite.

It takes half an hour to walk back to the camp. Every moment the snap and crackle of fire draws nearer. The air is hot from advancing flames and thick with belching, black, acrid smoke. Although the erstwhile warden is still on site, he immediately disappears in search of help. We await his return, helpless to do anything and fearing at any moment an explosion signifying the untimely death of one brand new single cab pickup costing several thousand pounds.

Would abandoning the vehicle in the face of advancing fire lay us open to a charge of negligence?

Eventually the warden returns with reinforcements, two ragged and impoverished individuals who may have offered to dislodge a stranded vehicle or simply assist him do away with its occupants. Not a single living person in Zambia, or indeed anywhere on the planet, knows where we are today except these four men, five counting the warden. With a silent prayer to the Almighty, we place ourselves in their hands and set off back to the stranded vehicle. Since there is no other vehicle on site, we must walk back through the encroaching fire once more.

Yet as surely as God put men on earth to get cars out of predicaments like this, he equally provided woman to get behind the wheel while the men do the pushing.

If only men pushed out babies half as well as they push out cars!

There is no question of proceeding further. Even the warden concedes this point. Instead it's back to base and a picnic of cold chicken washed down with Fanta orange with a picnic table and lake all to ourselves and nothing but the limitless cobalt sky up above and the sounds of nature all around . . . Oh, and the fire drawing ever nearer. But fear not, the car keys are safe in my pocket. Should the fire come too close, then I'm out of here.

One of the car pushers claimed he was the boatman and promised to take us out in the boat this afternoon. Yet 3pm arrives and there's no sign of him. Eventually he wanders along at a quarter past, shuffling his feet disconsolately in the dusty earth.

"You have come to take us out in the boat?"

He looks bemused. "For sure, you want to go out in the boat?"

Maybe he's bothered by an ominous hole in the boat, or the enormous crocs, or simply a lack of English. He shakes his head as if astonished at the weird demands of a couple of 'mzungus'. Then, clutching a matchbox containing one single maggot, which he delights in showing us, he clambers into the same boat and paddles off using one oar, out through the shimmering reeds and into the croc infested water.

Bob stands on the shore, rod in hand looking bemused. "Did I get it wrong, or did he get it wrong?"

"Let's just say it was a problem of communication."

At least the man in the boat doesn't catch any fish, but then neither does Bob fishing all afternoon from the shore. When the man returns, Bob attempts to explain that we'll come back in two weeks' time, and would like to go out in the boat, holes, crocs and all, if that is okay.

"You're crazy," I tell Bob.

"But the guide book recommends a boat as the best way to see birds here." Since we've not seen a single bird all day, the guidebook could be right, unless of course the crocs get him first.

All this takes care of Saturday, leaving Sunday still to fill. Back in Kitwe, there's just time before darkness falls for a quick recce of Kitwe churches in the hope of finding a suitable place of worship for tomorrow.

Behind the salmon pink edifice of the Edinburgh Hotel, sandwiched between Shoprite and the African bus station, stands a red-brick Anglican church which doesn't look inspiring. Nearby is a Catholic church, but we're not Catholic, and the UCZ church looks more like a building site mistakenly hit by a bomb. Various Apostolic and Pentecostal churches are scattered around Parklands and Riverside, Kitwe's only two affluent suburbs. Property there is ring-fenced and enclosed behind eight feet high walls with barbed wire or electric fencing on top and with double iron gates guarded by security guards and guard dogs. Which begs the question, which church would people who live lives like that attend? Yet it still doesn't provide us with a place to worship.

"If God is calling us," I argue, "then surely He'll lead us to the right place of worship."

On Sunday morning at the Church of Christ, not a 'mzungu' is in sight amongst people thronging inside. Not that that matters, though it crosses my mind . . . *would that people thronged into English churches in the same way!*

The Catholics are also crowding in. Since we haven't converted overnight, this leaves the Anglican church, but there is no sign of life there. A tatty notice board announces Sung Eucharist at 9am. Since it's now well past that time, we can only store this information up for future use. Lastly there is the spanking white, freshly painted Kitwe Chapel where the service has not yet started, but 'mzungus' don't appear to worship there either and the service is not in English.

Maybe it wasn't meant to be today. We abandon the search and seek distraction elsewhere. On the way into town a sign advertises a river lodge with hippos basking in the blue – *surely they are joking!* – waters of the Kafue River.

The car bumps and grinds down a dirt road which wends its way, even over the bare rock of a dried up river bed till eventually a second sign points through a rickety gateway onto private land. A couple of kilometres further, the road crosses an earthen dam wall where the car wheels balance precariously between two small dams. The road finally comes to an abrupt end in a small car park. There is no sign of life. One final sign points up a small kopje towards reception.

On top of the small hill, stand four simple chalets overlooking a dam on one side and the fast flowing but murky waters of the Kafue River on the other. Signs everywhere proclaim: *Beware of Crocs! Watch out for Hippos!*

Presumably these aren't there to amuse the clientele, not that we can actually see any. However, dotted about on grassy areas as well as down by the river and even on a small island in the dam are simple wooden picnic tables and braai stands, indicating eating of some description takes place here.

Eventually, a dumpy little man waddles up and assures us we can eat there. Since it's still early, he directs us towards a grandly named 'mountain trail,' although there isn't a mountain in sight. After following this trail through the bush and scrambling up a small kopje, we suddenly emerge on top of a viewpoint with a 360 degrees view of the surrounding bush, even back as far as Kitwe's smoke shrouded skyline.

For lunch we order peppered steaks which take forever to arrive. The dumpy little man, whose name is George, waddles backwards and forwards across the dam because we're the awkward customers who want to sit out on the island, which is only reached by crossing a small bridge. Nearby is a second bridge that would make his journeys shorter, but it is in pieces.

"In fact, the hippo came out of the river," George tells us, "through the first dam, then smashed its way through the bridge to reach the second dam."

Let's hope it doesn't charge back again while we're eating!

The food is worth the wait, steaks falling off the edge of oval platters and knives that cut through them like butter. George beams with delight at our clean plates. And for dessert?

George hangs his head sorrowfully. "Ah sorry, we don't have dessert but I can do tea?" And if it takes most of the afternoon, who cares! In this idyllic spot on the banks of the Kafue River, we're content to while away an entire afternoon.

"You know, we could even stay here," Bob eyes the lodges perched on the kopje.

On this our fourth trip to Zambia, we're already on our third accommodation option in Kitwe, this time self-catering flats. Other options, for reasons of security, noise or unsavoury on-site activities, have failed to please. Yet the prospect of returning here after a hard day at Kaputula, away from the smoke and grime of Kitwe, would surely be music in our ears. Along with details of the Anglican service times, we store up this also for future reference.

Driving back into Kitwe, the huge orange ball of the sun sinks behind the mine stacks of Nkana Mine, which belches noxious fumes day and night into the surrounding atmosphere. And some people imagine we spend our time here swanning around on palm-fringed beaches!

By the time we reach the flats, it's dark already. We dive inside trying to prevent an incursion of mozzies. Unfortunately, they still get in. I spray the entire flat with DOOM, which threatens instant death to crawling and flying insects, but also causes my eyes to stream for the entire evening. Goodness knows what's in it; it's more toxic even than what pours out the mine chimneys.

I'm not sure we actually found God today. At least not in the Anglican church, though maybe on the banks of the Kafue River. It was an incredibly beautiful and peaceful spot so close to Kitwe and the Anglican church remains a possibility for future trips. After all there'll be plenty more weekends up here and, if God is on the case, then the places He has in mind for us will turn out just fine.

CHAPTER FIFTEEN: MONEY, MONEY, MONEY
July & August 2004

After several trips to Zambia, one problem persistently fails to resolve itself, that of exchanging money. Previously we've run the gauntlet of dodgy exchange bureaus, as well as back-street dealers. This trip we're carrying £7000 of Starfish money for building programmes. Let any dodgy back-street dealer get a whiff of that, and we might never live to tell the tale.

The money is in $US travellers' cheques in the belief that banks here, as elsewhere in the world, will not only recognise them, but also exchange them. How wrong can we be! Kitwe banks demand 10% commission and refuse to exchange more than $100 per day. At that rate, over six weeks, we'd never succeed in exchanging enough dollars to buy sufficient pockets of cement to build a school. Then there's the question of personal finance to cover food, petrol, accommodation and car hire. After two weeks in Kitwe, these are already in urgent need of a cash injection. Thus desperate, that weekend Bob risks his credit card in a Lusaka ATM.

"Don't forget banks charge daily interest on cash withdrawals," I remind him. This doesn't deter him. In goes his Mastercard, which the ATM promptly spits back out again. Since our financial situation is desperate, I agree to him trying my card. In goes the card and pin number and out comes not K800 000 (about £100) but K80 000 (about £10). Did someone miss off a nought?

By the time we get the right amount, we might as well have traipsed around every bank in town with the travellers' cheques, though we do now have enough to see us through the weekend. Yet by Monday the cash situation is dire once more. Banks won't cash larger travellers' cheques because we're not customers, and hotels won't cash them unless we're staying there. What do we do?

Someone suggests trying Longacres Lodge, a modest hotel catering largely for backpackers and travelling salesmen. Its currency exchange bureau is apparently open to non-residents. We approach it with trepidation. Behind iron grilles sit two stony-faced tellers, while nearby the requisite guard dozes on a chair, slumped over his AK-47. One nod in the wrong direction and he could blow us all to bits.

"Yes?" demands one of the women.

"We'd like to change $520 please?"

The two women glance at each other, then shrug non-committally. Not so the guard. Aroused from slumber by the magic word 'dollars', his finger twitches on the trigger. Do they perhaps mistake us for Bonnie and Clyde?

Quite possibly, since somebody presses an alarm and a supervisor shoots out as if by magic from the rear office. We repeat our request.

"Sorry, we don't have the money, but perhaps if you come back tomorrow?"

What do they intend doing overnight, robbing a bank perhaps? But there is no point returning, since there's as little likelihood of them having money tomorrow as today. Instead we head for Manda Hills, Lusaka's one shopping mall. Since overseas tourists shop there, surely banks there will change travellers' cheques? But no, bank staff smile politely and give the same answer, "Sorry, no changing travellers' cheques without an account."

We stand outside, loaded with £7000 in travellers' cheques, yet with no means of accessing it. "I've had enough," I decide. "I'll draw what I can on my credit card, then, since the travellers' cheques are in our names, bank them back in the UK and refund the Starfish account. Simple!"

I approach the ATM confidently and insert my credit card. The machine accepts the pin number and agrees to give me K1m, enough for a few more pockets of cement then, without warning, aborts the transaction, spitting the card out in disgust. "This is becoming a habit!" I storm back inside the same bank, where staff have already refused to cash travellers' cheques.

"No problem," a polite young Zambian assures me. "The transaction was aborted."

"Yes, in that no money came out," I tell him. "Yet it accepted the pin number, so how do I know the money hasn't been debited from the account?"

"Ah, that can't be a problem."

"Not for you," I explain patiently. "But what about when my credit card statement shows a debit of one million kwachas? I need proof I didn't receive any cash."

"For that I must open up the machine and that I cannot do."

"There must be somebody here who can?"

Suspecting we may prove difficult to get rid of, he disappears in search of someone with the authority to open up the ATM. Enter a second person, who explains firstly he must shut down this machine, then stock a second one with money so people won't go without cash. Finally, he must locate the exact spot on a long roll of tape showing: *transaction aborted.*

"And I'd like that for my records."

"Ah no, that is for bank records."

"Then I'd like a copy, please, for proof," I persist.

For almost two hours we wait while he fills a second machine with money, locates the place on the roll, then photocopies the evidence that indeed we did not receive any cash from the first machine.

"Satisfied?" demands Bob when we are outside once more. He has spent the last two hours in embarrassed silence while I pushed bank employees to the brink. Meanwhile, we still haven't got any cash and only $100 per day each. Unless the car hire company accepts travellers' cheques? Management at the flats? Even the Kitwe NGO?

Bingo! Have we just cracked it?

The following weekend Ali and Thandi join us in Kitwe. On Saturday, we tempt them with a visit to Chembe Bird Sanctuary, after first passing by Kaputula to see the school we're building there. Though, after all the problems changing money, combined with community demands for extra money, there's nothing to show so far but a storeroom and markings for the foundation slab.

"Oh dear, problems already? I did warn you," says Ali.

Arriving at Kaputula, the sweet sounds of hymn singing drift across from the ramshackle SDA church. Mr Chipotoyo, alerted by the sound of a vehicle, wanders over, clad not in his work clothes, but in his Sunday best. *Or should that be Saturday best?*

"Mulishane!"

"Bwino, mulishane!"

We explain we wanted to show our family where the school is to be built. More beams, more smiles. Zambians love children and grandchildren, even better, they adore mixed race children.

"And this is your first-born grandchild? What is her name?"

"Her name is Thandi."

"Ah Thandiwe, the beloved one." Mr Chipotyo slaps my hand in a high five. "From now on, according to our custom, we must call you Bwanakula Thandi, the grandmother of Thandi."

"And me?" Bob doesn't wish to be left out.

Mr Chipotoyo laughs. "Ah for you, it must be bashikulu, the grandfather."

Bob clearly likes this name, since he keeps repeating it all the way to Chembe Bird Sanctuary, where the same warden is waiting to greet us, even though he probably hasn't seen anyone since our last visit. Bob sets off straight away for a spot of fishing from the shore, while we set about feeding Thandi who is loudly demanding her next feed.

Towards the end of lunch, the boatman unexpectedly appears. Either he recalls Bob's request a couple of weeks ago, or else the warden sent for him, or maybe he's just hard up. This time he offers Bob the boat trip.

"You're mad," we tell him, "even thinking about going out in a boat with a hole in it in crocodile infested waters!"

"But he reckons the fishing is better beyond the reeds," Bob argues.

"Where the biggest crocs are *and* where we can't see you because you're hidden by reeds!"

There's no dissuading Bob. Nevertheless, we keep the car keys with us. If a hungry crocodile does get him, then it's not getting the car keys as well. True, he returns safely, but minus any fish. But that's not what it's about. In

Africa it's man against nature, sitting out in a boat in crocodile infested waters convincing yourself you won't get eaten by one.

Next weekend, we head south to Lusaka since entry visas need renewing and the thorny issue of money has arisen yet again. The second payment is also due on car hire plus accommodation at the flats, while Kaputula is running out of cement. None of these can be resolved any longer on a $100 per day.

By now the dry season is well advanced and we marvel at the stunning array of colours in the bush, from earthy ochres and browns through to dazzling oranges, fiery reds, blazing yellows and shimmering gold. In Zambia, the coming of spring decks trees in gaudy colours as opposed to autumn in the northern hemisphere.

In town, we head once more to Longacres Lodge. Our entire stash of dollars cash has been used up in Kitwe, leaving only travellers' cheques. We are desperate almost to begging, "Do you have any money today?"

The woman eyes us suspiciously. This could after all be classified information. "Yes," she concedes grudgingly.

Goodness, it's harder than finding water in the desert. Yet, since she agrees to change our travellers' cheques, we sign every last one and push them through the grille. The woman makes a great show of counting and recounting, shuffling and reshuffling, before filling out the form. Financial solvency is finally in sight . . .

"Hang on, that's not right!" Considering the vast amount in travellers' cheques we've just given her, she has written down an abysmally low amount of kwachas. "What is the exchange rate?"

"Three thousand kwachas to the dollar."

I point to the display board. "Up there it says K4800."

"That is for cash. The rate is different for travellers' cheques."

Muttering darkly, we snatch up the cheques and head outside. Every last cheque is now signed. If we lose them, anyone could cash them . . . *providing of course they can persuade a bank here to do so!*

At least the ATM is more kindly disposed today. It swallows the card and spits out the money with the right number of noughts on the end. Have we got this sussed? Unfortunately no, the next day the same machine only gives K10 000 notes (worth just over £1 each), and only K400 000 (about £50) in total. Yet again, insufficient funds to solve a financial crisis, let alone build a school.

Sadly, problems do not end there. Over the weekend I go down with flu. By 5.30pm on Sunday I admit defeat and retire to bed.

"If that temperature's not down in the morning, you'll need a malaria test," announces Ali.

"What, have unsterilised needles stuck in me in a country where one in five people has Aids? I'd rather die first!" Should it be cerebral malaria, that may well happen anyways.

Monday is another day. Sick or not, there's a 250 miles journey back to Kitwe. My cough feels like a chainsaw is splitting my skull wide open. By the time we reach Kitwe, my temperature has rocketed yet again.

"Maybe you *should* take a malaria test?" Bob tries.

"Over my dead body!" I snap.

I struggle through the week, stubbornly refusing a malaria test and praying it's nothing more than a bad flu. Each bout of coughing leaves me totally exhausted. There is no cough medicine in our emergency medicine kit, so recovery is down to Paracetamol, Strepsils and a nightly dose of the God channel on TV.

By the weekend everything has become a gigantic effort, and yes, we're running out of money again. So far in Kitwe, where hardly a white face braves the streets, but where pickpockets, street kids, beggars and muggers abound, it's been a golden rule *never* to draw out cash from ATMs here. However, with no dollars left and not enough kwachas to see us through, there is no option. We must run the gauntlet of a Kitwe ATM, on the street and in full view of passers-by. The armed guard is nowhere in sight, but is around the corner chatting with friends.

Bob inserts his card while I keep a wary watch for anyone taking an unhealthy interest in two 'mzungus' using a cash-point. Yet Zambian ATMs persistently dislike Bob's card. I get out mine and insert it gingerly into the machine. It gives me K800 000 all in K20 000 notes. I stuff the huge wad of notes into my bag and, with heart hammering, scuttle back to the car, lock the doors and share the money between us.

"This will have to last," I declare, "because I'm not risking an ATM here again!"

As the day progresses, I go downhill faster than a skier on the piste. Yet Bob bizarrely decides I need a curry to help sweat it out. Too weak to argue, all I can manage is, "Make sure it's a mild one!"

Bob is gone so long that by the time he returns, I've not only forgotten what I ordered, but have fallen asleep. Roused from slumber, I tuck into the curry which smells good, yet is hotter than Hades.

Bob attempts to look innocent but confesses, "I mentioned you were sick, so the Pakistani owner said if it was your stomach, you shouldn't eat curry. I told him, it wasn't your stomach, your head was aching, your throat was sore and your sinuses were blocked." *Why don't I like the sound of this!* "He said they'd make you a special curry with extra chillies. But don't worry, I told them no extra chillies, only medium hot. Though maybe they put in extra chillies anyways."

The curry fails to do the trick. On Sunday, I admit defeat and head for a private health clinic. Formerly a house in colonial days, the white-washed building looks impressive from the outside, yet inside it's basic. A Zambian nurse clad in spanking white uniform laboriously records my details: aching head, sore throat, blocked sinuses. "For this you must pay," she announces, her voice even more starched than her apron.

"Er, do you take credit cards?"

"This clinic is fee-paying, cash only," she says frostily. "And you must pay before seeing the doctor or receiving treatment." Doesn't she realise I'm too sick to contemplate running off without paying? She takes my temperature and blood pressure, then weighs me. Only fifty-five kilos, clearly not a sign of good health in a 'mzungu' with enough cash to buy food. Assuming the same 'mzungu' can get cash out of a cash machine!

Dr Kangwa has a pleasant, smiling face. He records every miserable symptom, before deciding it is a viral complication, but they should take a blood test anyways to check for malaria, especially when he learns we're staying at self-catering flats nearby.

"Aieeh!" He rolls his eyes revealing eyeballs whiter than his doctor's coat. "You are not knowing those flats are beside the Kitwe stream, a notorious breeding ground for mosquitoes?" As he speaks, he brandishes a lethal looking implement my way.

I shrink back, shier than a violet caught in hot sunshine watching him select a needle and hoping it's from a sterile pack. He swabs my arm with what looks like antiseptic yet smells like neat brandy. Perhaps he imagines I'm terrified of needles, even that I can't afford to pay, yet my greatest fear is an infected needle. *Oh why, did I agree to this?*

Back in the waiting room, I await the results, praying I haven't contracted something worse than the virus I came in here with. There is no malaria, but a raised white cell count indicative of infection. I leave armed with antibiotics and £12 lighter for the privilege. Cheap at the price, yet it knocks another hole in the finances.

"There's nothing for it, it's the cash-point again," Bob announces with ne'er a touch of concern such as: *Never mind, dear, all that matters, is that you get better!* Instead, it's running the gauntlet of the Kitwe ATM yet again.

Ah Zambia! This week has been something of a trial. But life has its ups and downs, never having enough money to get by being one of the greatest. Yet even that pales into insignificance compared to the worry of what I might have picked up from an infected needle! What price peace of mind, hey?

CHAPTER SIXTEEN: THE MIDDLE OF NOWHERE
April 30th - > May 2nd, 2005

Although problems obtaining cash in Zambia will doubtless continue into the foreseeable future, we arrive in 2005 to find the national debt has been wiped out. Good news for Zambia, yet not quite such good news for us. The kwacha has strengthened, meaning less purchasing power and that will subsequently stretch both Starfish and personal budgets to the limit.

Thus, after a week spent in Kitwe kick-starting an ailing project with limited funds, by the following weekend we're ready for a break. Since Monday is a public holiday, there's no point staying in Kitwe. Back south we drive to meet our daughter and family in Kabwe, halfway between Lusaka and Kitwe. We're heading for a little known beauty spot called Mulungushi Dam. Since it doesn't even rate a mention in the Lonely Planet Guide, we have some reservations.

"Don't worry," Ali assures us, "a friend went there and says it's beautiful."

Would that be the friend of the overturned canoe on the Zambezi River? Indeed it would!

Of course, it would help if we could get away. Just as we're ready to leave, the car engine emits a sickening whine and refuses to start. Anxious to escape smoke-grimed Kitwe for the weekend, this hold-up wastes precious family time of which not nearly enough has been factored into this trip.

"It must have been last night, travelling back from Kaputula in the dark," decides Bob. "Using headlights all the way has flattened the battery."

The owner of the flats emerges to see what the persistent whine is all about as Bob repeatedly attempts to encourage the engine into life. "Maybe someone here can assist you," she offers.

Since the nearest garage is a long walk into town, I pray she's right.

Enter one of Zambia's new generation: middle class, overweight, sporting designer sunglasses and above all eager to demonstrate superior skills in starting reluctant engines. Possibly it's the same man who kept us awake last night, splashing around in the swimming pool at 10.30pm, making more noise than a hippo wallowing in a bathtub. However, these nocturnal antics apart, the man could yet prove our saviour.

I smile sweetly, "Do you have a set of jump leads?"

No, but he does have a spanner and a wrench. He removes the battery from his own car, a spanking new 4x4 with wheels to rival those on any tractor, and proceeds to jumpstart the car using this basic toolkit.

"All will be well now," he says with a cheery wave.

Trusting his judgment, we stop off in Kitwe to collect money and shopping. Big mistake! Firstly, the credit card machine, cause of so much grief already, again stubbornly refuses to accept Bob's card. He hovers helplessly in front of the machine. Return to the car for my card and he'll lose his place in the lengthy end of the month queue, yet if I get out the car, then luggage and possessions are left unguarded.

Not that it matters because, secondly, the car won't start again. We're now stuck in a fee-paying car park in the centre of town surrounded by a heaving sea of black faces . . .

Ha! We both spot her together, the white face of a Norwegian volunteer. Not only does she know where the nearest garage is, she also accompanies Bob there, leaving me shut inside the vehicle along with luggage, food, valuables and with every window shut tight and every door firmly locked.

It is 9am and already the sun is blazing brazenly from a cloudless blue sky. Inside the vehicle the temperature rises relentlessly one degree per minute. Five, ten fifteen minutes crawl by. By nine-fifteen the heat is unbearable. Five more minutes, then I will slip outside, braving pickpockets and street kids simply for one gulp of heavenly fresh air . . .

My hand is on the door handle, when Bob reappears accompanied by three Zambians bearing one battery, one spanner and one wrench. No point in asking if anyone has jump leads. Clearly they don't!

The whole comic process of restarting the car with a spanner and wrench begins again. Within seconds the car starts. This time we're taking no chances. Still without cash or weekend food, we set off for Kabwe ignoring an irritating beeper, which beeps each time we exceed the speed limit. Since we exceed it all the way to Kabwe, it beeps the entire journey until, with one final exhausted beep, we sweep into town to find Ali and family waiting impatiently outside the Hungry Lion.

"Don't even ask!" we forestall their questions. "We haven't got money or food!"

Big mistake number two. We decide to drive on to Mulungushi while they remain in Kabwe to buy food, because of course, without them, we can't find the road to Mulungushi. No problem, Ali told us, my friend's directions are very straightforward.

Hmmm, that same friend again? Indeed, yes!

Less than one hundred yards from the main road, we become enmeshed in the maze of an African township. The first person we ask, directs us back through Kabwe and out the other side to the Mulungushi Textile Factory. Do we perhaps look Chinese? Not long ago the plant was taken over by Chinese who worryingly seem to be taking over a lot in Zambia, road maintenance and the railway network to name but two major areas.

Back through town and out onto the dirt road once more. Every junction offers at least three options, yet not one is signposted to Mulungushi Dam. We stop to ask directions of a man who not only is drunk, but pokes his face inside the car window drowning us in an alcoholic soup, before giving yet more confusing directions. Next we try a gaggle of schoolgirls, but are forced to give up since their coy giggles clearly indicate they think we're trying to pick them up.

Eventually we come upon a long, straight dirt road seemingly heading nowhere. Dare we hope it leads to the dam? Not a single car is in sight. We even about-turn at one point, convinced we've missed a turning. Yet after one and a half hours instead of the estimated one hour, we reach a locked and barred gate with a sign proclaiming: 'Mulungushi Dam. Strictly Private!' Having survived this far, we're not going to let a little sign deter us.

In the distance, the waters of the dam shimmer enticingly. There is no sign of life and not a sound apart from the endless crinkling, crackling and chirruping emerging from the surrounding bush. This definitely is the middle of nowhere.

"One of us must stay here with the stuff while the other climbs the gate and tries to find someone," decides Bob. "Shall we toss for it?"

And Ali reckoned this place was so popular it could be overbooked! I toss up the odds, the stifling heat of the car versus the unknown. "I'll go, you stay."

I clamber over the gate and set off down the track, keeping Bob and the vehicle within sight. The scrunch of gravel underfoot must surely announce my arrival to anyone listening. Still nobody appears. Tossing one last glance back at Bob, I head out of sight around the corner. Another hundred yards and finally the sound of voices reaches my ears.

"Hello?" I call.

A lengthy silence ensues before two startled black faces, eyes round as saucers, peer around the wall of what looks like a kitchen area.

"We'd like to stay here," I tell them. "If you have any vacant chalets, so could you unlock the gate and let us in?"

"Oh yes, yes indeed!" The two men jump out from behind the wall, almost falling over themselves in their eagerness to sweep us inside, rather like the widow who lost her coin and is overjoyed to find it again.

So when did they last see anyone here?

Inside the gate, the hillside sloping down to the water's edge is dotted with chalets and simple rondavels, the better maintained ones clearly privately owned. However, they offer us two ancient rondavels, little more than circular tin shacks with rusty tin roofs. Inside are two iron bedsteads on a polished earthen floor but nothing else. Ablution blocks are either down the hill or up the hill, depending on which rondavels we choose. Ones lower down are nearer the ablutions, yet ones higher up are in marginally better condition.

Just then Ali and family arrive. Clearly they didn't get lost and made better time along the dirt road. We settle on two chalets up the hill since they are nearer to the pool and cooking area. Even so, a maid has to sweep them out since they've not been occupied for a long time. She also makes up the beds with our bed-linen, while the man gets the kitchen fire going for hot water and a barbecue for us to cook food.

Ah bliss, an afternoon relaxing far away from the rigours of charity work in Kitwe, a barbecue out in the open as the sun goes down and the first stars dotting the evening sky which has faded from turquoise through green to become an immense inky velvet heaven studded with nightlights.

Later we retire to our *rustic* accommodation. Spiders and other former inmates have not been at all deterred either by our arrival or the sweeping out, but have returned in force to spend the night inside. Some spiders are as large as the hand of a small child. Matabele ants in search of food, have also taken up residence, the ones that bite like hell. I try beating them with a shoe.

"You really love this life!" Bob stretches out on his iron bedstead surveying the slaughter.

"Once upon a time, yes. Now, I've the distinct feeling I'm getting too old for it."

Since the 'facilities' are a hundred yards downhill in pitch darkness, I've taken the liberty of providing myself with a bucket from under the sinks in the loos.

"You're not seriously going to use a bucket?"

"If you imagine for one moment I am going outside this chalet in pitch darkness, running the gauntlet of snakes, spiders, scorpions and whatever else, then you can think again. I am not leaving this shack until the hours of darkness are well and truly past."

I'm talking to myself. Sated with fresh air and good food, and lulled by the nightly orchestra of the bush, Bob has fallen asleep. I give the shoelace, which is all that is fastening the door in place, one final tug, then switch off the one naked light bulb and slip under the one thin blanket.

'Lord,' I pray, 'please keep us safe throughout this night from whatever danger lurks outside!' I close my eyes briefly only to snap them open again, "Plus… anything *inside* also!'

We wake safe and sound apart from the cold. Temperatures plummeted overnight, leaving me to root around in the dark unearthing jumpers and towels to put on the bed for extra warmth.

Yet this morning the sky is duck egg blue in the crisp light of dawn. First job is to creep down to the shower block and dispose of the incriminating bucket. Meanwhile Bob heads over to the kitchen block to make tea, only to find the two guys falling over themselves to do it for him.

Even with limited rations, breakfast is a mammoth affair that sets us up magnificently for doing not a lot all day. The men half-heartedly dangle fishing rods in the lake, but it's the cold season again and fish aren't biting. Would that the same could be said of the Matabele ants who, at every opportunity, feast avidly upon uncovered flesh.

The pool is verging on glacial. Nevertheless, the blue sky and sunshine encourage us into taking a dip.

"Brrrr! Can this really be Africa?" I squeal.

Indeed yes, because where else do sunsets rival the ones here? Our short break is nearly over, yet it's been a necessary respite from making hard decisions about the way forward in Kitwe. If it were not for times like these, allowing us re-harness our resources, we might even contemplate giving up.

The second night is even colder, feeling more like July than late April. At 3am an unmistakeable cry pierces the darkness. "Whoo-oop! Whoo-oop!" repeated over and over and far too close for comfort.

"Hyena," whispers Bob in the dark.

I envisage their ugly lopsided bodies prowling around and lolloping awkwardly right outside our door, still fastened with nothing more secure than a shoelace. One hard shove and it will break.

"What are they after?" I whisper back. "What about the others next door, would hyena attack if they scent a child inside?"

"I'm sure they're just picking over scraps."

"But whose scraps?" I persist. "Hyena are scavengers, not hunters. They scoff the leftovers of lion and leopard. What if they're around as well?"

Next morning there is no doubt the nocturnal visitors were hyena. Pugmarks score the ground around both chalets, continuing on down to the soft earth around the dam where the ugly brutes went to drink.

More worrying by far are marks that look suspiciously like leopard prints. Though maybe it's better if we don't confirm whether a leopard also was on the prowl last night. Years later we learnt hyena are also opportunists. They will circle a camp where there are children and will indeed attack!

Today we're heading back to the dirt and grime of Kitwe. As we drive out the gate, a pair of fish eagles soars high into the blue heavens. High in a tree perches an African grey parrot scoffing its breakfast. No time to hang around though; we need to reach Kitwe before dark to avoid draining the car battery again. Even though Bob has discovered a switch that supposedly charges the alternator and battery while we drive, we'd rather not take that chance.

Sadly, we're unable to leave a tip for the two guys who have looked after us here, lighting fires, keeping hot water going, digging for worms. With a guilty handshake and muttered thanks, we leave without giving them anything.

Some problems here refuse to resolve themselves. Getting our hands on enough money for essentials, let alone extras, being one of them. We've barely enough cash to fill the petrol tank for the journey back.

And what prospect does that leave in store for tomorrow? Yes, yet another battle with the infernal cash machine in Kitwe. Oh joy!

CHAPTER SEVENTEEN: ON SAFARI - BUDGET STYLE
August 20th - > 25th 2005

By August 2005 our second life here is not only well established, it has also moved up a notch. Half our family now lives here, while the charity work has grown beyond anything ever imagined. Add to that, we now own a Zambian licensed and registered vehicle and you could well ask, why don't we simply come and live here?

In late August, after eleven days' hard graft in Kitwe, we travel south before setting off with family to South Luangwa Game Reserve. South Luangwa is one of Zambia's biggest reserves, patronised mainly by wealthy tourists who fly into Lusaka, then board tiny aircraft which whisk them away to stay in luxury safari tents or lodges with hot and cold running water, en-suite showers and flush toilets. They eat from fine bone china, drink from crystal glasses and naturally can afford $300 or more per person per night for the privilege.

Not having the same budget, we tend to do things differently. In other words the hard way, travelling for two days in two cars from Lusaka, covering just over 600kms the first day as far as Chipata.

As we set off at 8am heading eastwards, early morning mists still linger in dips and hollows of the gently undulating landscape. There is little traffic. Nevertheless, at one point a seriously overloaded bus almost topples over on top of one car, while later both cars sandwich a bush pig between them, almost bringing it to an untimely end. Then a cyclist, who doesn't realise two cars are overtaking, also almost comes to grief. But then all that's par for the course on a road journey in Zambia.

One obstacle we are prepared for, is crossing the Luangwa Bridge. The bridge is heavily guarded by both army and police, both of whom are notorious for relieving drivers and passengers of anything they happen to fancy inside their cars.

Our daughter and family are in front as we approach the bridge with trepidation. Unfortunately, their recently imported car from South Africa doesn't as yet boast registration plates. The police immediately seize on this, scrutinising import documents and attempting to find something not in order. Meanwhile a soldier with his ubiquitous AK-47 stands to one side, finger itching on the safety catch until small money changes hands and their car is waved on. Will we be so lucky?

"Something for a drink?" As the soldier leans forward, his gun also slips forwards, tilting alarmingly towards Bob's face.

Bob reaches behind for a bottle of Sprite from the cool-box. The soldier eyes this paltry offering grudgingly. Clearly, he had something more substantial in mind such as cash, yet we're reluctant to flash around wallets or purses for once bulging with cash from a suddenly co-operative cash-point. Thankfully, he accepts his gift and waves us on.

"Lucky for us this time," comments Bob. "Yet we have to cross the same bridge again on the way back."

Are these words set to return to haunt us?

We travel 602kms to reach Mama Rula's Lodge, a tropical haven of tranquillity after eight gruelling hours on the road. And if the electricity dies at 6pm, closely followed by our one hurricane lamp, who cares! We dine by candlelight on butternut soup, curry and rice with salads and sponge pudding.

Next day a further one hundred kilometres lie ahead crawling over a treacherous dirt road riddled with potholes, rocks, loose boulders and bare earth to reach Flatdogs Camp. Previous dirt roads pale into insignificance as we average barely twenty kilometres per hour.

Flatdogs Camp is located outside the main entrance to the Luangwa Reserve. Not only can we not afford to fly there, we also can't afford $300 per night to stay inside the reserve. Fortunately, wildlife can't tell the difference between territory inside the reserve and outside, meaning we're likely to see as much wildlife here as in any upmarket camp inside, but for a fraction of the price. Having friends and family in the know has certain advantages.

At the camp, staff insist on driving us to our chalet. Apparently, it isn't safe to walk *anywhere*, other than within a 10 metres radius around the chalets, or else along the short footpath leading to the pool and dining area.

"So, some excitement in store then?" I joke with the guard.

He rolls his eyes heavenwards. "Aieeh, madam, elephant here roam freely. Even they rampage through the campsite area."

"Thank heavens we're not camping then," I respond feebly.

"You must be careful at all times. Even they poke their heads inside chalet doors or windows and help themselves to food."

Suddenly I'm feeling less enamoured of this place we've travelled three days and over 1200kms to reach.

"Baboons and monkeys also are a problem," the man continues, settling into his stride. "Chalet doors and windows must be kept closed at all times or they will help themselves to anything and everything."

Can there possibly be anything else?

"Then there are crocodiles in the river." He nods through the trees towards the sludgy brown waters of the Luangwa River slowly slipping past not one hundred yards away and where a huge pod of hippo lolls languorously on a sandbank.

"Ah, hippo!" I exclaim.

"Yes, but beware of them also," continues our guide, a killjoy if ever there was one. "They come out onto the bank to graze after sunset and during the night. Hippo can be very dangerous. Always remember animals belong here first. We are guests in their environment." With this, he finally departs.

That evening two armed guards position themselves strategically between our chalets while we set a fire going, not only to cook food, but also to scare away marauding animals. As we damp down the fire for the night, one guard sweeps his flashlight around in a circle, picking up mini red lights reflected in the eyes of hippo grazing not twenty yards away.

"But there were forty or more of them on the sandbank earlier," I say.

"For sure they are around somewhere." The guard obligingly beams his torch around in a wide arc, picking out not more hippo, but a herd of elephant trooping silently through the camp.

I inhale sharply. "If you hadn't shone the torch . . ."

"No, madam, you would not have known they were there."

This doesn't exactly make me feel any better!

The night is far from quiet. Grazing hippo grunt full throttle, baboons bark in chorus, interspersed with the occasional whoop from a hyena or trumpet from a passing elephant. The cacophony from this bizarre orchestra, resounds from double bass and bassoon through to French horn and of course trumpet. Not to be outdone, the dawn chorus bursts into song at 5.30am precisely.

As morning advances a second herd of elephant troops silently through the camp. Not wishing to miss a photo, Bob sneaks behind the chalets, unknowingly positioning himself upwind of them. Suddenly they veer off track, heading straight for the adjacent chalet where Ali is standing outside with Thandi.

Just in time Ali grabs Thandi and dashes inside before they're trampled in the stampede. She manages to shut the door but not bolt it and leaving windows wide open. Intrigued, a mother and baby elephant halt outside and peer in through the open window. Completely panicked, Ali snatches Thandi and retreats to the bathroom. Yet mother and baby elephant follow them round, then stand outside pawing their immense feet and snuffling loudly.

Meanwhile, we watch, helpless to do anything but silently pray for their safety. One false move and the herd could turn on us and charge.

"Got the picture you want?" I hiss at Bob. "Now we know why they told us *not* to go walkabout! From now on we stick together."

For once Bob readily agrees.

Later that afternoon, as the heat diminishes, we set off on a game drive. Because guided drives here cost a fortune, we take our own vehicle.

"Just keep between the gravel road and the river bank and you cannot get lost," the camp owner assures us.

Right from the start animals seem to be queueing up for viewing time: elephant, impala, red lechwe, waterbuck, baboons. Crocodile lie prone on riverbanks or hang suspended in the water, floating like partially submerged logs. The river teems with hippo, spurting lazily or else sunning themselves liked beached whales on the sandbanks, waiting for the sun to sink before repeating last night's shenanigans.

Back at camp, all is quiet until the guard on duty flashes his torch at yet another passing herd of elephant. "Ah but it is quiet tonight," he informs us. "Maybe the animals don't like the wind."

Praying he is right, we retire for the night.

The plan is to rise early for a game drive. Indeed, a hippo, munching outside the bedroom window at 5am, ensures everyone is awake. We pack a hastily assembled breakfast and head for the game park entrance. Dawn is breaking, streaking the sky a full spectrum of paint box colours. The animals are already up, feeding, socialising, looking stunningly wild and beautiful, yet this time skilfully managing to avoid all the best camera shots.

Straight away we encounter a herd of elephant, closely followed by a herd of buffalo, then a hyena skulking in the early morning shadows, thinking he can slope off without being seen. Later we come across a second larger male, less reluctant to run away. Then we spot his female crouched below a culvert guarding her young.

We head for Chichele Hill about 26kms from the main gate. Stopping and starting, it takes two hours to get there, by which time our stomachs think we have forgotten them. We sit atop the hillside like Karen Blixen in 'Out of Africa' enjoying breakfast with a view out over the vast plains of the Luangwa valley.

As the car lurches down a little used track, I remark, "These thickets look very much like lion country."

"As if we'd be so lucky . . ."

"Look, something moved right there, an ear or possibly a tail. Yes, it is, not one but a whole pride of lion!"

Bob lets the vehicle creep downhill, across a sandy riverbed and up the opposite bank where a female stands stock still in the dried up riverbed scrutinising our approach. Close by, sheltered by a scrubby thorn bush, another four females are lounging with cubs as curious to see us as we are to see them.

"Wow!" There is no other word for spotting lions in the wild!

Later, heading back to camp, we turn onto a side road to avoid following another vehicle. Sunning itself on the sandy road, lies a leopard. It rises slowly, unfolding its long, slender legs, stretches languorously before sauntering off with a, *'Now why did you have to interrupt my nap!'*

As it moves off, it startles an unsuspecting impala which barks in fright, then leaps away crashing through the bush. The leopard makes as if to give chase, yet loses interest and flops down on its distended belly. Clearly it ate well last night and can't be bothered to hunt again today.

Back at camp over lunch, the elephant reappear. We barely have time to barricade ourselves in the chalets before a young elephant comes right up to the window and noses inside. Clearly he doesn't like us staring back scared stiff at him and paws the ground, shaking his trunk as a warning before losing interest and ambling off to join the rest of the herd.

"Phew, that was close!" Finally, Bob is becoming as unnerved as the rest of us by the proximity of such large and powerful animals.

On our last full day at South Luangwa, we set off complete with picnic on a day trip to reach Kaingo Camp in the far north of the game reserve, though where we will picnic in a game park full of elephant, lion, buffalo and baboons, is another matter.

Game abound on the track northwards to the remote reaches of the park: stately giraffe, skittery zebra, stolid buffalo, gentle doe-eyed waterbuck, startled kudu and shy wildebeest. Lagoons teem with storks, pelicans and herons. Whenever a bird spots a fish, they repeatedly descend on the same spot, wings flapping and emitting raucous squawks of jealousy. The beating of so many mighty wings resembles the whirring of a jet engine preparing for take-off.

By noon there's still no sign of Kaingo Camp. Somewhere in this vast game park we missed the turning. Bob as ever remains optimistic, so we ask at Lion Camp which we've just passed and which is so new it's still under construction. The owners allow us to picnic on the veranda, which is an improvement on getting out the car in the middle of the game park. We sit munching hardboiled eggs, tomatoes, cucumber and crisps where doubtless, in a few weeks, rich tourists will dine in far greater style and on far richer fare.

With no hope now of reaching Kaingo, we return by a different route alongside the meandering river. The riverbank and water are thickly populated with inert hippo and crocs. Unless of course one of us should get out to spend a penny, when they might suddenly prove a lot more active.

The track is isolated and little used, yet suddenly we come upon a stranded family of Asians, their vehicle stuck in deep sand where they drove off-road. Allah must have been looking out for them, because the chances of another vehicle coming along this remote stretch are slim. Unbelievably the man is the engineer responsible for sinking the borehole at Lion Camp. Strange then, he didn't know not to drive off-road into deep sand.

No sooner have we sent them on their way, than we also are floundering, wheels spinning in deep sand that stretches almost one hundred yards. With a silent prayer to our own God that our newly acquired vehicle will automatically engage four-wheel drive, we slither and slide our way through it.

Four hours there and three hours back, yet we have covered barely 100kms today. There's no sign of elephant tonight, though they rampaged through the campsite earlier. We collapse exhausted into bed, praying for a quiet night, before commencing the long journey back tomorrow.

No such luck! In the depths of darkness . . . Crack! Snap! Was that someone after the car; worse is a burglar inside the chalet? I fumble for the torch and sweep its light around the room rousing a grunt from the other bed.

There it is again, an ear-splitting crack right outside the window. I beam the torch out into the darkness. Four immense elephants are enjoying a midnight feast ripping entire branches off the trees not twenty yards from the window.

I switch off the light and get back into bed. The noise continues for some time, until with one last trumpet, they trundle off around 5am. Peace and quiet at last? No, the hippo decide its time to make their presence felt with grunts, loud snuffles and honks until finally it's time to rise.

Three days travelling lie ahead, from here to Chipata, then on to Lusaka and finally back up to Kitwe. Just as well we don't know in advance just how eventful this journey will turn out to be or maybe, wild animals or not, we might have stayed right where we are.

CHAPTER EIGHTEEN: YOU HAVE COMMITTED AN INFRINGMENT!
August 2005

Problems obtaining money in Zambia will doubtless still bedevil us, yet they pale in comparison to the nightmare of hiring vehicles. Zambian roads vary between unsurfaced dirt and broken, potholed tarmac. In addition, the state of some vehicles and the competence of many drivers is questionable. Thus a sturdy, reliable 4x4 vehicle is not a luxury but an essential for safe travel.

Yet right from the first hired vehicle, problems have ranged from dud batteries to slow punctures, from missing wheel nuts to punctures in the spare wheel. Some came with no documents or with the wrong documents entirely. One was even a 'shunt' vehicle, where the front of one crashed vehicle is welded to the back of a second one. Prang one of those and the whole thing might well split in two.

Fairly early on therefore, we considered buying our own car and leaving it in Zambia between visits. After all, we were now travelling here twice a year and covering thousands of miles each visit. Fortunately, in Zambia there is a regular trade of second hand vehicles imported from Japan and driven up there from Durban or Capetown. It wasn't long therefore before we were offered a second hand Mitsubishi Sportsgear.

"It's not exactly a Hilux Surf," was our disappointed reaction, having become rather fond of their bulk and solidity when facing the rigours of driving in Zambia. Jeremy Clarkson once declared the Hilux indestructible. Yet fate, destiny or sheer bad luck landed us with a Mitsubishi Sportsgear instead, black in colour with tinted rear windows.

"You should change those tinted rear windows," advised the person selling the car. "Thieves might break in, thinking you have something to hide."

We never did change the windows, because a certain Zambian lady of traditional build and temperament was fond of travelling in the back seat. Secreted behind those same tinted windows, she could watch the world outside, while the world outside was unable to observe her. Because of its shape, size and colour, combined with a certain stubbornness, the car was soon nicknamed the 'heffalump', a name which stuck throughout.

We first acquired the 'heffalump' for the trip to Kitwe prior to driving to South Luangwa. But first its purchase entailed spending an entire day in Lusaka registering and insuring the vehicle, as well as obtaining a certificate of 'fitness' for the vehicle to travel on Zambian roads.

Later Bob reports this was a complete farce since the person who took him simply slipped the vehicle inspector twenty thousand pin and the vehicle passed without a second glance. This possibly explains the number of clapped out vehicles on roads here. Sometimes owners don't even bother to take the vehicle with them to the examination centre.

Little wonder also we risk life and limb driving here!

The new vehicle sails through the initial trip to Kitwe. However, during the trip to South Luangwa, the first niggles like burgeoning toothache appear when one wheel develops a slow puncture.

"Probably due to the appalling road surface," declares Bob, "most likely on the long drive up through South Africa and Botswana. Besides, a slow puncture's no big deal. All cars get them sometimes."

And if later one of its fancy fog lamps shakes loose somewhere along the dirt stretch between Mfuwe and Chipata, then other things are more serious than slow punctures or losing fog lamps in a country where there's never any fog.

However, on the return journey between Chipata and Lusaka, things start going badly wrong. But wait, there's that bridge over the Luangwa River to cross once more . . .

As before, we travel in convoy. Generally, our family is in front, but sometime on the second day, we reverse positions, putting us in pole position on the approach to the infamous bridge.

"You're looking remarkably happy," Bob happens to say as we zip along, slow punctures and missing fog lamps temporarily forgotten.

"It's been a fantastic week in the bush, the colours of the trees bursting into leaf, incredible blue skies every day and temperatures touching thirty degrees, maybe this is the life!"

"Though not quite as we remember it," Bob reminds me. "Remember, we've always reckoned Africa's bigger than us and . . ."

"Look!" I interrupt, pointing up into the limitless azure dry season sky.

Bob slows and squints upwards. A large bird of prey hovers overhead. Dangling from its beak, a live snake squirms helplessly. The sight sends a shiver down my spine. Is this perchance an omen? Bob was about to remind me that, just as you think you're in charge, Africa has an uncanny knack of reminding you just who is in control. Is Africa currently reasserting control?

We reach the Luangwa Bridge behind a white pickup. Of our family there's no sign.

"Shall we wait?"

Bob shrugs. "Let's follow the van over and wait on the other side."

We follow the white van onto the bridge. And no, there is no nasty troll concealed under the bridge, though a drunken soldier and an equally drunk and heavily made-up policewoman, cap perched jauntily askew atop her false hairpiece, wait on the other side.

The policewoman allows the white pickup to pass, then steps into the road, hand raised. "You have committed an infringement in that only one vehicle is allowed on the bridge at a time."

"Who says?" Bob blusters.

"There is a sign located on the approach to the bridge."

Sensing Bob's hackles rising, I lay one hand on his arm. "Well, I didn't see it and I didn't know about any regulation," he concedes huffily.

Ignorance, however, is not a valid excuse. The soldier and policewoman shake their heads as if he has broken every rule in the rulebook. "For this there is a fine of K200 000."

"You must be joking!" Bob explodes.

I fear the worst, we'll be arrested, shot . . . Suddenly I catch sight of movement. Another two vehicles are crossing the bridge both at the same time yet, to our amazement, the two of them allow both vehicles to pass unchallenged.

"Why didn't you stop those people?" I demand.

"Because they are our supervisors," smirks the soldier.

"What, mzungus in *both* cars and *both* your supervisors?" Bob's incredulity spits out like lava erupting from a volcano.

Sensing an affront to dignity, their faces suddenly change like wind veering to the opposite direction. This situation needs saving and fast.

"Officer," I try, "we are charity workers helping OVCs. Any fine will take funding away from OVCs."

"What exactly are OVCs?" The policewoman lowers her face and leers into the car, causing her cap to slip further down and settle at an even more rakish angle. The smell of alcohol on her breath is overpowering.

"Orphans and vulnerable children," I explain. "We are here in Zambia to help them."

"Aha!" Her voice rises midway between a laugh and a shriek. She thumps one hand against her ample bosom. "Me also, I am an orphan, so why don't you help me?"

To contest this would be risky, yet what to do? Just then a convoy of South African vehicles drives onto the bridge . . . *eleven vehicles all at once!* The policewoman and soldier turn to witness this manna falling from heaven. Now they can fine all eleven drivers.

The soldier moves away, however, the policewoman stays put and thrusts her head inside the car. "You have water?" she demands. "Then give me some water."

"How about a couple of beers?" In this heat, water is far more precious. I hand over two lukewarm beers. With a flick of one finger, she gives the go-ahead to drive on. Clutching her beers, she scuttles away to secrete them in the back of a dilapidated car parked at the roadside which, despite its condition, doubtless possesses a road fitness certificate.

Meanwhile every single vehicle in the South African convoy drives straight over the bridge without stopping and straight past the soldier, leaving him swaying unsteadily amidst a cloud of dust.

Not wishing to hang around we drive on at modest speed. The others have not yet appeared, so we decide to wait at the next town on the map. Unfortunately, we never make it that far. As we head up a long, slow incline, the car engine emits a long drawn out wail of anguish, "Whooooooooo!"

"I'm sure it's nothing serious . . ." Barely has Bob uttered these words, than a hundred yards further with a growl and a splutter, the engine falters and breathes its last. Slowly and inexorably the car grinds to a halt.

"That sounded pretty serious to me!"

We climb out. There is nothing around but endless bush, the middle of nowhere, somewhere between Chipata and Lusaka with not a sign of life or of habitation. As for cell phone coverage or roadside rescue, forget it!

"At least the others are behind," I say, grateful for one small blessing in a dire predicament.

Bob tries pumping the clutch pedal up and down but to no effect. He lies flat on his back on the tarmac and peers underneath the engine. "My guess is the clutch has gone."

At that moment Ali and family pull in behind. After lengthy examination by the two men and much discussion between all four of us, to the accompaniment of Thandi's screams of protest at this unwanted delay, we agree it is serious. Our son-in-law scans the surrounding bush and spies a sliver of smoke spiralling upwards from trees some distance away. The three of them decide to walk there to see if anyone can help, leaving Bob and me on the sweltering tarmac, debating what possible help might come from villagers living in mud huts . . .

"A chain!" I can't believe my eyes when they return with a man clanking a hefty chain. The man is willing to sell it, but only for an exorbitant sum of money. Yet a chain means they can tow us to the next town where possibly there might be a garage.

We negotiate the price of the chain downwards. It's still pricey, yet if it saves the day, it's worth every penny. Though that villager and his family will live *very* well for a *very* long time!

We hitch up the two cars ready for towing. But a Toyota saloon was never designed with towing a Mitsubishi Sportsgear in mind. As soon as the chain pulls tight, the 'heffalump' jerks forwards like a demonic kangaroo, leaping and bounding with no control over speed, steering or braking. Frantically I signal them to slow down. Immediately the chain slackens, dragging along the road surface and showering up dirt and gravel which hit the windscreen like mini golf balls. With the gears useless, the 'heffalump' continually runs forward threatening to bump their vehicle from behind.

This continues for forty kilometres to the next town which, fortunately, they crawl through in the hope of spotting a garage or accommodation where we might hole up for the night with our wounded vehicle. The others could travel on, then tomorrow send back a breakdown truck, even all the way from Lusaka. There is nothing.

"It looks like you'll have to tow us all the way to Lusaka." This suggestion is not well received. Yet, with no other option, it is indeed what happens.

"At least keep the speed steady," Bob pleads, before the nightmare crawl resumes behind the now struggling saloon car. Much more of this, and not one but two broken down cars will limp into Lusaka.

Eventually both drivers get the hang of towing. There is less pull from in front, while the chain stops jerking and dragging up gravel and Bob regains some control over steering and braking. Thus lulled into a sense of security, we come upon yet another police checkpoint and yes, out steps the inevitable policeman, hand raised. "You are committing an infringement," he announces.

Haven't we heard this already today?

Outside on the tarmac muttered conversation takes place between our son-in-law and the policeman whom I suspect is more interested in money than our current dilemma. We keep schtum, since we're being towed illegally by a vehicle with no registration plates. We are in the proverbial you know what, right up to our necks. Yet suddenly small money changes hands and we are waved on.

"I can't think what this will cost if every policeman at every police checkpoint between here and Lusaka has to be bought off."

"Never mind that, I'm far more worried what the repair will cost," retorts Bob.

We limp back to Lusaka. Darkness is descending as we crawl up the last stretch. We are back, but only just. Ahead lies the trial of getting the 'heffalump' back on the road. Tomorrow we're also due to travel back to Kitwe. Somehow, I don't think that will happen.

Next day, repairing the 'heffalump' takes precedence. At 8am Bob takes a taxi to Lusaka's one Mitsubishi garage, hoping they will provide a towing truck. However, they insist he gets the car to them. Since the alternative is allowing dodgy back street car mechanics to lay hands on our precious vehicle, Bob agrees to pay the cost of a towing truck, even though the price is outrageous.

Inside the stifling cab of the truck, it feels as if its engine is on fire. The towing truck is in an even worse state of health than the 'heffalump', yet doubtless it also possesses a full fitness certificate. It deposits the 'heffalump' inside the pristine premises of the Mitsubishi garage, run by Mr Tomito, all the way from Japan, simply to restore wounded Japanese cars back to full health.

Yet our family doesn't agree with this decision. They try to convince us mainstream garages in Lusaka are notorious. They will rip us off, return the car in a worse state than before, even remove parts from the engine. Unconvinced, we await instead the advice of Mr Tomito, not to be confused with tomato.

"We may be able to repair it," Mr Tomito hesitates. "But then we may not. In which case, we may have to send to Japan for parts."

"We said you should use a local mechanic!" says our daughter.

"What, let some dodgy mechanic get his hands on our car?" This comment is not well received, yet news later that the clutch has gone, is far worse. And no, they cannot get a replacement, not even all the way from Japan. The only hope is finding a second hand part in a car breaker's yard.

Unfortunately, family relations deteriorate even further. To allow the dust to settle, Bob and I decamp to a hotel to await further developments. As we enter the hotel, we recognise a guy from Flatdogs Camp in South Luangwa. Hearing our sorry tale of woe, he is adamant about one thing, "Don't let any back street car mechanic get his hands on a Mitsubishi Sportsgear!"

"So what do you suggest?"

"Man, I have my own workshop." He scribbles his name on the back of his business card. "Tommie knows where I am. Get him so send the plates round for skimming."

Talk about encountering angels when you need them most!

"For sure, the clutch will last another hundred thousand miles after that," he assures us.

Well, if namedropping combined with skimming gets us back on the road, so be it. What it doesn't do is restore family relations. Stuck in a hotel room, we await Mr Tomito's judgment as to whether the 'heffalump' can be repaired. Today, tomorrow, some day, or maybe never . . .

Finally, next day brings good news. The vehicle will be ready for collection at 5pm, a lot quicker than back street mechanics with nothing more sophisticated than spanners and screwdrivers might have achieved. Yet, since expressing similar thoughts has currently exiled us from our family, maybe they're best kept to ourselves.

At 5pm we take a taxi to the Mitsubishi garage where we kick our heels in a tiny waiting room. "You do take credit cards?" Bob suddenly thinks to ask the man on the desk.

"Ah, no," he replies. "Nor travellers cheques either, but we do take $US."

However, their exchange rate is so abysmal, we cannot consider using our precious dollars, nor can we change them elsewhere because we don't even have them with us. Besides, exchange bureaus and banks are now closed. The car must stay there another night while we return to the hotel and calculate how many dollars we need to exchange in the morning to pay over K2million for the repair.

Worse, there's *still* no communication with family!

Overnight depression settles in. Even the thought of collecting the car fails to lift dampened spirits. How long will this repair even last? To save time, Bob collects the car alone, while I pack the suitcases. When he returns, it is not with joy on his face.

"Mr Tommie himself gave the car a final test run," he explains. "He reckons the car was originally used as a rally car in Japan. That's why the clutch packed in; it also explains why it was fitted with those bizarre foot pedals."

From the start Bob has struggled with small foot pedals fitted so close together, he often pressed two pedals at once. Apparently, rally drivers do this to help them skid around corners.

"Surely there's *some* good news?"

"Mr Tommie himself tightened every nut and bolt and even fitted proper foot pedals free of charge. Then he gave us $10 back because the kwacha rallied overnight."

Finally, we set off for Kitwe three days late. Family relations remain fragile and whether the 'heffalump' will survive beyond this point, let alone the rest of this trip remains to be seen. We give the whole issue serious consideration, even making enquiries with the original safari company, with which we booked our first trip back in 2002, as to whether they could hire out the vehicle when we are overseas in an attempt to recoup some costs.

"We would be delighted," the manager assures us. "Your car will be well looked after. Indeed, it will only be hired to drivers who will be careful with it. For sure, it will only be hired out in Lusaka. No long trips at all."

With assurances such as that . . . w*hat possible reason could we have to doubt him?* What indeed!

CHAPTER NINETEEN: GOD MOVES IN MYSTERIOUS WAYS
April– >May & August– >September 2005

Previously in Kitwe, we searched for a suitable place of worship to attend when staying there. Since 90% of Zambians are Christian and most attend church on Sundays, there was plenty of choice. What was not so easy, was finding a church 'mzungus' attended, or one that started and ended at a convenient time, or even one that held a service vaguely recognisable by our then Anglican affiliation.

Since nothing suitable turned up immediately, for the first few visits to Kitwe we contented ourselves with encountering God via the medium of television. Well, He does use any channels, no pun intended, to get His message across. Indeed, in Zambia He has His own channel, TBN or Trinity Broadcasting Network, otherwise known as the God channel. Thus we began making daily acquaintance with such TV greats as T D Jakes, Paula White, Joyce Meyer and, like him or not, Barry Hinn.

We even began timing the evening meal to coincide with the evening's preacher. Besides, the God channel easily won against endless political debates on ZNBC and it was generally a different preacher each evening. Uncanny how, after failing to discover God in a local church, each evening He was now reaching us via the TV set.

However, in April 2005 we tentatively attend our first service at St Michael and All Angels, Kitwe, an Anglican church we'd located eight months ago. Anglican by name, but would it also prove Anglican by nature? 'Holy Joes' some folks back home had labelled us yet, like most people, we were happier worshipping inside our comfort zone rather than on its fringes.

Not wishing to be late, we arrive in plenty of time, though the 9am start suggested a lengthy session. From the outside the church is a nondescript, red brick building located to the rear of both the Edinburgh Hotel, a crumbling, salmon pink relic of the colonial era, and the strawberry and vanilla hues of Shoprite. The bustle of the African bus station is also close by, where blue and white minibuses cram the streets, their drivers touting out the windows for pickups. Not perhaps the quietest location for a church.

Inside the redbrick theme is continued ad infinitum along with copper fittings and large brass fans to keep the humid air circulating. Being the tail end of the rainy season, at barely 9am it's already sticky. Immediately evident is the altar dressed in red. Since we were in green time when we left UK, somewhere along the line, we've lost track that today is Pentecost.

As the service starts, the church is only half full, yet people continue trickling in. Time keeping is not Zambians' strong point. Only two other 'mzungus' are there. Many of the men sport the blue blazers of MAF, Men's Anglican Fellowship, while many of the women wear the distinctive white blouses with blue 'chitenges' of the Mothers' Union wrapped around their waists and with white scarves tied around their heads. Clearly people here wear their affiliations with pride.

On entering we're handed a much-thumbed Order of Service that at least has its roots in Common Worship, though Hymns Ancient and Modern, causes Bob to grimace. Still, the choir are already taking their places and tuning up with Gospel songs, mostly familiar but melded into the very different harmonies of African voices. In no time the congregation is singing and swaying, clapping and shaking to the music. What is there to do but sing and sway and clap as well, though we draw the line at shaking; we are English after all.

"Maybe not quite so traditional," I murmur as we take our seats.

This about sums the service up, Anglican in nature certainly to begin with, yet somewhere along the way the praise and worship erupts into African exuberance. Hands waving in the air, women ululate and swing, shaking generously proportioned hips. And all those smiling faces, oh that people smiled like that in churches in the UK.

"Maybe English people simply lack enthusiasm and exuberance for the Lord," I say, trying to make myself heard above the increasing volume. Someone somewhere has upped the controls.

"Could be," Bob mouths back.

Eventually the service picks up where it left off with more orderly worship as it heads for the notices. Even though a comprehensive notice sheet was given out as we entered the church, they still read out every notice on the sheet. Maybe because some people there can't read English, though a whole hour has vanished already and there's no sign of a sermon yet.

Prayers of intercession follow. If we occasionally complain these go on too long back home, they're as nothing compared to here. The intercessor, a small man, of humble demeanour, sinks to his knees in the centre of the nave in front of the chancel steps, clasps his hands tightly, then raises his arms heavenwards. There is, worryingly, no sign of a script to keep him on track.

He begins so quietly, we struggle to catch what he says. However, he soon gets into his stride as, voice rising and falling, he exhorts God to forgive us humble sinners. He lauds, praises and magnifies the Almighty in rising and falling cadences, at times so carried away, he lapses into his native tongue, Bemba. And, in a country where HIV AIDS, TB and malaria are rife, the list of the sick and dying brought before the Lord is seriously long.

Meanwhile, lunch slips ever further over the horizon.

Twenty minutes later, knees creaking in protest, we heave ourselves back onto the pews. And we still haven't had the sermon! Yet even as the preacher begins, it becomes apparent this is what the congregation has eagerly awaited. The sermon is excellently prepared, competently delivered and would put many UK preachers to shame. What catches us unawares, is the congregation's unashamed appreciation, which corresponds directly to the preacher's powerful delivery. They whistle approval, clap loudly in encouragement, with inevitably much ululating from the women. Finally, the preacher takes his seat to one last tumultuous round of applause.

The choir rises and launches into an exuberant rendering of: 'We shall enter his gates with thanksgiving in our hearts,' swinging and dancing in the aisles while the collection is taken and delivered to the front. The amount collected the previous week is printed on the newssheet for all to see. It is amazing how people with so little manage to give so much. Some of the congregation are clearly professional, however others are shabbily dressed. Nevertheless, tithing is both preached and practised by all.

Are we there yet?

No, we're not, there's still The Peace, followed by an enthusiastic welcome for visitors. Each visitor must stand and announce who they are and where they come from into a microphone, all to the accompaniment of yet more clapping. And since, there are several visitors today, they also burst into their special welcome song.

Are we there?

Yes, finally we are, except for one last hymn, 'When peace like a river', sung like most of the hymns today in beautiful melding harmonies and delivered at a funereal pace. How slowly can one sing such perennial favourites as 'Praise my soul the King of heaven', which started off the service? In Africa, very slowly indeed, is the answer.

True, they also sang modern songs to which most people knew the words. Just as well since Hymns Ancient and Modern certainly doesn't contain any modern hymns. Some songs and sung responses were in Bemba, but even without words, it was easy to sing along.

Two and a half hours later, we emerge into bright sunlight. Even as we leave this mammoth service, the choir is still going, keyboard, guitar, drums, tambourine all raising the roof in one final chorus, while singers clap and dance in a circle around the musicians.

Oh glory be!

Yet all is not over, tea and coffee await visitors in the resident priest's house. He laughs when we comment how services are somewhat longer here than in the UK and recalls in great detail his one trip to the UK many years ago.

"Did you find the service too long?" I ask Bob when finally we are back at the flat.

"Not really," he confesses. "I enjoyed it!" Which was apparent from the way he was singing and swaying along with everyone else. "Though I think people in UK might have been worried about their Sunday dinner burning in the oven."

After today, we both agree, people here come to church prepared to take however much time it needs to praise God and to the best of their ability. And they certainly don't cut any corners along the way.

Thus, August 2005 finds us back in Kitwe following the visit to South Luangwa with the trauma of the car breaking down, as well as the rupture of family relations. And, if that's not enough, things aren't going too well at Kaputula either. Not surprisingly, that first Sunday back in Kitwe finds us seeking solace in St Michael and All Angels.

Initially I'm reluctant to attend. "What will we find there, that we haven't already found by praying and reading our Bible?"

"This is the 'day that the Lord has made' and all that!" Bob's timely reminder rouses me from bed, though not exactly raring to go. Yet what is the alternative, but to remain here feeling miserable all morning?

What we do not know until we arrive, is that today is a healing service and the theme is 'Suffering'. Since some people leave the 7am service and go straight back into the 9am service, in a country where there is so much poverty, sickness and death, clearly suffering is a popular subject.

Or, did He to whom we've been praying earnestly all week for a restoration of family harmony and relief from the trials of charity work, by any chance arrange this subject especially for today?

This morning, the sermon is not quite so long arriving, maybe because there's a lot to get through what with a sermon as well as healing and communion. Yet as soon as the preacher starts speaking, an uncomfortable feeling stirs somewhere deep inside.

"There is someone here today who is suffering. Someone who is bleeding inside." She, for it is a woman preaching, pauses and sweeps her eyes around the congregation searching for that person. I keep my head lowered, but there's no escaping the raking eyes, the penetrating voice . . . "There is someone here today whose heart is breaking."

I sneak a peek sideways. Bob sits stony faced, though that's not to say his emotions are not also in a state of roiling turmoil.

I lean sideways and whisper, "How does she know what we're going through?" For know she most certainly does. A week, in which the Kaputula community has driven us to the brink, has also passed with no contact from family in Lusaka. Today, my heart is heavy with sadness.

The preacher presses on, confessing that, while writing this sermon, God spoke directly to her saying there would be someone in great need in church today. "And I know that person is here!" Her voice reverberates round the church.

My palms are sticky with sweat. I can feel myself going hot and cold all over. Much more of this and I shall surely faint or burst into tears. I consider

112

making a sudden dash for the door, yet imagine her voice calling after me, *'Stop, I know you are the one!'*

So I stay, willing this to end. But there is still the healing part of the service to come. So far Bob hasn't uttered a word. I have no idea whether he feels equally overwhelmed, yet my mind is made up. Even if I walk the length of that church alone, right up to the altar and with all eyes in the church upon me, I intend going up to receive healing.

I stand shakily, preparing to take the first tentative step when Bob slips into place beside me. I dare not look at him fearing resolve might crumble. Instead I focus on the altar and the woman waiting there. We reach her and kneel together in front of the altar rail. The woman bends low so our voices carry only between us. She lays a hand on both of us, "What is troubling you, my brother and my sister?"

Stumbling over the words, we tell of a family rift and of how troubled our hearts are, not only by that, but also by problems bedevilling the work of Starfish: the bribery, corruption, threats, irreconcilable differences, arguments and disputes that threaten to bring work to a standstill, of how the feeling grows daily we're too old, too weary to carry on any longer, alone in a foreign country without any backup or safety net to catch us should we fall.

Inevitably tears begin streaming down my face. I hold onto Bob who holds onto me and we both grip for dear life to the hands of this woman who appears to have been granted *supernatural* insight into our suffering.

Her voice reverberating loudly enough to reach heaven itself, she begins raining God's blessing down upon us, upon the work of Starfish and upon fractured family relationships. She rails against the forces of evil currently disrupting our lives. She calls upon the power of Almighty God Himself to drive away the demons behind it. She prays not only for us and our family, but also for our continuing work and for a renewed trust in the Almighty, because somewhere, in the midst of all this, we have managed to wander away from trusting in Him.

Still holding hands, we make our way back down the aisle to our seat. Every eye in the congregation is turned our way. They may never have seen the like from a couple of aging 'mzungus' before, but there's a first time for everything and it may well provide food for discussion later.

Not surprisingly today's service stretches into a three hours long marathon, and there are still cups of tea afterwards. Eventually we leave, thankful to have received so great a blessing from people who are not only total strangers, but also of a different race and culture.

Later that same evening Paula White is preaching on God channel. If we've not heard enough already today on the theme of suffering, then yes, the Almighty is hammering the message home on TV tonight.

"Rejoice in your suffering," Paula preaches from TV screen, "because of the opportunities it presents to you."

This may perhaps be one stage too far at the present moment. Nothing has changed since this morning, other than we both feel calmer and ready to let God take control. For sure, only one week of this trip remains in which to sort out problems here in Kitwe, as well as to get family relations back on a proper footing in Lusaka.

In fact, it takes all week to sort out the Kitwe end. At the end of it, we head south once more to Lusaka with no idea what to expect. Yet to our relief, all is forgiven, and forgetting will doubtless come with time. That evening Ali asks us to baby-sit while she attends a party.

On her return, she mentions she hasn't had a drink all evening. "Didn't fancy one," she shrugs.

"Strange," I comment to Bob later. "Ali's no drinker, all the same . . ."

"What are you suggesting?" he asks naively.

"Just that, if I were a betting person, which I am not, I wouldn't mind betting that pretty soon there'll be the patter of another pair of tiny feet!"

"Go on!" he laughs.

But I keep any further speculation to myself. The next few months will prove me right or wrong anyways. If nothing else, as we have been reminded this trip, God moves in mysterious ways His wonders to perform.

CHAPTER TWENTY: MISSION IMPOSSIBLE
February 2006

Trips to Zambia are invariably fraught with problems, of which the hassle of money: how to obtain it, carry it, keep it safe and not least, how to spend it wisely, remains one of the greatest. Yet, winner by a whisker is the issue of transport, because of risks inherent in hiring vehicles with hidden dangers and the disastrous decision to buy our own vehicle. This vehicle is currently on a last warning: *Break down again and you're in the knacker's yard!*

A third nightmare is that of finding suitable accommodation. In Lusaka we stay with our daughter. However, our charity work takes us 250 miles north to the copper mining town of Kitwe whose most notable feature is smoke belching from the mine chimneys. For this read: miles away from tourist or scenic attractions thus severely limited as to accommodation options.

To date we've tried Kitwe's one hotel, the Edinburgh, a crumbling relic of colonial days, plus several guesthouses catering mainly for single Zambians or 'mzungu' businessmen, both of whom occasionally seek diversions many would consider inappropriate. We've also tried self-catering, but this means running the gauntlet of queues in Shoprite, as well as cooking and washing up at the end of long and at times harrowing days spent at centres for orphans and vulnerable children.

So what other options remain as we land in Zambia in 2006? It's not the ideal time for a visit, since it's also the height of the rainy season. However, needs must. Right now, our daughter also urgently needs to find alternative accommodation. The sitting tenant of the house she's currently renting, is due back any day from the States and may not take kindly to someone else living in her house.

If all this is not enough, the Zambian economy has inexplicably rallied, creating an abysmal exchange rate of just over three thousand kwachas to the dollar. This has almost halved purchasing power both for personal expenditure as well as for the Starfish budget. Prices in shops, lodges, garages, everywhere have effectively doubled, plus a fruit-fly infestation of crops in South Africa has created a chronic lack of fresh fruit and vegetables.

Oh Zambia, how we miss all your trials during absences overseas!

With a view to trying a new avenue as regards accommodation, we agree to meet Dinah, a wealthy Zambian originally from Kitwe, now living and working in Lusaka. Dinah may be interested in renting out her private home in Kitwe during our time up there.

"It's a beautiful house," we're told, "very Zambian in style and with all mod cons." Zambian in style could mean anything from a mud hut to a concrete palace tastelessly decorated in lavender and black, or tiled from floor to ceiling in glittering ceramic tiles and with every knick-knack and gee-gaw imaginable. Nevertheless, we agree to meet Dinah to discuss the possibility of a rental.

Dinah is a large and traditionally built Zambian lady with an outlandish headpiece and a booming voice. She sweeps into the house, enveloping Thandi in a crushing embrace to which Thandi objects volubly. It is not set to be a quiet encounter.

In fact, the meeting is cagey, each skating around the other like first-timers on an ice rink. We have no idea what we're letting ourselves in for, while Dinah equally has no idea who we are other than Alison's parents. The question of rental costs is delicately avoided like a hole in the ice, though she seems happy for us to pass by her property in Kitwe. If we like it, we'll stay; if not, goodness knows where we'll go.

However, Kitwe is a few days away. For the moment, we must assist our daughter, now a single mum with a second baby on the way – *I was right about that last one!* Since she also has a full-time job, solving her particular housing crisis must come before our own needs.

Thus, two days after arriving in Zambia, we swap charity work in Kitwe for finding rental accommodation in Lusaka. First stop are adverts in the daily press for flats to rent. Flat being a ubiquitous term in Zambia for anything with four walls and a roof on ground level as opposed to an apartment in a block of flats. Anything with more than one storey is classed as a house.

Confused? So are we!

The search is complicated by a chronic lack of suitable properties in Lusaka. Most either go before the advert reaches the paper, or else never existed in the first place. Bogus adverts routinely appear in the paper with the aim of relieving prospective tenants of hard-earned cash.

By lunchtime on the first day we've only succeeded in viewing one dreadful flat. Two others still have people living in them. Not a good sign in Zambia where there's no guarantee tenants will move out when their lease is up. Already it's beginning to look like mission impossible!

But no, there's a semi-detached bungalow close to town which the owner is currently doing up. Moreover, it's within budget and, since the owner is on site, we can view it right now.

We bundle a protesting Thandi into the car. House viewing rates low in the priorities of a two year old. Not that it matters. The owner spots 'mzungus' and immediately hikes up the monthly rental from K2m to K3m, claiming there was a mistake in the advert.

We drive off in disgust. It's bad enough hiking up the price of cement in Kitwe, but doing the same with house rentals is appalling. However, Ali admits it wouldn't have suited anyways. Being so close to town, it was a complete no-no security-wise for a single mum with two children.

Later that afternoon we have an appointment to view another flat in Kabulonga, near where Ali currently lives. Arriving at the address, the guard on the gate appears strangely reluctant to let us in.

"There is no flat for renting here," he claims. This is a pity because the gated complex of garden flats is ideal security-wise. There is even a communal swimming pool. "But there is a property for rent further up the road," he reveals.

Since the supposed leasing agent for this flat is currently not answering his phone for reasons best known to him, we head further up the road. Outside yet another pair of eight feet high locked and bolted solid iron security gates, we are again denied entry. Anyone would think we were trying to get into Fort Knox!

Eventually persistence combined with white faces opens the gates, though the guard shows us nothing more than the outside of a flat similar to the one for rent but not the actual flat, because people are still living in it. Even though at this moment they're not in, as in not being there to open the door.

Confused? So are we!

Determined not to give up, Ali knocks on the door of an adjacent house. The door opens a crack and a black face peeps warily out.

"Aieeh, you must be careful," whispers this person. "Sometimes bogus agents do a deal with outgoing tenants to trick people into paying a deposit."

She does however reveal the name of the organisation authorised to rent out all the flats. Since it's now late Saturday afternoon, nothing can be achieved before Monday morning.

"At least I'm ready when that agent rings on Sunday offering to meet us at the first flat, even though he clearly hasn't any keys to take us inside," declares Ali. Dodgy dealing at its worst!

By Monday the situation is desperate. The American lady returns on Wednesday on the early morning flight and doubtless will be angry to find squatters occupying her house.

Back to the daily press and the same problems as before. Either the property doesn't exist, or it's still occupied or is over budget. Then a new obstacle appears, a demand for a £10 viewing fee. In the entire morning, we manage to see one property, in the wrong area and at the wrong price.

Eventually in the afternoon, we arrange another viewing in Kabulonga. This 'flat' is in the right area although over budget, but there's a chance of negotiating the landlord down in price. We arrange to meet the 'agent' outside his office in Cairo Road from where he will conduct us to the property. Does meeting him outside an office make him genuine? Who knows!

He directs us back to Kabulonga, from where we've just driven into town, back once more into Chila Avenue, past the turning into Sable, then Roan Avenue and onto the far end of Kudu Avenue, which just happens to be the road Ali lives on. True it's a long road, so the house we're heading for could be anywhere along it . . . But no, after going all around the houses, literally as well as figuratively, travelling the full length of Kudu Avenue, we end up outside a house on the plot next door to the one Ali currently lives on.

This 'flat' is a three bed-roomed detached bungalow on the side of the plot adjacent to the owner's larger house. It is clean, safe, secure, everything it should be apart from one thing, it's expensive, though the rental does include water, electricity, taxes and supposedly security. Since nothing else has come up, this seems the best option. We make appreciative noises to the owner and promise to bring our daughter back later.

"We're sure she'll take it," I promise the agent.

"Are we?" asks Bob when we're back sitting on the veranda next door.

"Not at all, but the agent doesn't need to know that!"

Unfortunately, the heavens open at 5pm releasing a downpour of tropical dimensions. In no time, the garden is flooded. Water runs down the road outside like a river. Negotiating the pathway between the two houses is like crossing a swamp, while the garden next door has become a swimming pool, though not of man's making. The sky has darkened, threatening more rain. Not the most favourable ambience for house viewing. While we recall its sunny aspect earlier this afternoon, now darkness and rain create a gloomy atmosphere.

"Actually, the owner wasn't over friendly," remarks Ali as we head back, picking our way through puddles. "Plus, with adjoining properties, if he doesn't pay his utility bills, I get cut off as well."

"At least it's nicely painted in cream," I try, "not lavender and black."

"Yes," Ali concedes, "but it was too large and *didn't* include security. The owner was adamant: the gate between the two properties stays shut at all times. Obviously, the security guard stays *his* side of the fence."

"Couldn't you employ your own guard?" I persist.

"Forget it, Mum," she responds wearily, "that house simply won't work."

Mission impossible *not* yet achieved and only one day left!

Next day is Valentine's Day. Lusaka is awash with red roses, yet romance is far from our minds. At 9am Bob and I set off for 'mzungu' run rental offices, this time with a revised budget *upwards*.

In the first office, everyone has gone to a meeting and no-one is available to help. The second, which claims to deal in desirable residences, has nothing desirable on their books.

"Except there might be one," concedes the receptionist. She agrees to phone us later. "For sure by the end of the day I'll have something for your daughter when she flies in from America," she says brightly.

What is the point in explaining it's not our daughter flying in, but the person in whose house she's living. If the rightful tenant is on tomorrow morning's flight, she could arrive as early as 7am.

On to yet another office which has a flat in Kabulonga, but unfortunately without security, though that could be added on for an extra K500 000 per month. In desperation, we agree to view, but it's immediately apparent that, even with the best security, any car left outside would be gone by morning.

Thoroughly dispirited we head back to tell Ali we've failed abysmally . . .

"Good news!" she beams. "The house next door's coming up for rent."

"But we visited that one last night . . ."

"No, another one right here on *this* plot!"

Ali lives on a plot containing four small bungalows, or 'flats' in Zambian parlance. Two are detached and two are semi-detached. All, to our knowledge, are currently occupied. Except, the guy next to the gate is behind on his rent and has apparently given notice.

"As of today?" I ask, since there are less than twenty-four hours left.

"Not exactly today," Ali hesitates. "More like the end of the month . . ."

Are we any nearer a solution? The guy in question is currently in South Africa. All his stuff is not just in the bungalow next door, but also in the one attached to it, which he was using as an office. We've taken not one step forwards, but two steps backwards.

"I think it's best if you two head off to Kitwe," suggests Ali.

"What, leaving you homeless with a two year old and another baby on the way?" This doesn't bear thinking about.

"I can stay with a friend till this guy returns . . ."

"And if he doesn't return?"

Fortunately, she's spared from answering by the phone ringing. One of the agencies has three flats all within budget to view tomorrow.

Since Ali is in meetings, Bob and I visit the flats. The first is out of town towards the airport, but that's not too great a problem. What is a problem, is sitting outside the property hooting the car horn for five minutes and no-one coming to open the gate until finally, the agent gets out the car and opens the gate himself, which means potential burglars could do exactly the same.

On to property number two, a detached house still under construction. The builders are still on site, so no point in asking whether it will be ready for occupation by the morning.

This leaves property number three, an ugly redbrick building with as much appeal as an army barracks. Not that it matters since yet again, we can't get inside until the agent gets the keys later. Despite its exterior, the flat is pleasant inside yet has one major hazard. At the top of the stairs is an overhanging balcony with spaces between balustrades that a two year old could squeeze through, falling twelve feet onto solid concrete down below.

Decision time has arrived. But first we view the house on the same plot that's supposed to be vacant at the end of the month. Since both landlady and defaulting tenant are 'mzungus', there is some likelihood it will actually become vacant on the proposed date. And, more importantly, it ticks all the boxes!

"Shall I risk it?" asks Ali over lunch.

"It's your call," we respond. "But it means two weeks staying in someone else's house."

"Meaning you two can head off to Kitwe."

Ah yes, and all the uncertainty awaiting up there, deciding between Dinah's Zambian-style mansion or yet another guesthouse with problems of outside drinking and solicitation, even putting up with self-catering again. Maybe house hunting in Lusaka is an easier option after all.

In the end, Ali opts to spend two weeks at a friend's house to await the return of the guy from South Africa. At least then she'll be moving back into a house on the same plot as she's moving off. When the landlady agrees to sign a written agreement, it clinches the deal.

Mission impossible achieved? Who knows! The end of the month is still two weeks away and a lot can happen in two weeks in Zambia.

CHAPTER TWENTY-ONE: HOW THE OTHER HALF LIVES ZAMBIA STYLE
Feb – > March 2006

Next day, first priority is evacuating the house before the American lady returns to find squatters in situ. Having removed the bulk of stuff the night before to where Ali and the girls are staying for the next two weeks, we escape by a whisker.

All that remains then is to head north to Kitwe and the uncertainty of a private rental awaiting us there. Apparently, Dinah has informed staff at her house to expect us. But where are they? We sit outside yet more locked iron gates and ten feet high walls mounted with razor wire and electric fencing, tooting the car horn for someone to let us into this mini Fort Knox. When finally we are inside, the garden is a verdant oasis of peace and calm. Two housemaids plus gardener greet us, while a night guard will appear later.

This begs the question, what exactly is Dinah guarding here?

The two maids, Prisca and Juliet, are anxious to please. They show us around the house switching on and off, or off and on, every light bulb and appliance and pointing out every single security switch and alarm. A Zambian once said it's not worth having too much in Zambia, because the more you have, the more people will try to steal it. Dinah's exaggerated need for security perhaps proves this point.

Eventually we convince Prisca and Juliet that, after five hours in the car, what we need is a toilet, lunch and a swim, preferably in that order. The first presents no problem; the second proves a minefield. Both maids follow me around the kitchen watching every move. As soon as I put anything down, it's picked up, washed, dried and put away. Even the tea-towel is meticulously folded and hung back up again. When we finally reach the swimming pool, the gardener opens the gate, wipes down the chairs and sweeps the concrete surrounding the pool.

"Such cosseting means only one thing," I call across the turquoise waters of Dinah's private pool to Bob prostrate on a sun-bed. "We're staying!"

Later we explore the house alone. There are three bedrooms all en-suite, each in different pastel shades, plus a master suite for Dinah and her husband who is currently away on business.

"That's not to say he won't turn up at any time," whispers Bob as we peer around the bedroom door at unashamed opulence in a country where people are dying of poverty, starvation and HIV AIDS.

Ashamed of our nosiness, we creep back to the main lounge which is midway between a funeral parlour and the inside of a chief's palace with heavy black and gold brocaded drapes and burnished brass and gold fittings.

Would we even dare to sit on the plush leather suite, let alone put feet up in front of the TV? Thankfully there's a separate smaller and cosier TV room.

In contrast, the dining room looks as if it's come straight out of a bridal magazine, with dining chairs draped in white covers and windows and table festooned in white lace. Double china cabinets are filled with gleaming china and sparkling crystal. In one corner somewhat incongruously stands a large white chest freezer, filled with packages of bloodied meat.

"Frozen village goat, if I'm not mistaken." Bob drops the lid with a bang.

The kitchen is the only room resembling anything familiar, albeit circa 1970, with faded cream cabinets ornately trimmed with gold veneer and gold handles and crammed with china and oddments dating back to the colonial era, almost enough to serve the entire Zambian army at one sitting.

Outside the kitchen is a laundry room, then a fitness room beside the swimming pool. Detached from the house is a guest cottage, presumably where the maids sleep, since Dinah said someone would be on site at all times. Two further residents remain, ferocious guard dogs, caged up at the rear of the house, from where fortunately they cannot access either the front garden where the pool is, or the side of the house where the car is parked.

"Are they safe?" I ask the maids.

"No, they are not safe." Prisca, or else Juliet, implies these brutes are trained to kill. "Even the gate between the front and back garden is unlocked every evening at 8pm and they are let loose so they can patrol all night."

"But the guard?"

"Ah, they know him. However, they don't know you, so you must not to go outside when they are loose. In the morning, when I feed them, they go back into their cage."

I only pray they do so obediently!

Grand tour over, we sink exhausted on loungers beside the pool. Such luxury is very different to what we're used to in Kitwe. But can we live with all this security, not to mention dogs that might eat us alive, servants to wait on every whim and furniture we dare not sit on? Even the lap of luxury comes with a hefty price tag!

Ah bliss, the peace and quiet of staying in a real house . . . er, not quite! Music blaring from a radio wakes us at 1am. At 5am loud voices rouse us once more. Clearly the pink bedroom with matching en-suite is rather too close to next door's servants' quarters.

Juliet, who has set up breakfast in the bridal dining room, informs us, "The owner of the house next door keeps erratic hours. However, maybe you could move into the bedroom next door." This seems a good idea, since the blue bedroom, also with matching en-suite, overlooks the gardens and swimming pool as opposed to a brick wall adjacent to an inconsiderate neighbour. However, first Juliet must ask the madam who, apparently, phones each day, partly to check the maids are still on site, but also to check we're not wrecking her house, or emptying her freezer of dead goat meat. The whole arrangement smacks of a blind date, based on a thin sliver of trust.

"Madam says the security guard must go next door to request the neighbour to make less noise," reports Juliet at lunchtime.

So, no blue bedroom, just a prayer this resolves the problem. At least there is good news from our daughter. The tenant of the house she's moving into, has agreed to depart next Tuesday, meaning a return to Lusaka next weekend. Even better, all our stuff can stay here instead of having to lug it down and back again.

Today Juliet, whether from vigilance or curiosity, follows me around the kitchen like a lapdog. Since she is the only maid who's turned up today, I ask her to prepare a salad then stew some guavas bought yesterday from a roadside seller, since the dearth of fresh fruit and vegetables in shops continues without relief. Juliet is clearly bemused as to why 'mzungus' would eat something that falls from trees and is sold cheaply by the bucket-load at the roadside. However, I tell her to wash them, peel them, quarter them, then poach them gently in a little water with sugar until they're soft, then leave then to get cold.

"You want them cold?" The logic of cooking something only to eat it cold, is beyond Juliet. Surely the point of cooking food is to eat it hot? Clearly a 'mzungu' in the kitchen will take some getting used to. Guavas duly stewed and left to cool, she now watches preparation of pasta and vegetable sauce with something approaching awe.

That evening, being Friday, we decide to eat in a nearby restaurant, except one thing must be made *very* clear. The guard must *not* let the dogs loose until we're back inside the house. To be absolutely certain, we confirm it with him as he stands to attention by the gate, saluting as we pass.

"Heavens, does he think we're royalty?" Bob jokes.

"Just as long as he keeps those dogs locked up until we return!"

In the restaurant, we sit by open veranda doors gazing out into the velvety blackness of an African night. After a couple of glasses of wine, Africa becomes magical once more. It's possible even to forget we live cosseted behind security walls, electric fences, security guards, dogs, all necessary to keep man and property safe on this dark continent.

It still doesn't detract from the magic!

Back at Dinah's house, the security gates swing open in response to the car horn. The guard salutes as we sweep in, before locking and bolting the gate. As for the dogs? I open the car door a crack. But they're locked in their cage with bones to keep them happy till we're safely inside.

We scuttle in then follow the routine Juliet explained on the first night. Every single door to the outside is locked and bolted and keys removed. Proceeding backwards from the front door to the pink bedroom, we shut and lock with a key every internal door as well.

"I'm not sure we sleep any more soundly for all this palaver," I say as we settle down for the night. "Or how safe we are! We lock up at night, removing all the keys from the locks. All the windows are shut and barred with burglar bars, then we lock every internal door behind us as we go to bed, then finally lock ourselves inside the bedroom."

"Meaning what exactly?"

"If there was a fire, how would we escape this death trap?"

"Just as long as that infernal radio doesn't come on in the middle of the night!" Bob turns over and falls asleep.

Since we're returning to Lusaka at the end of the following week, we remain in Kitwe over the weekend hoping to relax by the swimming pool. But first we need to convince Juliet she doesn't need to do *everything* for us. Perhaps because it's the weekend, she tries doubly hard. But does she have to watch Bob's daily aspirin dissolving in water?

We are eating lunch by the swimming pool, when Prisca approaches to say she's knocking off. Her puckered expression resembles that of a camel with the hump. "I should have knocked off at twelve, but since I did not start until 8 o'clock I have remained until two o'clock."

Was that because we didn't open the door until eight this morning!

"Also, there was a problem with the freezer in the kitchen which only now I have finished dealing with."

Apparently, while we were out shopping, the kitchen freezer stopped working and flooded the kitchen floor which Prisca dealt with by removing our frozen meat and dumping it in with the dead goat in the dining room freezer. Thanks a million, Prisca!

Feeling generous, I tell Juliet also to knock off. Yet her dismayed expression indicates madam has told her to watch the 'mzungus' at all times. Eventually she concedes defeat, but only after finishing the ironing, washing the dishes and going around the house drawing all the curtains, meaning either we have to draw them all back again or else sit in darkness. Oh, the trials of having housemaids!

By Sunday Juliet finally accepts we don't need watching all the time. We are not going to run off with the family silver or the dead goat. Prisca, on the other hand, understands perfectly and disappears to wherever maids disappear to on Sundays in Kitwe.

Unfortunately, the weather deteriorated yesterday and it rains almost non-stop for twenty-four hours. After a day stuck inside watching relentless rain falling in torrents, we retire to bed thoroughly depressed. The one thing we pray for is a peaceful night. Alas the radio begins blaring again at 5am on Monday morning. Finally, Juliet concedes we should move from the pink en-suite to the blue en-suite.

"I just hope Dinah doesn't mind," I say as we sink into bed that night.

"All that matters is an undisturbed night before the journey to Lusaka." Bob reaches for the light cord. Suddenly noise explodes fit to waken if not the dead, then at least the noisy neighbour. Deafening reverberations echo and re-echo filling the darkness and booming out into the night. The guard dogs, hungry to sink their teeth into an intruder, begin barking madly.

"Waa-woo! Waa-woo!" The hideous racket continues relentlessly.

"Whoops! Did I pull an alarm cord instead of a light switch? Maybe if I pull it again . . ."

"DON'T YOU DARE!"

Eventually the racket stops. Since neither the police nor security firm turns up with reinforcements, Bob switches off the proper light switch and we get some sleep before the long drive tomorrow.

Meanwhile in Lusaka Ali has spent two weeks at a friend's house awaiting the move, meaning we have nowhere to stay. Unlike Kitwe, the problem with Lusaka hotels is not lack of choice, but being able to afford them. Because of all the international business plus donor money floating around the capital, hotel accommodation in Lusaka is not cheap. We settle on the Chrismar Hotel, not so cheap as to be shoddy, yet given the cost of cool drinks beside the pool, not even cheap at all.

Next day, we head out to where Ali is staying to spend an hour playing with Thandi, though it's also an excuse to see how wealthy white expats live on their small farm covering twenty acres. First obstacle is getting past a speak-easy on the electronic gates. Inside, four of the twenty acres are walled and surrounded by electric fences. There is also a panic alarm system inside the house wired up to a rapid response system, even more sophisticated security than at Dinah's house.

We sit on the veranda sipping cool drinks and surveying verdant gardens, manicured lawns, swimming pool, tennis court and beyond that stables and eating chocolate cake baked by the cook, while nanny baths the children. Bob lies back replete, chocolate smeared from ear to ear.

"I could be tempted by this life," I confess in a moment of reckless abandon. "It certainly frees a woman up for other things."

Strangely the man of the house doesn't appear impressed. What does he suppose I'd do, *have an affair?*

Back at Chrismar, things are warming up for Friday evening with a jazz band playing in the open-air bar cum dining area. Since our room lies midway between pool, bar and car park, goodness knows what the night will bring.

These fears are well founded. Music blasts till gone midnight, while patrons consume an ocean of alcohol. When the music finally dies down, they begin shouting and phoning outside, then chasing shrieking women up and down the passageway. Meanwhile out in the car park, car doors slam and voices are raised in arguments over women or lost keys or both.

Finally, at 3am all quietens down, yet we must be up at 6.30am for the removal. Firstly, we head for the farm to pick up Ali, then back into town to meet a removal truck, which of course is not there, though someone called Tennis promises faithfully to come up with a truck. Meanwhile we do a couple of runs to the new house where a new maid called Dora awaits. Dora is skeletal and wearing more makeup than a fashion model, yet quickly proves herself a gem. She's already inside and has started scrubbing down walls and washing windows and floors. There's only one fly in the ointment, the previous tenant is still buzzing around and has left a double bed in the main bedroom, clothing in cupboards, a locked cupboard full of private stuff, a pile of boxes in the living room and two rabid dogs, one with tumours dangling from its belly.

No sooner has he removed his stuff, than the truck trundles in belching thick black smoke and piled high with Ali's worldly possessions. Zambians leap off the truck and begin crawling over the house like busy black ants. Furniture is offloaded and brought inside faster than I can call out where to put it. Dora and her bucket are swept aside in the haste to get everything installed. For a while all is chaos till a semblance of order is achieved by lunchtime when Ali fetches Thandi to see her new home. With her is Sandra, mother of Dora and Thandi's new nanny. Let's hope she doesn't let Thandi wander back into the house she left two weeks previously and where the American lady is now re-installed.

Mission finally achieved? Pretty much so!

In no time, we're back tooting outside Dinah's house, waiting for the gate to open. Home from home, except Dinah's husband is also expected to arrive for a funeral. Hopefully he won't object to strangers sleeping in the blue bedroom not the pink one.

The first night passes with no sign of him. The maid thinks he may have stayed over in Ndola or else returned to Lusaka. Just in case, Bob doesn't go into the kitchen in his underpants to make early morning tea, while I don a housecoat for breakfast in the bridal room. Yet, returning later after an arduous day in the bush, shattered, hot, sweaty, dirty, with the car splattered in red mud, the elusive husband is waiting to greet us dressed in his neatly pressed funeral outfit and with a brand new shiny Pajero sitting on the drive.

The days slip by, drawing ever closer to the end of another trip. And if a falling out between Juliet and Prisca, because the absence of the 'madam' and the return of the husband to Lusaka, leads Prisca to think life has become one long holiday, don't for one moment imagine life here is nothing but lazing beside swimming pools in lush tropical gardens. Actually, the fall out between them worsens. They start arriving later each morning, then cease locking and unlocking doors, even drawing back the curtains. If we don't do it, the house remains in darkness most of the day. Even the breakfast table is not cleared.

"Was it something we said?" I put to Bob.

"No, when the cat's away the mice will play and they've simply fallen out." Such wisdom from a man, on things female, whether black or white!

Whether Bob intentionally attempts to resolve the situation or not, but he sets fire to his toast on our final morning, forgetting it's not a pop-up toaster. Smoke fills the kitchen and pours out the back door setting the dogs barking and causing both maids to come running from wherever they're hiding. For sure they're not at that moment in the kitchen watching the toast burn.

Just as well we weren't locked in the bedroom, or that could have been the end of us!

But that's not all. Since we're leaving that morning, the gardener decides to 'bathe' the car. Instead of using a hosepipe, he pours bucket after bucket of water over the bonnet to get rid of the mud. Thus, instead of winging us swiftly down to Lusaka, the 'heffalump', which has already spent ten days out of thirty this month in dock, is yet again back in the garage.

Oh, the joys of Zambia! There you are imagining we've finally got it sussed. No such luck, Zambia still has more than a few tricks to pull on us yet!

CHAPTER TWENTY-TWO: ONE DEATH TOO MANY!
July- > August, 2006

"There are a lot of Cookes on this flight," says the man at BA when, in July 2006, Ali phones to add newly arrived Becca onto her ticket.

"Yes," agrees Ali, "and please could we all sit together?"

"No problem," he assures her.

Why then at check-in, are Ali and the two children in one part of the plane, has Bob been bumped up to World Traveller Plus, and myself allocated an unreserved booking, meaning I may not get on the plane at all?

"You could put us all in World Traveller Plus?" The man behind the desk is not amused. Possibly because Becca is squalling, while two year old Thandi has emptied out the contents of her hand baggage onto the floor and is currently removing all her clothes.

Eventually all is sorted. Bob renounces his upgrade and is given an extra legroom seat instead. Ali and the children are given bulkhead seats with the promise of a bassinet for Becca, while I end up sitting cramped behind them, but at least I'm on the plane. A ten and a half hours night flight lies ahead with two fractious children, before landing in freezing cold temperatures. It may be sweltering in the UK with gardens bursting with raspberries, strawberries, blackcurrants, lettuces and tomatoes, but in Zambia it's midwinter and a chilly seven degrees.

We arrive to a spotless house and Sandra and Dora waiting to get to grips with two exhausted children. Just as well, since the rest of us feel like zombies. And so begins another trip! Our daughter is now a single mum with two young children and hopes to return to work soon. Charity work must take second place since hands-on grandparents are required. Besides, it's a public holiday weekend, so there's not much point in dashing north to the smoke and grime of Kitwe, because nothing much will happen there before next Wednesday at the earliest.

Yet, when the time comes to leave, Thandi doesn't understand why, after three months together in the UK, we must now part. I promise to bring her a lollipop back from Kitwe. Frankly, there's not a lot else to buy for her there. Certainly not a stick of Kitwe rock!

We return to Lusaka in mid-July. Ali wants to try a couple of days in work before returning full-time. What my role is, is not clear. Dora arrives each morning at 6.30am to dress the children, make the beds, clean through the house and do all the washing and ironing before knocking off at 2pm.

Meanwhile Sandra arrives at midday to look after the children in the afternoon, then stays until 6.30pm to help with bathing and suppertime.

So, what is my role? Oh yes, grandma, of which Thandi is very good at reminding me usually at 5.30am when she races into our bedroom and jumps onto the bed shrieking, "Wake up, Gamma! Wake up, Gan-dad!" And so, another day starts.

Monday is a trial day back at work. At 5.45am, Ali and not Thandi pokes her head around the bedroom door. "Have either of you seen the bit of rubber off my breast pump?" This baffling paraphernalia is required in order to express breast milk, which Dora gives to Becca in a bottle. However, neither of us has seen the missing part without which the apparatus won't work.

"Perhaps Dora threw it out with yesterday's rubbish?" I suggest. Dora probably hasn't a clue what it's for, since most Zambian babies take milk from the breast, even up to four years of age.

"Then I'll have to search the entire rubbish heap," Ali groans. She could have done without this on her first trial day back at work. Lusaka, as yet, does not have regular rubbish collections. In most housing complexes, a pit is dug towards the rear of gardens, where rubbish is either burnt or buried. Not the most sanitary solution, and definitely a magnet for rats and other vermin.

"Unless the night guard picked it up," suggests Bob. "He rummages through the rubbish bags every evening when he comes on duty."

"What possible use would a guard have for a rubber ring from a breast pump?" retorts Ali. What indeed except, being so poor, he searches other people's rubbish for pickings to eat or sell for small money. Maybe there's a market for breast pump rings here?

Six o'clock in the chill morning air, we stand around the rubbish pit trying to identify which bags came from Ali's house yesterday, then tip them out on the ground to find . . . *I just pray she sterilises it before using it again!*

What to do for the rest of the day? Aunty Dora busies herself with housework all morning, while Aunty Sandra turns up at lunchtime to look after the children in the afternoon. The two maids are addressed as 'aunty' since Zambian tradition doesn't approve of young children calling adult non-family members by Christian names alone. All that's left for Grandma and Granddad is to catch up on Starfish business in the morning, then spend the afternoon passing a restless baby between nanny and Grandma, then back again.

The second day does not go quite so well. Still without a clearly defined role, I plan to paint my nails. No sooner is the top off the nail varnish, than Becca begins squalling and refusing to take milk from a bottle, even if it's the same breast milk as at every other feed. Should I step in? Becca's frustrated screams are increasing in volume by the minute.

"Give Dora a minute or two," advises Bob. "After all, she has to cope when we're not here."

But does Becca fully understand this, since she's wriggling and squirming in Dora's arms? In spite of possessing perfect café au lait skin, her face is growing redder by the minute. Dora looks completely fazed. After all, Africans simply sling their baby on their backs allowing them unlimited access to the milk supply as and when they want. I reach for the bottle and the wriggling, squirming bundle. A pair of molten chocolate eyes gaze up into mine, contemplating whether to continue the battle. But no, Becca relents and begins sucking with gusto, all the while fixing her liquid pools on mine. My heart melts; I know why I'm here.

The rest of the week Ali is still officially on maternity leave, so we plan days out, even if inevitably to the same places. On Saturday, we revisit Kalimba Reptile Park to show Thandi the crocs. She's old enough now to find them fascinating, though worryingly they might find her equally appealing, albeit for different reasons.

"That one looks just like Gan-dad!" She points to a twelve feet giant with a belly bulging at the sides. Unfortunately, she's right. Food where we're currently staying in Kitwe consists of a diet to die for, of which more later. For the moment, Gan-dad's belly indeed resembles that of a well stuffed croc, though maybe he doesn't need reminding.

Today is the stuff of which memories are made. Yet it's back to Kitwe in the morning and an unhappy face from Thandi, because Gamma and Gan-dad are leaving. For two pins she'd be in the car with us. But how to amuse a two year old in Kitwe, that's the question?

We return to Lusaka for my birthday. On the day Thandi is raring to go from 5.30am, that being the time birthdays clearly should start. She runs into our bedroom and with a flying leap lands on my swollen stomach. "Happy Birthday, Gamma!"

Ali and the children have bought me a silver necklace threaded with malachite beads. There's also a huge birthday cake with a number two candle on it. "That means you are two, Gamma!" shrieks Thandi, who wants to cut the cake right now.

Bob disappears mid-morning on a mysterious mission and returns with three dozen red roses. Zambia is awash with red roses at the moment. They almost swamped the president on TV the other night and they were giving them away at church the other week. Someone is making a killing growing red roses here.

As for Becca, birthdays are of little consequence, as long as the milk supply holds up. Yet she refuses to settle tonight, which is worrying, since tomorrow is Ali's first full day back at work and Aunty Dora's first day coping alone, though we're also here should the system break down. Dora's novel take on childcare involves putting Becca in a baby bouncer with wheels, then pushing her round the floor with one finger, crooning as she polishes and shines. Becca thinks this is wonderful, until it's time for afternoon milk. She can't understand why the 'boops', as Thandi calls them, returned at lunchtime but aren't around now when she wants them. I intervene yet again.

But what happens next week, when we're back in Kitwe?

Unfortunately, as the week progresses, Bob falls sick. Since the owners where we're staying in Kitwe this trip, have all recently had malaria, concern grows. If the diet doesn't kill him, we wouldn't want cerebral malaria to succeed instead. He spends the whole day sleeping in a chair, shivering, even with a fleece on. Yet overnight his condition worsens, meaning a visit to a private clinic, where he must pay up before being seen by an Asian doctor wearing what looks like white pyjamas. He suspects a viral infection and prescribes antibiotics and sufficient Benalyn to turn Bob into a zombie for days, but at least it's not malaria.

Possibly due to the amount of time he spends sleeping off Benalyn, Bob recovers in time to spend the weekend out of town on a farm north of Lusaka. This involves packing and ironing for five people, as well as sorting enough clean clothes to last us for fifteen days in Kitwe where laundry also is proving problematic. What with food for the weekend and bags for two children plus three adults, plus a pram, Moses basket, toys and books, we could be emigrating instead of travelling fifty miles outside Lusaka. I just pray with a two year old and a new baby, the weekend away works!

We're staying on a working farm, although no-one else seems to be either staying or working there. We choose two lodges close to barbecue, dining room and kitchen, since everything has to be ferried to the kitchen area in order to prepare it, then ferried back in order to eat it. Try explaining that to a two year old who wants 'foodoo' and *now!*

The night is cold and pitch dark, though not very silent thanks to frogs croaking, crickets chirruping and guards mumbling near by. We wake to a chilly dawn. It's freezing walking over to the kitchen to make a cup of tea, cold sitting outside to eat breakfast and colder still showering in a bathroom with gauze over the windows and a freezing wind blowing through the open mesh.

And this is Africa!

One thing is immediately apparent: shoes must be worn at all times. The ground is carpeted with three inch long acacia thorns as thick as a darning needle. Get one of those in a bare foot and it would be very painful.

That evening we prepare to barbecue. Michael and Donald are on hand to collect firewood, light fires and help in the kitchen. Donald helps Bob, while assisting me in the kitchen is Michael, slightly the worse for drink, yet determined to relate his life story as he peels the vegetables.

"Ah Madam, I used to be chef at a restaurant in Arcades." Arcades is Lusaka's newest shopping mall. Could a fondness for drink explain why he's no longer there? "Even Donald was manager along the road from here." That being at an upmarket place we visited earlier today.

"So why isn't he there now?" This question permits the story to proceed.

"He was having a disagreement with the boss about an 'unauthorised' loan to a friend."

I take that to mean the 'unauthorised' loan came out the till. Hmm, the background of these two leaves a little to be desired and perhaps explains their low paid jobs on an out of town farm. Yet not so low as that of night guards in rural areas, who rank about the lowliest there is where pay is concerned. Today, the place where we had lunch, hosted a seminar with all expenses paid for Ministry of Finance delegates. Oh, that some of what was spent on them reached people like the guard in Lusaka, forced to pick through bags of rubbish, or the guard here hanging around outside hoping to glean the leftovers from our plates.

Sunday is our last full day together. Tomorrow Ali and the girls head back to Lusaka, while we head north to Kitwe the following day. Maybe Thandi suspects we're leaving and thus forgets about keeping shoes on at all times. Suddenly an almighty screaming erupts. A three inch long acacia thorn is buried up to its first spur in Thandi's foot. It comes away clean, but requires a goodly smear of Grandma's 'pop-pop' (Savlon) to make things better.

Next morning the others head back to Lusaka, leaving us alone with Donald and Michael, maybe not the most trustworthy characters. In the evening, a second guard appears. Word of the bountiful food falling from our table must have spread. Still, it's comforting to know we're now guarded by, not one, but two guards. Or is it? Should wind of our isolation become known to people who'll stop at nothing to get their hands on the wealth of others . . .

Oh dear, maybe we should have travelled to Kitwe today after all!

However, this particular stay in Kitwe is not destined to last long. After barely a week a text arrives to say Dora's eighteen months old baby has died suddenly. Since the baby was also Sandra's grandchild, Ali's childcare collapses into chaos. We drop everything and return at high-speed to Lusaka.

"The baby fell ill last week with diarrhoea," Ali says. "They kept thinking it would get better, only it didn't. Then on Friday night, they appeared on my doorstep with the sick baby wrapped in a blanket." She pauses. "It was grey and looked really sick. It was dehydrated and not even crying which is always a bad sign. I tried giving boiled water, but there was nothing I could do."

"So what happened?"

"Sandra stayed with the girls while I took Dora and the baby to the hospital. Apart from diarrhoea, the baby was suffering from malaria, pneumonia, malnutrition and was dehydrated. Even so, they reckoned it might pull through. On Saturday, it seemed better, then last night Sandra phoned to say it had died." There's a catch in Ali's voice. "To think, I held the baby on Friday, yet by Sunday, it was gone."

"So what happens now?"

"The funeral, which can last up to five days." Meaning without childcare Ali will be unable to work. Grandma and Granddad to the rescue, though I wish the circumstances were not so tragic.

The funeral takes place quickly, yet neither Sandra nor Dora is fit to return to work, though Sandra turns up at the house, pain furrowing her features so deeply as if a tractor had ploughed across them. She requests an advance on her monthly wages to pay funeral costs. I put one arm around her shoulders, helpless to know what to do, unable even to invite Jesus into the situation, since Sandra is a Jehovah's Witness. I give her something towards the funeral costs. She thanks me profusely, tears streaming down her face.

It is a long week, not because of looking after the children, but because of the painful situation. Sandra reappears towards the end, but reveals she also has diarrhoea. She blames the funeral food. Apparently, relatives turn up bringing goodness knows what in the way of food, which then lies around for days. However, she quite possibly has the same bug as killed the baby, so we send her away, gaunt and grey to grieve her loss and to recover, while we hold the fort, uncertain when we'll get back to Kitwe.

Yet Sandra returns the following week, grim-faced but composed. When Bob expresses sympathy, she merely shakes her head saying, "It happens."

"Do you have other grandchildren?" I pray the answer is yes.

Sandra eyes become blank with pain and loss. "There was another grandchild, but he also died."

"Ah Sandra . . ." To lose one grandchild is bad enough, but to lose two . . . I feel utterly helpless.

Despite her grief, Sandra is determined both she and Dora will return to work on Monday; it's her way of coping. "But will Dora cope?" I ask.

"Madam, what else can she do?" Zambian fatalism at its worst!

Thus, on Monday, they return and life goes on. What else can happen? Heavens, after two months here, the inevitable is happening, we're finally becoming Zambianised! Yet inevitably, the time also comes for us to leave for the UK.

"Are you sad you're leaving?" asks Ali.

"In a way, though strangely Zambia now feels like home." Actually, every which way is home these days, constantly moving between two countries and two cultures with family here and family there. So where is home any more? But there is one problem . . .

"I'm coming with you, Gamma and Gan-dad," announces Thandi the night before we fly out. It takes some persuading that might not be such a good idea, however much we might want it. But never fear, Thandi, we'll be back.

CHAPTER TWENTY-THREE: A ROOM WITH A VIEW, ALBEIT WITH A DIET TO DIE FOR!
July - > August 2006

Despite family affairs occupying much of this trip, we still reach Kitwe where the question as ever is where to stay. This time, even though Bob keeps pointing out staying there could differ from spending the day there, we're trying the riverside lodge where we've spent many enjoyable days.

Unless someone's getting cold feet?

Still, there's the view to die for from the veranda as the sun sinks below the horizon. The glorious sunset colours are mirrored in the two dams in front, while the murky Kafue River slips silently by on the other side. In the distance, a lone hippo barks in welcome, causing Bob to sigh blissfully, "Yes, definitely the right choice!"

Cold feet temporarily forgotten, let's see what's for supper before jumping to conclusions. The first night produces tomato and avocado salad followed by chicken, but only tea and biscuits for afters.

"Is there any fresh fruit?" I try.

George, whom you may recall is supposedly a former high court judge turned chef, indicates the tea and biscuits. "No, only this."

Hmmm, time will prove whether location is indeed everything.

Next morning, chilly dawn mist shrouds both dams and river, while on the far side of the dam, early morning sun burnishes the treetops orange. We leap out of bed to gaze in wonder until gradually the mist shrinks away and the rising sun lends warmth to the day.

At 6.45am George knocks on the door with early morning tea. He's fifteen minutes early but we haven't the heart to tell him. After all, he still has both breakfast and packed lunch to get right. Pure Joy orange juice and cornflakes appear as requested, while two fried eggs congeal on cold plates alongside doorsteps of barely toasted bread. Last night there wasn't any fruit, yet this morning two red apples inexplicably appear. I peek inside the packed lunch and discover huge beef-burgers inside white baps, destined to be soggy and inedible by lunchtime.

Oh dear, not such a promising start!

During the first week, a pattern emerges of packed lunches containing sodden pies, pasties, samosas or burgers, followed by hefty meat-laden evening meals. Breakfast vaguely resembles what we ask for, but with unpredictable variations. We stock up on fresh fruit at Shoprite and begin substituting lunchtime meat with boiled eggs or peanut butter sandwiches from breakfast, passing unwanted meaty fare to Messrs Mbai and Chama who think such bounty is wonderful.

"Ah, you are not liking meat, Mrs Cooke?" asks Mr Chama tucking into yet another meat pie.

"I do, Mr Chama, just not three times a day!"

Yet grave damage is being done. At the end of the first week, Mrs Tembo at Kaputula exclaims, "Mrs Cooke, you are putting on weight!" This may be a compliment since increased weight proves not only can I afford to buy food but also, in a country where so many are HIV positive, my vital signs are looking good. Realistically, all it proves is the damage this diet is doing.

Yet all hope of escaping it over the weekend vanishes with the morning mist. Since we're not travelling to Lusaka, we must survive here. On Saturday, after a breakfast of fried ham and eggs with white toast - no cereals, no fruit, no fruit juice - Bob collects a can of worms to go fishing in the dam with the crocs for company, while I settle down with Starfish accounts and the view to die for. By the time he returns minus any fish, it's time to eat again: enormous beef-burgers in buns *with chips*, and a mere dab of coleslaw on the side.

"Whatever happened to five portions of fruit and veg a day?" I groan.

We retire to the pool, determined to swim off this excess, while admiring the view to die for out over the vlei. Tall grasses sway gently in the breeze. Brightly coloured birds dart here and there and only the occasional drift of smoke from a bush fire mars the eternal blue of the dry season sky. As the sun sinks in a huge orange ball, it balances precariously on the rim of the horizon before slipping away for another day.

But there's another meal to face: massive T-bone steaks with salad and enough boiled potatoes to feed an army. Bob leans back, his stomach distended. Time to recall what happens when Bob overeats. We emphasise to George, no cooked breakfast tomorrow, just juice, cereals and toast.

Yet a hidden agenda is also at work. What George serves depends not only on our choice, but on what madam who lives on the kopje gives him to cook. In which case, we're stuffed, literally as well as figuratively. Therefore it's no surprise to find the breakfast table groaning under the weight of juice, oranges and cereal along with four immense frankfurter sausages, fried eggs, toast, jam and peanut butter.

Oh George, if only you realised what this is doing to us!

"There's more to this than meets the eye," I mutter darkly as George disappears behind the tatty curtain which conceals his miniscule kitchen.

Dismally Bob surveys frankfurter sausages with which his digestive system has a particularly bad relationship. "What's that then?"

"The more George cooks, the less we can eat, so the more there is left for him and Dennis, the barman as well as the night guards. Thus, since everything disappears, madam imagines we're doing justice to the food, so keeps sending down more and more for him to cook!"

Today all is peaceful. At lunchtime, we retire to the island in the middle of the first dam, reached by crossing a lone rickety wooden bridge, the other bridge having been demolished by a hippo barging through to the second dam. We order a bottle of Autumn Harvest, a grossly underestimated South African sparkling white wine that in a blind testing could pass for champagne. Okay, maybe not good champagne! Inevitably there is yet more meat.

Come suppertime, George waddles along to ask what we'd like to eat.

"Just tea, toast and maybe an egg." George's expression registers shock, closely followed by dismay at the prospect of meagre pickings, merely confirming our suspicions as to the fate of any leftovers.

The dining room also houses the lodge's only TV set which tonight has been swapped from a black and white set to a colour TV. The World Cup has reached even remote corners of darkest Africa. While we demolish toast and eggs, George, Dennis and the night guards watch Italy play France, inexplicably cheering for Italy, even though none of them has ever been there or has any knowledge of or affinity with the country. Come 11pm, they're still closeted in the dining room cheering every penalty. Oh dear, what about security tonight? As for early morning tea, forget it!

Nevertheless, breakfast still surprises. Having ignored frankfurter sausages yesterday, four more appear on Monday along with four eggs, six slices of toast and two oranges. No cereals, no juice.

"Are these yesterday's frankfurters?" I poke one tentatively.

"Well, George and co are welcome to them," responds Bob. "And where's today's packed lunch?"

I peer around the tatty curtain to find George dozing on a chair after watching late night football. A few minutes later the unappetising aroma of onions frying drifts around the curtain. Enormous beef-burgers yet again, awash with fried onions and accompanied by two cartons of orange juice. The missing juice from breakfast perhaps?

By the second week, trouser belts have given all they can. We start off on Monday by ordering fish for dinner.

"Ah sorry, madam has already cooked meat and rice," George says. Clearly madam is trying to impress two newly arrived guests with her unrelenting meat diet. At least they only stay one night.

On Tuesday, we try again, requesting vegetable samosas for lunch. A flustered George approaches us out on the island. "The samosas are frozen so I cannot tell which are vegetable and which are meat. However, I will cook one of each so I can tell which ones are meat and which are vegetable."

And this man was supposedly a high court judge?

Yet watching him waddle back over the earthen wall between the dams, he has a certain demeanour. And yes, George produces five enormous vegetable samosas *each* for lunch. That afternoon we walk them off strolling to a fishing camp upriver, where a sign warns: 'Beware of hippo!'

Fortunately, none are around, nor the leopard that lives hereabouts, nor the twelve foot croc, supposedly caught by a poor white relative of the owners. Unsure what to do with it, he roped it up, put it in the back of his pickup, then drove to the farm of a whacky neighbour who collects crocs and dangerous snakes. Unfortunately, the croc escaped and now lurks in the river until the poor white takes out a motorboat, then tries to overturn the boat. We beat a hasty retreat lest the croc can't tell one poor white from another.

Tonight, two Afrikaners have arrived. The table groans under whole bream served with roast potatoes, fried aubergines, watermelon and two cream puddings. Naturally the full works appears for breakfast, followed by the inevitable meaty lunch, then gargantuan pork chops, chips and coleslaw the following evening, after which the Afrikaners want to settle up. Enter madam muffled in scarves to tot up how many beers they've consumed along with mountains of food, which they're paying for with wads of rands, dollars and kwachas. They may be leaving, yet we must survive two more days.

The Afrikaners depart at 4am the following morning, leaving the cold water tap running in their chalet. Instead of showering in lukewarm water because the night guards have run off all the hot, this morning we shower in scalding water because the Afrikaners drained the cold water system dry. Since water is heated by a log fire underneath an outside boiler, it's a wonder the whole system didn't blow sky high.

Next day we return early bearing the gift of a live chicken which pooed copiously all the way here in the back of the car. George is flustered at our early reappearance plus requesting veggie burgers for lunch and worms for fishing this afternoon. Oh, and the chicken killed and cleaned for transporting to Lusaka tomorrow. Information overload perhaps? He waddles off shaking his head.

We wait ages. Finally, George reappears to say the cooker has blown up, meaning all food must now be cooked in madam's kitchen up on the kopje. Just as well we're leaving tomorrow, but not before another steak meal with biscuit pudding to follow. Quite how anything appeared tonight with a defunct cooker plus the disturbing news that the young madam has cerebral malaria. Worrying indeed, since we've also been copiously bitten by mosquitoes while here. Cerebral malaria or a diet to die for, what a way to go!

Ten days in Lusaka provides a welcome respite from the diet to die for. So much so that, on our return, we order T-bones with chips and salad for lunch. I sneak off for a quick swim before lunch, only to find a couple of near naked Zambians canoodling in the pool. Apparently, the old madam caught two stark naked in there on Sunday and ordered them off the premises.

"No morals!" the old white boss thunders.

No swimming costumes more like!

In the late afternoon, we stroll along the riverbank, noting fresh hippo prints the size of dinner plates and deep scratches gouged out by crocodile claws and catching the unmistakeable whiff of leopard. All this merely whets the appetite for immense cheese and ham toasties made from thick wedges of white bread. George and Dennis are delighted we're back; daily rations will increase once more.

Just don't tell madam where all the leftovers go!

Drawing back the curtains next morning to see mist shrouding the dam, it feels remarkably like home. This time we're determined to eat meat only once a day. Such resolutions are all very well, keeping them is another matter. By lunch next day there's already a problem.

"There are no vegetable samosas," announces George. "Would you like sausage and mash?" When we arrived in Lusaka, Ali commented we both *looked* ill. At this rate, we *will* be ill!

However, an afternoon by the pool, admiring the view out over the vlei and I'm already wishing I could take this back to England. Later as the sun sinks in a fiery ball, I sit alone on the veranda with nothing but the sounds of the surrounding bush for company. Crickets whirring and birds tuning their evening chorus, while I'm thinking, *'Gosh, I really love this place!'*

George spots me sitting alone and waddles along with hot water and tea bags. His old-fashioned service and courtesy are something to which one easily becomes accustomed. Yet later he reappears, hopping from one foot to another. "I am thinking there are samosas for supper," he says.

Strange since there weren't any for lunch!

"Actually, we'd prefer bream," I say. George waddles off shaking his head. Between madam up on the kopje and madam in the chalet, life can be very trying.

Next morning, after delivering morning tea, George announces, "Sorry, there are no cereals. Will Jungle Oats be okay?"

More than okay! We approach the dining room with light steps. Porridge yes, but with *juice, bacon, eggs, toast and jam!* Two days back and the diet is disappearing faster than water down a plughole, anti-clockwise naturally, since we're in the southern hemisphere. So much for resolutions *not* to eat meat three times a day!

And so it continues throughout our second stint here. Meat blocks our guts, fat clogs our arteries and the pounds pile on relentlessly. At least until Wednesday when George goes on leave and Dennis is left in charge. Apart from a chronic stammer, making prolonged conversation awkward, Dennis is newly arrived from a village beyond nowhere. Although he won't cook for us, he will wait at table, take orders and bring morning tea.

Dinner is a hit and miss affair. Since everything is cooked up on the kopje, the food arrives cold and portions are noticeably smaller. Next morning tea fails to arrive, while breakfast is a measly affair of one orange, a small bowl of cornflakes, one boiled egg and toast. A packed lunch eventually arrives of congealing veggie-burgers topped with processed cheese and oozing ketchup and mayonnaise.

Oh George, how we are missing you!

Over the next twenty-four hours Dennis holds the fort tenuously. He manages the inevitable T-bones for supper, but we wait in vain for dessert. But you've heard this story before, about the ice cream melting in the fridge, which Dennis reckons madam said was for *tomorrow* night.

Mercifully, George returns by Friday night in time to ask, "What are you wanting for supper?" His expression suggests he's prepared for anything,

"What is your speciality?" George looks completely fazed. Should I have said: *signature dish?* "Can you cook curry?"

The thought has probably never entered his mind, yet he reckons he can cook curry. Curry it is, followed by chocolate cupcakes, and a bottle of Autumn Harvest. What a way to go! Though after all we've been through and since the young madam has indeed succumbed to cerebral malaria, this rather begs the question: *dare we even come back here to stay?*

Yet ten days later, we're back, because we can't afford anywhere else. In the afternoon, we stroll along the riverbank to the rapids keeping a wary eye out for hippo, crocs and leopard. Grasses lining the riverbank obscure the view. As we cross the bridge to the rapids, suddenly something crashes into the water. Instantly we freeze . . . *that was no fish!* Since Bob actually saw the croc, we beat a hasty retreat lest it fancies a couple of impoverished but well-stuffed whites.

Tonight, Dennis is in charge and struggling. George is on leave after spending ten days cooking for Congolese missionaries who, having escaped here from violence in the Congo, have eaten all the food and drunk all the drink, which so far no-one has replenished.

"Is there any fish for dinner?" we ask Dennis.

"No, the young madam is not buying fish because fish in the river are dying. She thinks maybe something is poisoning them." This is the longest sentence Dennis has ever managed. "However, there are fingers of fish."

Fish fingers it is. However, because George is away, everything is again cooked on high and arrives stone cold. At least Dennis doesn't attempt to conceal the ice cream, since we already sussed that one. Tomorrow we need an early start, so I write on a serviette: TEA 6.30AM, BREAKFAST 7.15AM, PACKED LUNCH 7.30AM.

Next morning, in perishing cold, George reappears. Tea is on time and the packed lunch waits on the table, but no eggs, no toast. George waddles off up the hill to fetch eggs and half toasted bread. After an age eggs start sizzling behind the curtain.

Yet this isn't a temporary blip. Next morning again, there are no eggs. One of the guards has gone to Cedric's Farm for eggs, but has not returned. This doesn't mean he's run off with the eggs, simply he hasn't arrived back yet. Cereals and toast won't be so bad, but there are also no Sprites, no fish, no chicken, no eggs, no samosas and our room and toilet stink of urine.

True, eggs arrive in time for lunch, but the only choice for dinner is T-bone or pork chops. The monotony is getting us down, yet there's no-one to complain to. They're all either down with malaria or have vanished. We retire to bed disgruntled, both suffering stomach problems due to a chronic lack of fruit and vegetables plus the discomfort of a meat laden diet.

Somehow, we survive till Friday night when George announces there's no chicken. Or rather, there is chicken, however it's frozen but could be ready by 7.30pm. It's now 6.45pm. What does the chicken go through to produce watery curry by 7.30pm? For dessert, an enormous do'nut filled with artificial cream appears which I eat, then immediately feel unwell. Earlier today someone commented, "For sure God will reward you for what you are doing!"

With a diet that won't wipe us off the face of the planet, please!

We consider returning to self-catering. Yet decamping from here would take all day, not forgetting battling with Shoprite on Saturday. So we stay. Not an easy decision, since guts now require close proximity to base at all times. We try consoling ourselves that location is everything . . . *well, maybe 90%!*

In the event, the death of Dora's baby provides a much needed respite from dietary purgatory. Yet one week later, we're back to a rapturous welcome. Dennis and George grin from ear to ear. Management turns out in force to greet us, perhaps fearing we wouldn't return for more of the diet to die for. And it's good to be back, even if supper is immense beef samosas and there are no cereals for breakfast, only cold bacon, hot eggs and dry toast. But we're used to it now and heck, location *is* everything, isn't it?

However, there's *still* no fresh fish. Apparently, the mine poured effluent into the Kafue River killing all the fish. There are however delicious breadcrumbed fish fillets from the freezer. I compliment George on the dinner.

"Ah sorry, madam!" What *does* he mean, sorry they're nice, or sorry he didn't serve them cold or ruined?

Huge chocolate snowballs follow that taste disgusting, but we eat them anyways. We're becoming Zambianised. Stop complaining; accept what comes, you can't change it anyways. At least not if you're Sandra or Dora, or the leper begging outside Shoprite, or the teacher at Kaputula who's living in a storeroom because he's nowhere else to live, least of all low paid guards in rural areas.

Not surprisingly, the night is diabolical, yet there's a full English breakfast followed by a launch ceremony the next day. Still, two days and we're out of here and on a plane to the UK.

Today's launch ceremony produces another live chicken that spends the day pooing inside a cardboard box in the back of the car. We hand it over for killing and cleaning to a delighted George who keeps the 'sausages' or intestines, as well as the feet for himself.

Unfortunately, it's also George's night off, leaving Dennis to cook the first fish Bob has caught here as a starter for supper. Except Dennis doesn't understand the concept of starter and serves the whole dinner of pork chops and chips together with the fish. Chocolate ice-cream appears for dessert, the only dessert Dennis is trusted to serve up. How will he cope with breakfast tomorrow when we've yet another launch ceremony? Not well I fear, frazzled eggs and cold toast, and that with a day at Kaputula!

That leaves one dinner, comprising yesterday's chicken now cleaned. "Do you know how to cook chicken?" I ask Dennis.

"Yes, madam, also chips and salad."

"But no sprinkle," we warn him.

Dennis does the business. Clearly someone has been teaching him, yet hopefully not to step into George's shoes quite yet.

Our last morning dawns. I rise at the crack of dawn and tiptoe out onto the veranda for one last look at mist shrouding the water and the sun rising beyond the vlei. My heart fills to overflowing at the beauty.

Dennis manages breakfast, though boiled eggs and toast come first followed by cereals and juice. Still, it's finally goodbye to the diet to die for, and the place where location is almost but *not quite* everything. That is if you can also survive hippos, crocs, snakes and the ever-present danger of malaria. Time alone will tell whether we have indeed survived the latter.

CHAPTER TWENTY-FOUR: THE CAR THAT TRAVELLED BACK IN TIME
May 2007

In spite of two major breakdowns, in May 2007 the troublesome 'heffalump' is *still* in our possession. But only just, since we frequently threaten to get rid of it. Yet that raises the question: w*ho'd have it anyways?*

However, there is a need to recoup the small fortune it costs us in maintenance, insurance and repairs, as well as save it from rusting away. Therefore, the safari company that organised our first trip back to Zambia five years ago, now rents the car out in our absences overseas. At the start of each trip, we collect the car, praying it's none the worse for this experience.

"All's well?" Bob asks the man behind the desk as we wait for the keys in May 2007, nine months after we left the car in their care.

The man's deadpan expression flickers momentarily. "Indeed yes, except one rear seat belt is missing."

Bob frowns. "So what do you intend doing about it?"

The man spreads his long black fingers flat on his desk. "I have not yet been able to contact the man in whose charge the vehicle was."

"You mean the man who hired it?"

"Not exactly . . . the man in whose charge it was."

I sense Bob's hackles rising. "But your company will replace the belt?"

"Naturally, I will inform you when we are able to fit a new seat belt."

The 'heffalump' awaits in the car park. As we approach it Bob says, "Why would anyone remove a seat belt?"

To me it's abundantly clear. "Why, to tow the vehicle of course!"

He stops dead. "You are joking?"

Oh, that I was!

Inside, the car reeks as ever of Mr Sheen. Before starting up, Bob gets out his little black book, in which he records trivia such as when he fills the petrol tank, how much petrol costs, how many miles we travel, plus mileage on the clock when we hand the car over for rental and when they return it.

"Well I'll be damned!" His fist thumps the dashboard so hard, the car rocks. "There are less miles on the clock than when we handed the car over nine flipping months ago."

"Well it can't have gone very far, nor have been hired out much."

Is that steam emerging from my beloved's ears? "They could've driven it to Mongu and back, ten times over. Someone's turned the clock back!"

Bob prepares to storm back inside, but halts. "First let's see how much they reckon we've earned. If there are any earnings from a car that's apparently gone backwards, that will prove they're up to no good."

Yet over the next few days driving around Lusaka, the car once more begins making terminal sounding noises and threatening to breathe its last. Not trusting the safari company's mechanics, we head for Mr Tomito again.

"Ah, you are back," he welcomes us like old friends.

After a run around the block and much revving of the engine, he decides it's not serious and he can fix it for around £75. Great news, except that will eat another hole in our personal budget because the garage still doesn't accept credit cards.

"Aha!" Mr Tomito greets us next day. "Your car is sounding healthier. I have replaced a gasket in the exhaust and managed to get the revs back up so it is no longer stalling all the time." This sounds better except . . . "Your air-con is on the way out and there is a problem with the timing belt."

Apparently, a timing belt is vital to the running of the car. At some time it's been changed, but he's not sure when or how much longer it will last. The belt could break at any time, but to replace it, he would have to send to Japan. For all the use the car is, it might as well go back there as well. And we have a journey to Kitwe tomorrow.

"This car has to go!" I say as we head north on the morrow. "It's been nothing but trouble since we bought it."

"But how do we dispose of it?" responds Bob. "Who else would want it?"

But that's not all. Because someone interfered with the wiring, the petrol gauge also is not working. There's no way of knowing how much petrol is in the tank. To be safe, we fill up at Kapiri Mposhi.

"Aieeh, your petrol tank is leaking!" The petrol pump attendant bangs on the car window. Petrol gushes out over the forecourt, as if someone has cut the car's jugular and it's bleeding out. The attendant helpfully indicates a shack over the road where we might get it fixed.

But hang on; the crisis may already be over. Bob checks to see if the haemorrhage has stopped or whether the 'heffalump' continues to bleed to death. And yes, the pump attendant tried to squeeze every last drop in and flooded the tank.

We proceed cautiously to Kitwe and the lodge on the banks of the Kafue River where, for reasons of economy, we're returning to the diet to die for. However, all is not well. George is on leave, Dennis has left for the heady lights of Lusaka and a young lady called Grace in charge, even though management previously vowed not to employ young women, because they chat up male customers and make assignations on the side.

Perhaps Grace came highly recommended, yet she can't tell vegetarian spring rolls from ones with meat in. Later she serves chicken and boiled potatoes with Zambian style cabbage, saturated with oil, onion and tomato. All too soon, we're doomed to putting on weight yet again, worse, to fall ill, in spite of requesting in advance plain breakfasts, meat free lunches and vegetables or salad with dinner followed by fruit.

Next morning the table groans under the weight of fruit juice, oranges, cereal, fried eggs, fried ham and six immense slices of toast. They served what we asked for, but with a fried breakfast! Yet Bob tucks in as if he's not seen a cooked breakfast since last we were here.

Maybe management is stoking us up to cope with car problems. On Friday it returns to the Kitwe garage that got it back on the road after a spectacular breakdown en route to Chilumba.

"Ah, it's you!" Owner Johnny grins broadly. "I remember your car, even your registration plate!" But can he fix it? Johnny assures us he can. We book the car in for Monday and request a Chep vehicle so we can continue with our programme.

On Monday, the car is in the garage by 8am so mechanics can fix it by the end of the day. A Chep vehicle will take us to Kaputula, but not back to the lodge. Johnny assures us it will be ready by 5pm so, no surprises, that, after a trying day, the car is not ready.

"Ah sorry, we were unable to fix your car today, but we replaced a missing wheel-nut and also bathed the car." Meaning the car must return tomorrow to have the work done they didn't do today.

Tomorrow is always another day, even if Grace's indigestible chicken has kept sleep at bay. Then a bird perches in a nearby tree at 6am and kookaburrers incessantly. And, even if we feel like catching the next plane back to the UK, there's still a car to be repaired, after un-toasted bread and cold fried eggs, followed by cocoa pops and sugary orange squash.

Today the garage wants the car later, saying they will repair it while we wait since it won't take long. Three hours later we're still imprisoned in a box sized waiting room in a garage beyond the fringes of Kitwe with nothing nearby but an African township. The office doorbell ping-pongs every time someone enters, while the neighbourhood cockerel thinks it's dawn and crows constantly outside. Soon both noises are driving us to distraction.

There is only one consolation, no, two. Firstly, the repair costs a fraction of what it would cost in Lusaka. Secondly, the mechanic confirms problems with the fuel gauge were caused by someone turning back the clock.

"Somebody in that safari company will swing for this!" thunders Bob, as we head back to the lodge, hoping for a late swim.

Yet the sky darkens and it rains in the middle of the dry season. Once upon a time such an event would have had Zambians running outside to see if the world was coming to an end. Nowadays, with global warming, it's less uncommon, so they simply carry on with what they are doing. In Grace's case preparing immense T-bone steaks served with greasy chips and chopped beetroot with onion. There is no dessert, just tea and biscuits.

"Maybe we should consider staying elsewhere for our last stint in Kitwe?"

Do the dining room walls have ears? Next morning there's an all out effort to get everything right: hot water for showering and yet another mammoth breakfast, because madam up on the hill *still* thinks we eat everything and rewards our efforts with yet more of the same disastrous fare.

On the way into town, a hideous knocking develops underneath the car, so back it goes into the garage for the entire day. We've lost count of how many times that makes this trip, though it's currently spending more time off the road than on the road.

At least there's a highlight on TV tonight to relieve another of Grace's unappetising offerings. The snake, croc, reptile and danger-loving nutcase who lives nearby, is on TV capturing and talking about species native to Zambia most of us would rather avoid, yet which make for fascinating TV. Tonight, he's on the trail of rock python and captures two of them. Pythons squeeze their prey to death as opposed to delivering a lethal bite, yet they possess over one hundred teeth. Although their bite isn't toxic, it can still do considerable harm.

While capturing rock pythons, our hero gets bitten twice. This doesn't deter him. Holding each python aloft with blood pumping down his arm from his wounds, he enthusiastically informs the Zambian public about the finer points of the sex lives of rock pythons. Fascinating stuff . . . *especially when trying to eat indigestible food!*

As we finish, the owner's son enters the dining room. "So where do you see yourselves going from here?"

Did he perhaps overhear us mention decamping elsewhere? Or is he referring to the future of Starfish as opposed to literally where we're going from here. Silently we reflect on how sometimes we long for a simpler life. Yet isn't there secretly part of us that, like the snake man, relishes the notoriety that goes with being just that little bit odd?

Tomorrow we're attempting the impossible, Chilumba, Kafubu and Kaputula all in one day in a car that some days barely reaches Kitwe before breaking down. We've failed twice already to accomplish this round trip all in one day. So, third time lucky?

Amazingly we succeed and, since time allows, we check out other accommodation options. Sadly, rates elsewhere remain beyond our means and there's no discount for impoverished charity workers. Thoroughly disheartened, we limp back to the lodge, praying at least for a decent meal and a glass of wine before travelling tomorrow to Lusaka for the weekend.

Yet Lusaka has trials of its own. The end of the road has finally been reached with the 'heffalump.' On Monday, with heavy hearts, we place a 'For Sale' advert in 'Zambia Post.'

But first we need the spare keys back from the safari company. And secondly, the vehicle would look a lot better with two rear seat belts instead of one. Even if in Zambia hardly anyone, children included, wears a seat belt. This time the director of the safari company awaits. Formerly an employee, he's been promoted, though not presumably for honesty!

"An employee was suspended regarding damage to your vehicle. In fact, the people who hired the vehicle took it to the Kafue National Park . . ."

"But you said it wouldn't be rented out of town?"

"Ah, we were not knowing where they were heading."

Are we supposed to believe this?

"When they realised the vehicle was unsuitable for the terrain, they requested another one. A driver was dispatched with a vehicle and instructed to drive your vehicle back to Lusaka. This he did, arriving . . . *four days later!*"

The urge to throttle him is strong, yet worse is to come. Not only did this driver rip out the seatbelt, and yes it was to tow the vehicle, but he also turned back the clock to conceal evidence that he'd gallivanted all the way to his village near Mwinilunga and back!

"And the spare set of keys?"

"Regrettably these are still in the possession of that driver."

This is one excuse too many. "Altering the clock is a criminal offence," thunders Bob. "Should the keys not appear, it will be a matter for the police."

There we leave it, allowing the new director time to reflect. Barely do we reach our next port of call, then he calls to say the wife of the offender has dropped the keys back into the office.

Not surprisingly this ends our relationship with the safari company. There is the matter of what we owe them for registering and insuring the vehicle, but equally there is the matter of a missing seatbelt plus what they owe us in income from a vehicle that travelled backwards in time. However, we have our vehicle and keys back, while they keep their reputation . . . *but only just!*

And there's still a knackered and useless vehicle to dispose of!

We return for a final stint on the banks of the Kafue River to a rapturous welcome. Perhaps management genuinely fears losing their most loyal customers.

Tonight, we eat out on the veranda under the stars. ZESCO is meddling with the electricity supply again, threatening to cut off power unless the owner pays vastly inflated bills. Plus the dining room is being repainted and the paint fumes are so toxic they could kill anyone who inhaled them. Dinner is an improvement, while breakfast exceeds expectations, leading us to suppose they overheard what we said about checking out other places.

One problem remains, the car must go into the garage again in order to fit a new timing belt before selling it. Even though as yet, no-one shows any interest in buying it. Johnny assures we will have the car back that afternoon so we can use it tomorrow.

Aha, don't jump to conclusions! They do skim the brake pads, but don't fit the new timing belt, in spite of telling them we needed the car tomorrow. So how do we get back to the lodge with no car? For that, they must reinsert the engine, which they've only just taken out with heavy lifting gear. No point in screaming . . . *why did you take it out at the end of the day, when there wasn't enough time to complete the job?*

At the end of a long and tiring day with another long day ahead tomorrow, we wait two hours while they reassemble the engine. Meanwhile, the irritating electric bell ping-pongs incessantly, and the equally infuriating cockerel crows endlessly outside.

It is almost dark when we return to the lodge. Not a good time to be on rural roads in Zambia. And we've missed the crocodile man on TV. Still, it's cool and pleasant out on the veranda under the stars. And, with George back in charge, even the food is passable.

Next day we have a launch ceremony for which we don matching 'chitenge' outfits. Since I struggle to zip up mine, the inevitable is happening, I am putting on weight! Bob gets off more lightly, his voluminous shirt hides a multitude of sins, extra weight being one of them.

But where is Mr Mbai, our project manager? There is no sign of him, so Bob sets off with a Chep driver to yet another garage, which might fit the timing belt. As they drive out the gate, unfortunately Mr Mbai spots the car and, thinking we've left without him, gives chase in a taxi.

"Wait Mr Mbai!" I call after him in vain.

Unfortunately, the garage can't do the work today, so they drive around half a dozen more garages with Mr Mbai in hot pursuit until finally he catches up with them and realises, "Oh, you have not gone without me . . . but where is Mrs Cooke?"

Back they come to pick me up, still without the timing belt fitted. Maybe it's as well since we acquire two very live chickens that spend the rest of the day pooing in the back of the car before we hand them over to George for cleaning and freezing down.

That night we sit in the newly painted dining room, its walls now deep chocolate. Still, it compliments tonight's colourful dinner of pale pink chops, white potatoes and bright red beetroot, followed by bright yellow banana fritters served with chocolate sauce and mint green ice-cream.

Next day another garage assures us they will fit the timing belt that day. This time we return carrying a female goat purchased from the Kaputula community as a wife for Kushuka. The petrified goat urinates all the way there in the Chep vehicle, then again out to the lodge in our car.

"Is your car fixed?" asks the owner of the lodge.

"Time will tell," we respond. Time however has an uncanny knack of playing tricks these days, especially where the car is concerned.

"My brother in Lusaka can fix any car. Just take it to him and he'll fix it." But we've heard this so many times before and besides, who wants it fixed? All we want is rid of it!

Yet the car develops a hideous vibration combined with starting problems en route to Lusaka. We consider the relative of the lodge owner, yet in the end plump for Mr Tomito. Being Japanese, he understands the car like no-one else. Yet even Mr Tomito can't discover what's wrong, so keeps it in overnight. Over the thirty days this trip, the 'heffalump' has spent ten of them off the road. Proof indeed, it must go.

Next day Mr Tomito is still unsure what's wrong, hasn't got the parts to fix it and would have to send off to Japan for them anyways. He suggests trying breakers' yards, graveyards for defunct Mitsubishi Sportsgears. But this would take time, which we haven't got, because time this trip is up.

We pass briefly by the relative from Kitwe who eyes the 'heffalump' with interest. "Leave it with me, and I'll see what I can do, but no promises." We decline the offer.

In desperation Bob tries a dealer who advertises for all makes of car to sell, but not apparently ours. He never touches them, which rather says it all. I doubt we could even give it away!

In the end, we abandon the car on Ali's drive. "If you come across anyone who wants to buy . . ." But Ali also wants nothing to do with it. After all the trouble we've had, it's more than her reputation's worth to sell it to anyone.

We leave with a prayer to return to finish what needs doing, then add: *And dear Lord, a reliable vehicle would be good!*

Postscript:
After returning to UK, the relative of the lodge owner emails to say he's interested in buying the car for his wife. He duly appears at our daughter's cash in hand and removes once and for all the troublesome 'heffalump' from our lives, which his wife then drives around Lusaka for some years. Yet that leaves one big question: what do we do for a car next trip?

CHAPTER TWENTY-FIVE: ONLY ONE PROBLEM, NO TWO ACTUALLY!
November 2007

Having pretty much exhausted Kitwe's accommodation options, this trip we try a new guesthouse recommended by the secretary of a car hire company. The 'heffalump' having finally departed, we're also hiring *not* buying another vehicle, though not from the same company as before. Safety plus reliability must now be our priority.

"You must try the Courtyard Guesthouse," advises the secretary when she learns of our many trials finding suitable accommodation in Kitwe.

"Is it quiet?" I ask.

"For sure!" Her enthusiasm all but dislodges her false headpiece.

"No problems with er . . . *solicitation or outside drinking?*

She understands perfectly. "No, you will not have any problems, you will be very happy there."

Thus, in November 2007, we turn into the Courtyard Guesthouse. First impressions are okay. The main part housing reception, bar, kitchens and dining room was formerly a large detached house of the colonial era. This has been enlarged at the rear to accommodate a dozen bedrooms around a grassy area complete with swimming pool, currently pea-green in colour. Though to be fair, the colour does match the lawn.

However, once out the car, our ears are assailed by loud music and raised voices emanating from the bar. In reception, we find Michelle. No point in beating about the bush. "When we spoke on the phone, you assured us there was no public bar here."

"Ah no, there is no public bar here."

"Then are the people making that racket staying here?"

"No, they are just going."

Letting this pass, we follow Michelle to our room. It's perfectly clean, though rather Zambian in style. All is well apart from one problem, two actually.

"It's quite close to the bar area and we requested a twin, not a double."

"There is no twin available at this time."

We let this also pass, albeit resolving after a late lunch to scout out alternative accommodation, and that after an early start plus five hours travelling. But there is no joy; Kitwe has suddenly become popular, meaning we're stuck here unless . . .

"Back to the diet to die for?" suggests Bob.

"No way!" I retort. "In the rainy season, the road there will be treacherous. Let's give it a couple of nights, if there are problems, we move elsewhere." Even though nowhere else currently has vacancies.

By late afternoon all is quiet. A timid waitress called Jessie trips across the emerald sward to present an impressive menu, everything from sweet and sour pork to prawn curry and more besides. We are not easily fooled.

"Do you actually have everything on the menu?" I ask.

"Ah no, only T-bone, rump steak, pork chops, chicken and Hungarian sausage." Jessie hangs her head sorrowfully.

Yet served with chips, rice or 'nshima', that makes fifteen combinations as opposed to what we've been used to. We order chicken and chips with salad, followed by fruit salad. The chicken and chips duly arrive but with fruit salad. Of the mixed salad, there is no sign. We ask again for mixed salad.

"Ah, you are not wanting the fruit salad?" Jessie's face droops. She may look on the verge of tears, yet possibly she's made of sterner stuff. Quite probably she has a full secondary certificate of education and this is the best job she could get.

"Yes, we do," I explain patiently, "just not *with* chicken and chips!" Jessie scuttles away. "Oh dear," I say, "can things get any worse?"

In Zambia sadly, the answer is not only yes, but also a great deal worse.

The first night is quiet. However, since there are no mosquito nets, we are copiously bitten and have to get up in the night to plaster on Deet. Why, when there is nationwide publicity that sleeping under a mosquito net could eradicate malaria forever, do hotels and guesthouses still fail to supply them?

Breakfast is a mish-mash affair: cornflakes, two apples – *in case one is bad* - orange squash and two slices of white bread each. Bob's toast comes a full five minutes before mine, whether because I'm struggling to peel an apple with a table knife – *sorry, there are no sharp knives* - or because they only have a two-hole toaster, who knows!

And where's the milk for cornflakes? Bob trots back along the veranda to fetch the immense jug of milk that arrived with early morning tea, perhaps draining the cow dry.

We arrive back late that afternoon, hot, sweaty, sticky and extremely tired to find . . . "They've changed the double bed for twin beds!"

"And look, a mosquito net!"

There is only one problem, no two actually. The only position two beds will fit is with their backs to the window. And try as we might, one single mosquito net won't fit over two beds. Besides, it's full of holes!

Whoops, does that make three problems?

As for a swim, forget it! Not only has the gardener just filled the pool with chemicals, but also a storm of tropical dimensions is brewing. In early November the rains have already settled in. Outside Kitwe the bush is turning green and farmers have begun planting early maize seed. Let's hope they haven't started too soon. Should the early rains tail off again, fragile seedlings will not survive.

Next morning, we are running late and do not need tea and toast *first* followed by juice and cornflakes. Yesterday morning there was no milk. Last night there was no bream and this morning there is no fruit. What will they run out of next? Clearly crisis management rules the day here.

That afternoon we visit an internet café recommended by Mr Mbai, who omits to mention a lack of secure parking there. For that read: not chained off or with a guard in attendance to deter chancers from breaking in regardless of whether they can spot anything left in the car or not. On our return, we notice youths paying close attention to the car. One is partially hidden on the driver's side to the rear. The same thought crosses both our minds at once.

"Quick, take the backpack, then jump in!"

Bob thrusts his heavy bag containing cash, credit card, camera at me and, with a click of the button, unlocks the door. I dive in my side throwing his bag over the back, while he leaps in his side, locking both doors before driving off at speed. A narrow escape from yet another of Kitwe's many hazards!

Back at base, the pool has turned an enticing turquoise ready for use. And there is bream for supper.

"The manager went all the way into Kitwe to buy it for you," Jessie tells us eagerly.

Maybe they're trying, but then maybe not. There are no serviettes at breakfast next day and when we return early for lunch, we wait over an hour for sandwiches, while that evening, returning hot, sweaty and sticky, we find three Zambian men filling the swimming pool with their bulk. The temperature has risen over forty degrees today, while humidity has rocketed off the scale.

Suddenly two females materialise from nowhere, dressed like gaudy butterflies, yet clearly not here merely to gather pollen. They settle beside the pool fluttering their gaudy wings. The receptionist appears with a third woman who sashays across the emerald lawn, hips clad in a sheath-like skirt and bosoms bursting from her skimpy top.

"My friend wants to meet you." The receptionist simpers to the men in the pool. "Maybe you could join her in the bar after your swim?"

Bob is clearly uncomfortable with what's going on. Yet quite possibly, if he was here alone, he also would have been offered a 'friend'!

Life goes on much the same until Friday, when the chef fails to appear to cook breakfast, leaving Jessie rattling around preparing and serving breakfast as well as making sandwiches for packed lunch. This all takes a very long time.

Today we've a meeting at Kaputula. Since meetings there invariably leave us drained, we're not in the best mood when we return late afternoon to find noisy drinkers ensconced outside our bedroom window, chain smoking and downing beers like breweries in Zambia are about to run dry. Voices grow ever louder with each round of drinks, till eventually we're forced to head elsewhere to eat, in the hope they'll either quieten down or else disappear. Oh, that we could afford to stay in places where management discourages such practices.

During the evening, the heavens release what has been building all day in menacing thunderclouds, heightened humidity and feints of lightning searing the darkening sky. Something Africa manages on a grand scale. The one blessing is, the rain drives the noisy drinkers inside.

Before returning to our room we tell Jessie, "No early tea tomorrow, it's Saturday."

Does Jessie understand? Too well, since no tea at all arrives. Bob potters along the veranda to find out where it is.

"Ah sorry," Jessie says, "there is only one tea tray and, until we find it, there's no tea." By the time they do, it's time for breakfast.

Today there are things to sort out in Kitwe. There is only one problem, no two actually. Though we carry everything with us when visiting projects, because invariably Zambians accompany us, Saturday alone in Kitwe is another matter. Leaving valuables in the bedroom is not an option, because there's no safe and the door key must be handed in for the maid to clean the room. The other day she left the door wide open.

Whoops, that makes three yet again!

The safest option is carrying everything with us, though that risks someone making a grab like the other day. In the end we leave all valuables, apart from money belts and bum-bag, locked in the car in the hope the car alarm will frighten off would-be thieves. Again we park in the unsecured car park outside the internet café because, unbelievably, during all this we're also keeping tabs on a house sale back in the UK.

A ragged looking African brandishing a filthy face cloth approaches. "Shine your car, boss?" he asks hopefully.

"Sorry, the car was cleaned, this morning."

"Then I will guard your car, boss." The man touches his cap. True, he'll guard the car while we're inside and anticipates a tip for doing so.

At lunchtime we return to the guesthouse where a crowd is gathering for another bout of serious drinking. Three people have again settled outside our bedroom window. Not that we intend spending the afternoon in bed, although sitting on the veranda might've been nice. Instead we head for Mindolo Dam, Kitwe's one beauty spot, which supplies both copper mine and town with water. Smoke belches constantly from the mine chimneys, while traffic growls and machinery rumbles nearby. Not so scenic, nor too idyllic either.

As the sun sets, the sky darkens yet again. A pre storm wind is already blowing as we head back under a lurid yellow and black sulphurous sky. Suddenly we drive into a blanket of dust-filled rain blowing in from the bush. The wipers are powerless against it.

By the time we reach Courtyard, rain is teeming in torrents. Yet a welcoming committee in various stages of inebriation awaits. Undeterred by rain, they're under the veranda or crowded under shelters in the garden and clearly here to stay. Some are even out on the emerald sward canoodling in the rain. Loud music thumps incessantly from the bar where windows are wide open.

I gaze at Bob in dismay. "It's how I imagine Sodom and Gomorrah!"

He shrugs helplessly, "Let's go out again."

Even where we ate last night, all is not bliss. Roused by the rain, mosquitoes are out in force. Since French doors stand wide to the heavens, they feast on exposed flesh like famished carnivores. One waiter kindly surrounds the table with burning mosquito coils, yet they swiftly breach these defences to feast afresh.

Returning late to Courtyard, cars are littered everywhere, on the drive, out on the roadside, spilling over every inch of parking space. The combined noise of music and drunken revelry has not abated one little bit. Eventually, at gone midnight, I thrust a skirt over my nightdress and head for reception to rouse a yawning waitress who at least quietens the last three drinkers still imbibing outside our bedroom window.

"Enough is enough," I declare as peace descends. "If you agree, we're out of this den of iniquity tomorrow."

Overnight resolve doesn't weaken to escape from here. Yet only one alternative exists: back to the diet, albeit with the view, to die for. There's only one problem, no two actually. No-one is around to inform we're leaving, nor to make up the bill other than the barman, not yet sober enough to tally up accommodation plus meals and drinks.

Enter Christina who dealt with our original booking query with the assurance, *'For sure, this is a quiet hotel.'* At 7.45am on Sunday morning Christina is wearing a black floor length evening dress complete with costume jewellery.

"I have been to church," she informs us, though she looks more like she spent the night in the Cinderella Nite-Club. We tell her we would like to settle our bill. "Ah, you are leaving?" she feigns surprise.

"Yes, because it's not quiet and we're not comfortable with what goes on here."

"Ah me, I am very surprised!"

"Even other places in Kitwe which encourage outside drinking have had serious problems, even shootings. It's only a matter of time before this place also gets targeted by armed robbers."

The one blessing is we won't be here when it happens. That is if we can agree the bill, because Christina tries to charge for vast amounts of food and drink. Perhaps for what three men plus 'lady friends' consumed?

"We are sorry to see you go," is her parting shot.

Not as sorry as if we were staying for even one more night!

The welcome at the lodge is overwhelming. George beams his one-toothed grin. The latest addition to the family must be cooed over, before lunch of steak and chips served out on the island. And, even if the sky darkens after lunch, it's good to be back. Other people are here for the day, yet by 7pm they have vanished back to Kitwe and peace descends. Apart that is from unnerving rustlings in the brush behind the chalet.

"There's a rock python living up behind," the owner tells us.

That would be the one that squeezes its prey to death and has one hundred teeth, so glad we didn't miss that!

"I am wondering what you want for supper?" George waddles along the veranda.

"Just some eggs would be good, George."

"Ah sorry, madam, there are no eggs."

Maybe the hens didn't know we were coming or forgot to lay, or nobody went to Cedric's Farm to collect them, or they went and haven't yet come back. We have bacon sandwiches instead. They come decorated with cheese squares, salad and crisps and followed by ice-cream. Oh well, it's only for three nights!

Our remaining days pass swiftly at the lodge where location is everything. We succumb meekly to the diet to die for, while listening to the night-time accompaniment of crickets whirring, frogs croaking, while the rock python slithers not so silently behind the chalet each night in search of prey.

Hardly surprising then that Mrs Musungaila takes great delight in complimenting me yet again, "Ah Mrs Cooke, I see you are putting on weight!"

And so ends another trip, during which we've breached the gates of Sodom and Gomorrah, yet have emerged unscathed to see another day and maybe even another trip.

Yet one problem remains, no two actually. Where to stay in Kitwe next time. Oh, and how to hire a reliable vehicle . . . and how to keep ourselves and our money safe?

Whoops, that makes three, possibly four problems? We simply cannot win!

CHAPTER TWENTY-SIX: THE LIGHTS GO OUT IN ZAMBIA!
September - > October 2008

"Ah Zambia!" sighs Bob as we head northwards to Kitwe in September 2008.

"What on earth do you mean?" But there's no response, other than the unspoken question that haunts each trip, *'What trials lie ahead this time?'*

Yet none more so than returning to what feels like a strangely rudderless country since the untimely death three weeks ago from a stroke of President Levy Patrick Mwanawasa. Nowadays many middle class Zambians have abandoned the traditional diet of 'nshima' and vegetables in favour of a western diet rich in saturated fats, salt and sugar, resulting in escalating numbers of wealthier Zambians dying of strokes, heart disease or diabetes.

And yes, we're headed for the lodge on the banks of the Kafue River because yet again, it's all we can afford. As we cross the earthen wall separating the first two dams, it almost feels like a homecoming ...

"Hang on, what's that in the water?"

Bob stops and we watch a lone croc spearhead its way across the dam where he usually goes fishing. It's not a large one; nevertheless, crocs are partial to other delicacies apart from fish.

Crocs aside, there's another irritation this trip. Zambia is running out of electricity, whether because of increased demand or underproduction at Kariba power station, no-one seems sure.

"It's the Zimbabweans' fault," claims one, "for not maintaining the supply or dealing with malfunctions and breakdowns."

"No, blame the South Africans," rants another. "Buying cheap electricity from us when we haven't enough for ourselves!"

"The ruddy Chinese are to blame!" rails another. Which group currently gets blamed when anything goes awry in Zambia, not least because they're digging a trench all the way from Livingstone to the far north of Zambia.

"But what's this trench for?" we ask our good friends, Mbai and Chama.

They shake their heads, "Ah, that we don't know."

"Better watch out," we warn them. "Before you know it, little green men might leap out the trench and begin colonising Zambia!"

"Ah, those Chinese will take us over for sure!"

Certainly, the current hike in the price of cement is partly due to the Chinese building everywhere. Yet no-one seems willing or able to stop them. Meanwhile, South Africans are building football stadiums like crazy ready for the World Cup and also buying up Zambian cement. Yet whether these two nations between them have indeed caused the power to go off, is not certain.

What is certain is, it goes off at any time due to 'load-shedding'. So, although we retire to bed on the first night with electricity, it goes off around 4am. Not to fear, there's a generator on site. Sales of generators have rocketed, along with tales of people importing them illegally from neighbouring countries. Though quite how anyone hides a generator in the back of a car, because it's not something eagle-eyed customs officials might miss.

On the first morning, the generator kicks in at 5am, upping the odds of a hot breakfast. Some hope! Cold bacon, tomatoes and onions along with lukewarm eggs and half-toasted bread appear as ever.

Welcome back, it's like we've never been away!

Unfortunately load-shedding colours this trip from the start. Although the whole country suffers, it's rumoured some parts suffer less than others. In other words, privileged or wealthier areas of both Kitwe and Lusaka. Yet, since the lodge lies outside Kitwe close to high density townships, power there frequently goes off all day or all night.

On our first day back, we return for a late lunch to find there's no power until 5pm. Not surprisingly obtaining food becomes even more problematical than usual. Meals are either cooked up in 'madam's' house, or else on a tiny charcoal brazier in George's miniscule kitchen where he zuzzes up such delights as raw onion and tomato slopped on top of *al dente* pasta for lunch.

Next day electricity stays on all day, but goes off as George is about to cook dinner. He tussles for an hour with pork chops on a tiny brazier, while vegetables cooked 'on high' arrive lukewarm. What with deceased presidents, hungry crocs and load-shedding, this is not set to be the easiest of trips. And that's without struggling to cut chops charred to a cinder on the brazier.

Certainly crocs are much in evidence. Two of them took up residence in the dams in the dry season when the river level fell, while a third larger one also occasionally appears. Most evenings strolling around the dams, the unmistakeable v-shape of a partially submerged croc arrows across the dam. Unnerving, since a small boy comes down each evening to collect water, trailing a can in his hands in the dam.

Equally unnerving is the discovery of a human skull washed up on the bank at the fishing camp, empty eye sockets staring blankly out. A murder perhaps?

"More like a croc or a drowning," declares Bob.

Dead men tell no lies. For now, the Kafue River guards its secrets, though the fishing camp is renamed, 'Place of the Skull', at least until increased water levels next rainy season wash the skull further down to another isolated spot.

That evening George cooks bream from madam's freezer for dinner. Unfortunately, there's a dead spider glued to the underside of my fish. I call George from behind his tatty curtain to show him.

"Aieeh, sorry madam!" George almost falls over in the profuseness of his apologies. "It must have fallen accidentally into the cooking oil."

Like the skull into the river perhaps?

That evening Rupiah Banda, acting president since the death of Levy Mwanawasa, appears on TV to address the nation. Formerly vice-president, he now hopes to become elected interim president in the forthcoming presidential by-election. Just as Banda gets into his stride, George announces the generator is going off, meaning no electricity until Zesco switches the power back on again which could be a very long time. On tonight's news they announced Zesco had inexplicably severed the main electricity link with Zimbabwe, thus heralding the biggest power cut Zambia has ever known.

In pitch darkness we stumble along the veranda to our room praying for light to return before bedtime. Texting remains possible, yet stumbling up a rocky pathway to the pool in order to send them when a rock python is on the loose is a no-no. Just as all hope vanishes, George appears with a candle stuck in a beer bottle which must suffice until electricity returns next morning as the rising sun evaporates mist from the dam. At least there's warm toast for breakfast before a day of trials at Kaputula.

That evening Bob attempts to catch a bream large enough for dinner, but instead attracts the attention of a croc. Each time he casts his bait into the water, the croc torpedoes across, homing in on its prey faster than Jaws.

"Be careful!" I call from a safe vantage point. "You don't want to end up another skull on a lonely stretch of riverbank!"

Later the lodge owner informs us crocs eat every part of their victim apart from the skull. Apparently, skulls are too hard. He warns us to take care walking around the dam. So few people come there now, crocs have taken to lying out on the footpath round the dam. Indeed, a couple of nights later we surprise one warming itself in the last rays of the sun in the middle of the path. It slithers with barely a ripple into the murky waters of the dam, then hangs suspended, watching our every move.

So busy are we watching him, we miss what's happening behind in the river. Suddenly, with a loud splosh, a huge black face surfaces midstream peering short-sightedly our way. The first hippo we've spotted here, though they're often honking not far away upriver. With less people around, they also are braving waters further downriver. We retreat to the bar veranda overlooking the river and watch its huge black bulk swim off downstream. Hippos, crocs, pythons, baboons, leopard, all very exciting, but sometimes just a bit scary.

As days progress, meals become more problematical. More food is cooked on high as they run out of charcoal for George's brazier. Rumours abound of a national charcoal shortage. Sales of braziers have soared. What with the trials of load-shedding combined with increasing age, George struggles to cope with running up and down the 'kopje'. Food arrives in varying degrees of warmth and in whatever order he remembers to fetch it.

Sadly no-one is on hand to help him. We've no idea how old he is, he could be forty going on seventy or just plain seventy. We wouldn't presume to ask. Though his increased forgetfulness and inability to cope, poses the question, if we stayed here again, would George still be here to look after us?

Yet during that first week, a diversion temporarily distracts us from these trials. One of our partners introduces us to a fresh-faced young Canadian girl, brimming with enthusiasm for her involvement in one of the organisation's projects near Solwezi.

"Even they've built a house for me in the village," she enthuses, "so I can live like one of the community."

'They' being members of the local community, already struggling to cope with HIV AIDS, poverty, disease, malnutrition, and the last thing they need is a well-meaning but misguided young 'mzungu' woman landing like an alien from outer space and dabbling in an Africa she neither knows nor understands. We ask how she became involved.

The girl's innocent blue eyes gaze out from a fair complexion already dappled red from over-exposure to tropical sunshine. She brushes back filthy dreadlocks that haven't seen shampoo in weeks. "My friend and I were backpacking, and kind of fancied seeing what things were really like," she drawls in a lazy Canadian twang.

Zambia is not geared to backpackers, unless you're prepared to live and eat like a Zambian. Nor is it cheap, either to stay or to travel around. Besides, living like a Zambian carries a hefty price tag: the risk of contracting malaria, TB, dysentery, typhoid, cholera and a whole host of other nasties.

She ploughs on regardless, "We like got a list of organisations in Lusaka, then phoned here and the director says like straightaway, why don't you come up here and see for yourselves."

I look from her to the pale, insipid young man standing beside her, who's almost falling asleep on his feet. "Both of you?"

"Heck no, my younger brother just arrived on this morning's flight. No, a girlfriend and myself saw what was happening and decided we *had* to do something to help. She returned to Canada to raise money, while I stayed to oversee building work. It's truly amazing, we're like building this school." She tosses this gem out as if no-one has *ever* built a school in Zambia before.

"The Cookes have already built a school here," says the director in that phlegmatic tone Zambians manage so well. "Maybe they can advise you?"

But where should we start? *Don't pretend you're a Zambian or can live like one, when you aren't and can't!*

Not that she'd take any notice. More likely she'll end up marrying a local man with no intention or means of supporting her. Maybe her folks sent the brother out to find out what's going on? Still, the director's face says it all, totally disenchanted with the whole business! Secretly I suspect it will take more than big brother's arrival to halt this potentially destructive avalanche.

That weekend, the two of them appear at the lodge as we're eating lunch on the veranda. We invite them to join us.

The girl rubs her gut ruefully. "Sorry, upset tummy."

Something picked up in the village perhaps?

"It's like so great having this opportunity to live with Zambians," she continues. "They like *so* appreciate what I'm doing for them." Clearly an upset tummy hasn't dampened her enthusiasm.

Her brother, however, eyes our omelettes enviously. Perhaps he's already tasted what lies ahead food-wise in the village next week, meaning sister has started as she means to go on: 'nshima' with kapenta or vegetable relish. Not only is it filling, it sets like concrete in the gut. How long before he also succumbs to something nastier than run-of-the-mill gut rot?

Yet that same weekend, we also succumb to upset stomachs, possibly because both the fridge and freezer at the lodge are off more often than on. Food deteriorates rapidly causing germs to thrive. From a hygiene point of view, we're currently no better off than the Canadian girl in her mud hut.

Yet her situation continues to cause concern. Next week we raise it again with our partners. That is after a breakfast with no eggs, no toast and no orange juice.

"Ah sorry, madam!" George rubs his hands sorrowfully, "it is the electrics again."

"But George, we need cold drinks today." Not for ourselves, but a treat for sponsored secondary pupils.

George waddles off to the bar. Deciding he may need assistance, I follow him along the veranda. "Look George, there is orange juice!" I point to cartons in the chiller cabinet.

"Ah me, I am blind!" Dismay clouds George's features. "It is because I am needing glasses. Maybe you can give me yours when you go?" Poor George, such things cost more than he will possibly earn in a lifetime.

"So what's happening with the Canadian girl?" we ask our partners later.

The assistant director shakes his head. "That one is causing problems. Even we have serious concerns for her safety. She does not realise that, should she get into trouble, it will reflect on our organisation."

"Is there nothing you can do?"

"Our director spoke with the parents in Canada. For myself, I spoke with her, also I tasked responsible people in the community to keep a watchful eye out that she does not get into a situation she cannot handle." He eyes us hopefully, "Perhaps if you . . ."

But the girl has already returned to the village, while on the morrow we head for Lusaka. We can only pray she comes to her senses before falling victim to Africa's many pitfalls.

We travel south to Lusaka for the weekend in a still rudderless country where no-one knows from one day to the next whether power will go on or off. In theory each area has scheduled shutdowns, but in practice it remains unpredictable. Lights, phones, traffic lights, petrol pumps, shop tills, businesses, all grind to a halt without warning creating chaos in their wake.

In an effort to satisfy a burgeoning need, charcoal sellers line the road all the way south from Kitwe to Lusaka. Zambians are desperate for fuel to feed hungry braziers. Yet if they continue chopping down trees at the rate they're doing, they may cause an even greater crisis.

Has no-one told them, trees are essential to the survival of the planet?

Bob, in his turn, adds to chaos in Lusaka by causing a flood. As if having no power with two young children in the house is not already enough, he attempts to replace a leaky tap washer by removing the bathroom tap. Water gushes out, flooding the bathroom floor and pouring down the passageway.

"Is there a stopcock anywhere?" he yells.

"Search me," responds Ali. "I've never had a flood here before!"

Bob stuffs a rag in the hole while we await the arrival of a plumber in a country where currently nothing is certain, least of all the lights going on or the election of a president. Yet this crisis merely adds to other trials.

"I'm not sure we should return to the lodge," Bob announces when upset stomachs stubbornly fail to respond to Lomotil or Immodium. "Power cuts lasting fifteen and a half hours are doing us no good!"

Pity there weren't plumbers for leaky guts also!

In the hope of regaining control over food, we return to self-catering in Kitwe and a warm welcome from Patricia, who formerly cleaned our flat. Recently she's been promoted to housekeeper, so no longer wields the Mr Sheen, but capably oversees a small army of maids and cleaners.

Unfortunately, self-catering means running the gauntlet not only of Shoprite to buy food, but also of street kids desperate to grab the trolley merely to earn five pin for pushing it from the shop door to the car. Then there are beggars desperate to milk the last drop of human kindness from our depleted fount. Not to mention keeping bags, purses, car, shopping and sanity safe from the grasp of thieves and pickpockets.

Yet power cuts follow us here. Evening food must be cooked by 5pm. No lights or TV are allowed after that time. They are however more organised. The first morning back the chef has a veritable armoury of braziers blazing both inside and outside the kitchen. Hot water outside is boiling for cups of tea, while bacon and eggs are sizzling inside. These last days in Kitwe become not only bearable, but also allow damaged guts time to heal.

Back on the job, Chilumba's second in command updates us on the situation regarding the young Canadian girl. "Our director has gone to the village to talk with the Canadian girl. In the absence of the girl's parents, she feels she must act like a mother and warn her to take care."

We can only pray that works and the girl comes to her senses.

And so another eventful trip ends. We leave Zambia not only to elect a new president in a presidential by-election, but also to restore light and power to the nation.

"Even they are bringing electricity to Chilumba," announces our partner on our last trip there.

"So when will it arrive?" we ask.

"Ah, that we don't know," he answers despondently. "Each time there is an election, the party seeking re-election puts up a few more electricity poles, yet when it will reach Chilumba, nobody knows!"

Sadly Chilumba, like everywhere else in Zambia, remains in limbo. Nobody knows when if ever the lights will go back on. Though in the meantime, perhaps they'd better a watch out for little green men!

Postscript:
The Canadian girl entered into a 'village' marriage with a local man and convinced locals to sever connections with the aid organisation, causing programmes to grind to a halt. Later her friend returned, declaring she was in love with the same man and became pregnant by him. The community was torn in two. To date no school has been built and local orphans are now without support. A warning indeed to: 'Be careful what you sow, lest you reap in tears!'

Rupiah Banda was duly elected interim president of Zambia in the elections, but only served until the next full presidential election when he was defeated.

CHAPTER TWENTY-SEVEN: LIFE'S FULL OF SURPRISES!
May 2009

You'd think by now we'd be used to Zambia's many surprises, yet it still has a few in store. Arriving in May 2009, it's colder than expected. Winter has arrived early and guess who hasn't brought enough warm clothes! At least one person isn't bothered by the cold. Thandi jumps up and down with excitement because we're back and has had Mummy up half the night lest she forgets to go to the airport. *As if!*

However, time with family is preciously short before heading for Choma to catch up on the completion of a rural health clinic there, where our field of operation has now expanded. Except Choma is in the south-west, two hundred miles from family in Lusaka and six hundred miles from Kitwe. And, as our one trip to Choma last November has already revealed . . . Choma looks set to raise a whole raft of problems of its own.

Last November we stayed at a family run lodge where chef Eugene rustled up delicious dinners served by candlelight under a thatched 'nsaka' before retiring for a peaceful night disturbed by nothing other than the chirrup of crickets and the whirr of cicadas. However, the owners have since relocated to Vic Falls taking Eugene along and leaving behind only a skeleton staff who will look after us, as long as we see to our own food. This suits well enough.

The lodge is five kilometres from Choma and is simply a cluster of thatched chalets plus a large kitchen with open thatched dining area. Staff live close enough to clean, light fires and keep hot water topped up. Yet as the car turns into the car park, the first thing that's apparent is an air of dereliction. Not a sign of life, no-one to greet us.

"Hello?" I call. "Is anybody here?"

Eventually a disgruntled maid appears. Welcome is the last expression on her face. Hearing we're booked to stay, she disappears for ages before returning with an elderly 'mzungu', presumably the owner's father. Clearly he's not expecting us either, but concedes grudgingly, it will be okay. Even he'll get someone to light a fire for hot water later.

Last November it was forty degrees every day here, yet it's currently even colder than Lusaka. Neither of us intends stripping off tonight to wash. The morning can take care of itself, which it does, by turning even colder. However, by lunchtime, the lodge has finally woken up. Since it's warmer outside than inside, we sit out to eat, entertained by a gardener singing as she weeds and waters, occasionally glancing our way to check we're listening.

Suddenly this idyll is shattered as a blazing row erupts in the staff quarters, every sentence punctuated by foul obscenities in English. The little black nightingale stops singing to prick up her ears. Has someone been sacked, caught with their hand in the sugar tin? Things have certainly changed here, proving yet again nothing in Zambia is ever what you expect!

However, a couple of days brings an about-change. Out of the blue the owners turn up from Livingstone. The old man makes his presence felt and the gardener sings her tuneless heart out. We however are off for a weekend down at Lake Kariba.

The plan is to meet Ali and the girls en route and travel in convoy to Kariba. Just short of the junction we stop for lunch and are standing outside munching food on plastic plates when suddenly a man lurches towards us. Not a soul is around, worrying since he's wielding a hefty club with an axe head on the end and looks menacing. True, he could have returned from the fields, yet suddenly his slow amble becomes a purposeful lumbering trot . . .

"Quick, back in the car!" I thrust my plate at Bob, tipping salad all over his lap, and leap in the car. Then I'm out of there, spinning the wheels in gravel lining the roadside. Who needs surprises like that!

At Siavonga we meet up with Ali and friends for the weekend. Bob and the three boys may be outnumbered, yet he has the prospect of several eager young fishing companions. The two oldest boys intend camping, while the rest of us are in chalets. Yet by 9pm on the first night two shaken boys return to the chalets, freaked out by hippo grunting right outside their tent.

On Saturday Bob takes the two older boys fishing. Thandi and the youngest boy also want to go, then three year old Becca also toddles along. Five boisterous kids but only one Granddad, means Ali also gets roped in. The other two ladies disappear shopping, leaving me alone by the swimming pool. Yet it's not long before the first defector loses interest and joins me by the pool, where the water is chilly and there's no temptation to linger long.

After lunch we walk along the lakeshore. "Stay away from the water!" we warn all five children. "There are crocs in there!"

"Huh, no-one *ever* got eaten by a croc here," one boy boasts bravely.

"Except the owner's dog!"

"Oh yeh?"

"Oh yeh!" End of conversation!

After a weekend at Kariba, we're loathe to travel 500kms north to smoke-grimed Kitwe. Not least because of the endless accommodation problems there. Yet such gloomy thoughts fail to prepare us for what we encounter en route. On a straight stretch of road, one of the many high-speed buses, which now ply the route between the Copperbelt and Lusaka, has knocked down and killed a young schoolgirl. They are just covering the body as we drive past. Her schoolbooks and one shoe lie scattered in the road.

Surprises like that, we can do without!

At the Kitwe flats, we pray as ever for a peaceful stay. Usually it's me complaining about the lack of a good night's sleep in Zambia, yet this time Bob can't seem to get a night's rest. He blames everything from decaffeinated Ricoffy bought by mistake, to dogs barking incessantly and too much meat passing through his gut. We even temporarily turn vegetarian to allow the weekend's surfeit of meat to pass through the system.

Yet all is not peace and harmony at the flats. Management have relaxed their ban on outside drinkers. Not a problem if drinkers stay in the bar, yet on the first night a group settles in front of our veranda drinking, laughing, texting and telling inane jokes. This doesn't bode well for a peaceful stay.

All the same, staying at the flats does have pluses. Apart from largely having control of our food, there's also the God channel on TV plus a cooked breakfast arrives each morning at the flat door, generally on time and generally exactly what we ordered. *And* laundry is included in the price!

But is this latter really a plus? Each morning I note what's gone in the laundry basket, lest washing starts unaccountably disappearing. With twelve flats, remembering which laundry came from where must test even Patricia's skills. However, after a few days I realise the washing's not coming back.

"What, not at all or just each day's washing?" Bob is not awfully clued up about how such matters operate.

"Both. Because of dirty washing from Choma, I've been slipping a bit extra through each day."

"Maybe they need more time, or it's not dry or ironed?" Bob has limited interest in the fate of his underpants.

I mention the unreturned washing to the maid. The backlog then returns, but not that day's washing. With the weekend ahead, I'm not happy with washing being be left out overnight. I decide to investigate. The drying area is in a narrow alley between the back wall of the bar and a breezeblock wall dividing this plot from next door. With winter approaching, the sun advancing northwards means the south side gets progressively less sun to dry the washing and may explain why . . .

"Agggh!" I leap backwards in fright. The drying area is also behind the kitchen area. My sudden arrival has startled half a dozen huge rats, which scuttle for shelter. The laundry problem can resolve itself; I'm out of here!

The second week in Kitwe starts much the same as any other. On the first day, I'm driving as we leave town via the second class trading area. Approaching a barely visible STOP sign at a T-junction, I stop before turning left, straight into a police roadblock.

Instantly, a young policeman leaps out, hand raised bringing the car to a halt. Police in Zambia are getting younger like everywhere else, yet this one is still wet behind the ears. "You have committed an infringement in that you failed to stop at the stop sign clearly displayed at the junction."

Would that be the one twenty yards back from the junction, paint peeling off it and leaning to one side because somebody ran into it?

"Ah officer, you are wrong!" Mr Chalwe pipes up from behind.

The young policeman turns to Mr Chalwe. "Are you telling me the wheels of this vehicle did stop?"

"Precisely what I am saying!" Mr Chalwe is angrier than I've ever seen.

"Even though I am observing that the person driving this vehicle failed to bring her wheels to halt at a halt sign before proceeding around the corner?"

"But the sign is twenty yards back," I try. "I stopped, but in order to see anything coming, I had to proceed forward to the junction."

"Where in fact you failed to halt!"

"This is preposterous!" explodes Mr Chalwe. "I recall myself the wheels came to a halt."

"I must warn you, sir, if you say anything further, you also may be charged and put in a cell. Even these people will be taken before the court."

Mr Chalwe finally decides silence is wiser. The young policeman, however, is just getting into his stride. "This person is disputing my judgement," he announces. "An infringement is an infringement."

"Officer, you cannot treat these persons like this!" Normally placid Mr Mbai joins the fray.

Even Mr Chama joins in. "These people are from the UK. Even they are helping the people of our country."

The young policeman is having none of it. "Everyone in this vehicle is in cahoots. I have no alternative but to ask you to proceed to the police station. Myself I will accompany you there." The officious young policeman opens the rear door and squeezes into the back seat. Just as well he is small, it's already crowded in there. "Drive on!" he commands.

By now, I'm shaking. "Are you . . . *arresting me?*"

"Indeed, yes, that is the case."

I can't trust myself to drive any further. "Then my husband can drive." I get out the vehicle slamming the door and we swap places. I only pray Bob doesn't lose his rag, worse, offer the policeman twenty pin to forget the matter. Police often don't get paid at the end of the month, yet now is not the time to slip him twenty pin. But there is an even bigger fear . . .

Dear God, please don't let them lock me up in a Zambian prison cell!

Silence reigns all the way to the police station, where not a 'mzungu' is in sight. A second policeman behind a desk records name, age, address, vehicle registration along with *alleged* offence. To say anything further at this point could result in all of us behind bars. Bob has been inside a prison here and reported they're grim places where prisoners receive no food unless relatives bring it in. Frequently prisoners rot inside for years. There is no evidence to suggest we would receive anything other than the harshest treatment routinely dealt out to criminals in this country.

The young man disappears with the charge sheet, presumably to seek authority to relieve us of precious cash. My stomach is churning. I feel sick. Yet we must see this through to the end.

Mr Chalwe, however, is made of sterner stuff and approaches a door labelled Superior Officer where he knocks and disappears inside. I just hope he doesn't make matters worse. Though, can they actually be any worse?

After a few moments, Mr Chalwe summons us in to face a senior officer, older and hopefully wiser than the youngster who arrested us. He says nothing, yet his expression speaks volumes . . .

What on earth do I do with a couple of mzungu prisoners in their sixties?

However, Mr Chalwe turns out to be the man of the moment, displaying such eloquence as he pleads for leniency from the senior officer who listens intently, all the while fiddling with his pen, his phone card, shuffling papers on his desk, while he contemplates how to resolve an awkward situation without losing face. Just as well he doesn't realise, I write down every last thing that happens in Zambia then publish it. If he did, it would be the cells for sure!

"So, this couple are here doing charity work?" he plays for time.

"In fact, yes, that is the case." Mr Chalwe is never a man of few words when half a dozen are better.

"Maybe because *she* is new here, *she* is not knowing the rules of the road, that in Zambia *she* must stop at a road sign?"

Best not to inform him that, not only has *she* driven for a number of years, but also we have been coming here regularly for the past seven years and driving regularly here. Some things are best left unsaid. My supposed ignorance could become my get out of jail free card.

Eventually he summons a minion and scribbles something on a piece of paper. "Take them to the payment officer," he says.

The female payment officer's hat is titled at a jaunty angle and there's enough slap on her dusky features to qualify her for a Bollywood movie. She silently scrutinises the paper before announcing, "Okay, you can go."

We don't hang around, but scuttle outside and into the car.

"In fact, we were lucky," announces Mr Chalwe.

That rather depends on what you call luck! I feel pretty sick, a feeling that persists all day, all evening and into the night and is still there next day. So sick, I could get on the next plane back to the UK!

None of which makes our last few nights in Kitwe any more pleasurable. Outside drinkers, as well as nightly power cuts, are both increasing. Come the end of the week, we're not sorry to leave Kitwe. Quite frankly, if I never see Kitwe again, that might be a day too soon!

Yet there's still whatever returning to Choma holds in store. Certainly, even colder weather as a cold wind blows constantly and then, in the middle of the dry season, it rains. A cold, grisly front is passing over South Africa, its tail end catching Zimbabwe and Southern Zambia. Zambians must think the end of the world is coming. Those with long memories cannot recall winters like this. They wrap up in coats, scarves, gloves, blankets, parkas and stand huddled, shivering on street corners or going about their business, heads bent against the appalling wind.

Our lack of suitable clothing is much apparent and we resort to wearing everything at once: vests, T-shirts, sweaters, shoes, socks and jackets. Since there's no heating in the chalet, the nights are miserable. I pile thin towels on top of thin blankets for extra warmth. Still we shiver.

After a miserable few days, it rains again, then finally the wind blows itself out. As if it had never been hiding for days, the sun reappears, the sky turns blue and normal dry season weather reasserts itself. The singing gardener unwraps herself from rags and tatters she's worn over the past few days and starts singing again as she goes about her work.

Unfortunately, the sun reappears just as we're due to leave Choma. That is if we can find someone to pay for our stay here. The owner's father has vanished and the maid, another Patricia, rules the roost. She has taken to sunning herself outside on chairs for guests' use and using guests' washrooms. Otherwise, she does little apart from shout. In fact, everyone here shouts. They shout from one end of the farm and guests' accommodation to another.

Patricia wears a black curly hairpiece skewed atop her head and shouts louder than anyone. Probably she was the one shouting on the day of the argument. Maybe I should shout at her right now. We have $10 credit from our previous stay, because the old boss had no change. Can I persuade Patricia to knock $10 off our bill? No, I cannot! I offer her $230 instead of $240, but she isn't happy, so we stand arguing outside the back door to the main house, where Patricia also holds sway. She doesn't invite me inside.

"If you are paying $10 less, then what shall I tell the madam?"

"That we had $10 credit. Look, perhaps if I spoke to the madam?"

"Madam is not here, she is in Livingstone." Patricia bars the door, perhaps fearing I will barge inside to search for the madam.

"Then may I use the house phone to speak with her, because unless I phone her, you and I will stand here all day."

Patricia allows me into the house to use the phone, but stands guard. What's she afraid of now, I'll run off with the family silver? Or perhaps I'll tell madam what goes on in her absence, such as Patricia cooking her food on madam's stove in madam's kitchen.

"Ah, sorry, madam is out of the country," a disembodied voice in Livingstone tells me. Currently this person is my only line to sanity. I relate the entire saga of the $10 credit to her. Does she get it?

"So you are saying that you are paying $10 less?"

"Yes, because we have a $10 credit!" Goodness, at this rate the phone bill is going to cost more than $10!

But Bob has had enough and is ready to return to family and sanity. "Let me see what you have in change," he says to Patricia. He plonks $300 in her hand and takes $70 back, exactly the same as if I'd given her $240 and she'd given $10 change. However, as we didn't have the right money and Patricia had no $10 notes but did have $50 plus a $20, we are quits ... *I think!*

For now, we're off to Lusaka, then on a plane back to the UK. This time we've had enough of Zambia, its not so pleasant surprises combined with its unfailing ability to catch us unawares. We've also outstayed our welcome at this lodge, so won't be back here.

"So where *do* we stay next time in Choma?" asks Bob as we pull out onto the tarmac heading for Lusaka, but that's supposing there is a next time. For some reason, a question mark seems to have appeared as to whether we return or not. Oh well, time alone will tell.

CHAPTER TWENTY-EIGHT: CRABS IN LUSAKA ... NEVER!
September - > October, 2010

After last trip's trials, I swore I would *never* return to Zambia. Yet fate, fickle as ever, decreed it would be eighteen months before we travelled there again. Time enough to put those horrors behind us.

Thus, September 2010 finds us once more outside Lusaka airport, complete with luggage and entry visa wondering where on earth the family have got to. Have they slept in, forgotten about us, had an accident ... Just then Ali appears puffing and panting with two excited children in tow.

"Shouldn't you two be in school?" I joke.

"What, miss Grandma and Granddad arriving, you *must* be joking!"

And so begins another trip, doubtless with trials, pitfalls, surprises pleasant and not so pleasant all of its own. First surprise, Ali has moved into another garden flat, an end bungalow on a gated complex owned and rented out by the nearby New Apostolic Church. It's somewhat smaller than before, though it does boast a larger, more private garden. Albeit a garden rather more flush with water than expected.

"There's a leaking pipe somewhere," Ali tells us. "But don't worry, the church people will fix it."

Arrival day is always a matter of surviving until a night's sleep restores sanity. However, this bungalow adjoins one next door, meaning our bedroom is adjacent to next door's kitchen. Not a problem if they keep the same hours, except they don't. They're outside on their cell-phones at all hours, plus one of them smokes but clearly not inside the house, so add to that a back door that squeaks every time someone goes in or out. Already on the first night it is apparent ... we're not going to get much sleep here.

None of which prepares us for surprise number two. "I'm thinking of leaving Zambia," announces Ali.

I don't even get as far as, *'Are you thinking of returning to live in the UK?'* before she adds ... "I'm applying for jobs elsewhere." She pauses, aware disappointment has leeched its tentacles into the room. "Mozambique, possibly Somalia or Tanzania."

I rein in my disappointment and attempt to keep my emotions under control. "So when's this likely to happen?"

"I need to get a job first, but hopefully early next year."

Still unsure where all this is leading, my mind hops aboard a roller-coaster of racing thoughts. What will happen to our charity work if our family no longer lives in Zambia? Their presence not only brought us back here in 2002, but has kept us coming back. Not to mention their presence here provides a much needed bolthole for when times get tough. Without family here, would Zambia be the same?

"What I wanted to know . . ." Ali pauses. Instantly my radar is on red alert, unsure what's coming next . . . "If I get offered a job, say in Mozambique, would you be willing to help with the move, Mum?"

Instantly I'm struggling with the enormity of this request. "You mean . . ."

"Come out for a few months, help settle the children into a new country. Are you up for it?"

Recently I've gone through a double operation on my right leg, which now looks as if one of Zambia's larger crocs took a chunk out of it. In the event I've only just made it to Zambia, since the dermatologist who removed a malignant melanoma was of the opinion, *'Why would anyone jump out of the frying pan into the fire?'* Now Ali wants me to accompany her to . . .

"But Mozambique's uncivilised, violent, they had a revolution? Or was it a coup? Anyway, it's out of the question."

"Is that your final answer?" Heavens, that sounds like a certain Saturday night quizmaster!

"Yes, I mean no, no way am I going to Mozambique!"

Yet, as we've already discovered, the word never isn't in God's vocabulary. Nor apparently should it be in a mother's. Perhaps a week staying in the beautiful surroundings of Chisoboyo Farm near Choma mellows my perspective. I return to Lusaka in a more open frame of mind.

We arrive on Friday afternoon for a family weekend before facing the trials of Kitwe. Is it my imagination, but is Ali looking strained? We sit in a drier part of the garden in the late afternoon sun watching the girls play on their swing.

"Any news of Mozambique?" I hazard.

"I've an interview there in a couple of weeks . . ." There's that pause again, pregnant with meaning. "I don't suppose you've changed your mind?"

"You're definitely going through with this?"

"If I get the job," she sighs. "At least say you and Dad will look after the girls while I go for the interview? I'll be away three nights, and frankly, I don't want to leave them with maids."

No hesitation in agreeing to this, yet it still raises the question, "And if you get the job, what then?"

"I thought of asking Sandra to accompany us, perhaps for three months, but she's getting on in years. Sometimes she looks so tired."

I resist the temptation to remind Ali, Sandra is younger than I am. Nor do I reveal Sandra was fast asleep on the settee this afternoon while the kids were watching a movie. Since the girls were nodding off too, this perhaps explains why some nights they won't go to sleep.

"All I can do, is cross that hurdle when I get to it." Her tone brightens. "Anyhow, fancy a Chinese take-away this evening?"

Yes, like swimming in crocodile infested water! I adore Chinese food, but the feeling is not reciprocal. However, since I already feel I'm letting our daughter down, I agree to a take-away, which Ali goes to collect, leaving us with the girls watching TV.

"Is Mozambique going ahead?" asks Bob.

"Seems like it," I respond. "Ali's thinking of asking Sandra to go with her, however, I doubt Sandra will agree so . . ." I take a deep breath, "I'm going to offer to go with them."

Bob looks at me as if I'm insane. "Do you know what you're doing?"

"No, but I'm going to offer. She's a single mother; who else does she have? It's not Sandra's place to go, it's mine. However, I shall tell her *before* downing a glass of wine and *before* eating a Chinese take-away!"

Barely is Ali over the doorstep, than I blurt out, "I'll come with you." At first Ali doesn't register, so I add, "To Mozambique, if you get the job."

She dumps the take-away bag and flings her arms around me. "I thought you were never going to agree!"

"Mummy, why do you look as if you're going to cry?" asks Thandi.

"Because, if Mummy gets the job, Grandma has just agreed to come to Mozambique with us. Frankly I don't how I'd ever cope without her."

"Where's Mozambique?" pipes up Becca. "Is it in Zambia?" Oh dear, information overload for a four year old. Grandma, meanwhile, needs that glass of wine, but a Chinese take-away, not so sure about that!

My first thought on waking is, *'Did I really agree to accompany them to Mozambique?'* It appears I did. Just as we thought we were finishing with Africa, Africa is not quite finished with us. Maybe because we're Africa people! Nevertheless, it's all so far outside my comfort zone, it doesn't bear thinking about. So I don't, but will deal with it as and when it arises.

As we head north to Kitwe on Monday, another thought enters my mind, "If Ali does go to Mozambique after Christmas and, if we don't return to Zambia, this could be the last time ever we travel to Kitwe, Kaputula or anywhere else here."

"It was always going to happen one day," responds Bob.

"All the same . . ." A lump chokes my throat. Maybe God does do *never* after all!

Two weeks later we return to Lusaka before Ali flies to Mozambique on Sunday morning. She's bought The Lonely Planet Guide to Mozambique plus CDs and books to learn Portuguese.

"We've been to Portugal," I tell her. "The language resembles a cross between Russian and Serbo-Croat. We couldn't understand a word."

"So I'm discovering," agrees Ali. "Yet, I'm expected to address them in Portuguese!" *Better her than me!*

Later I dip into the guidebook to see what delights Mozambique offers, only to discover dire warnings about malaria, car-jackings and dodgy areas of

Maputo to be avoided at all costs. Yet elsewhere it waxes lyrical, describing it as the place where the Mediterranean meets Africa, with continental style pavements and street cafes.

How could I not want to spend three months there?

That evening Ali drops another bombshell. During our last week, she has to travel with work. Grandparents to the rescue again, even though currently we don't know whether we're coming or going. Though going seems the strongest possibility.

If that's not enough, Becca's nursery class has been learning about families. What better than to invite real, live grandparents into class on a hot, airless Friday lunchtime to talk to four and five year olds about the good old days, since we're the only people old enough to remember that far back.

Meanwhile Ali is either buried in her Portuguese books or has headphones on, gabbling away in a language none of us understands. Since this occupies every minute of her day, we spend our day amusing the children. We do this so well, they collapse into bed exhausted and fall straight asleep. *Oh, that they do the same while Mummy is away!*

Not so Grandma and Granddad. Apart from the nightly racket from next door, it being Friday evening, the New Apostolic Church is holding a gospel service to which, if volume is anything to go by, the entire neighbourhood is invited.

We retire to bed hoping to get some sleep. Some hope! It's already apparent this plot has a serious drainage problem. Parts of the garden resemble a swamp where mossy, water loving plants thrive as opposed to sprightly zinnias or stately chrysanthemums. Frogs have taken up residence and right now are croaking full throttle. The noise is deafening.

"Something needs to be done about that ruddy swamp!" I bury my head under the duvet in sweltering heat, yet blaring music, squeaking doors, mating frogs, all break the sound barrier more effectively than Concorde!

At ten to five on Sunday morning Ali's alarm goes off. Within half an hour she's off to the airport. Since both children are wide awake, they join me in bed, leaving Bob to decamp to Ali's bed in the living room. And so grandparent duty begins.

Sunday passes relatively well but, although we're exhausted after a sleepless night, there's still another night in which to do battle with mosquitoes buzzing, doors banging, frogs croaking, and music yet again, this time a disco in the Agricultural Showground.

Monday dawns bright and early. Both children must be in school by 7.25am. Since our budget doesn't allow for a hired car while in Lusaka, we walk there. Today it's hot and windy, though maybe not quite so hot and windy walking down the road at 7am as it is at 1pm when we collect them. By then, both heat and wind have become unbearable.

During the morning, a water engineer appears to assess the situation in the garden, but is completely baffled as to why there's a swamp in the middle of a garden in the middle of Lusaka. "Maybe there is an underground stream they were not knowing about when the house was built," he decides.

As in a river running through it?

"Frogs are breeding in there," I tell him.

He shakes his head. "The situation is dangerous. The whole area could collapse into a gigantic sinkhole. The children must be kept away at all costs."

So, am I supposed to keep them inside all afternoon in this heat?

"We will dig along the pipe and locate the problem, maybe a leak or a broken pipe," the engineer decides. Great! Since pipes criss-cross the garden carrying water to other houses, half the garden will be dug up. Ali *will* be pleased when she returns!

That night the children go straight to sleep, but don't stay asleep. As we settle, a little voice cries, "I want a drink! Where's the light? I want Mummy!"

Becca joins me, meaning Bob is again banished to the living room where security lights blaze all night. Meanwhile, I lie sleepless in the dark listening to Becca's steady breathing along with infernal creaking from next door's kitchen door.

On Tuesday, it's up again at 5.55am. Supposedly it only takes five minutes to walk to school, but Becca drags her feet all the way in a howling gale that's turned Lusaka into a dust bowl. It's only September, yet already rain would be welcome. It takes fifteen minutes each way. No sooner are we back from the first run and have made the area around the sinkhole safe, than it's time to head back to the school in the wind and dust.

In the afternoon, the wind worsens. The choice is sweltering inside with doors and windows shut, or braving the wind and dust outside. By bedtime the wind is howling around the house and yard, banging doors and gates, lifting anything that isn't nailed down. At least it deters the frogs from their nightly courtship and even blots out the noise from next door.

Gosh, Africa can be so savage at times!

Amazingly we enjoy our first night's sleep this trip. Even the children sleep in until 6am, which means hurrying down the road so they're not late for school. But what's this? The wind drops and it turns freezing, just as the hottest month is due to commence. And we think we have global warming!

Not that it matters because, after dropping the children, we're off to Choma. Ali is due back later today, so the two maids will hold the fort. We're no closer to knowing whether we're coming or going. There's no news about Mozambique, though we're still needed for grandparent duty during the last week of this trip.

A week later we return as the hot season starts in earnest. Temperatures soar above forty degrees, though nights remain bearable. Of Mozambique there's still no news. Not that Ali's brief sojourn aroused any great desire to take up a post there. The kids are happy to see us, but are unhappy about Mummy being away yet again. And so to bed for a peaceful night's sleep . . .

"Grandma, I had a bad dream!" comes the first little voice.

"Grandma, I'm scared in here by myself!" Bob is banished yet again to a single bed in the living room, while Grandma shares a bed with two little ones who nowadays aren't quite so little. Oh, and Pooh Bear comes too.

I lie in the dark with Pooh Bear shoved up against my face, reflecting how when we arrived, we weren't sure how to fill this last week, yet Lusaka with its attendant crises has taken care of that. The swamp is still in the garden and the frogs' nocturnal chorus still shatters the night-time peace and quiet.

Earlier this afternoon out in the garden Becca was bitten on the toe. Her screams rent the neighbourhood. "A crab bit me!" she shrieked over and over.

"Nonsense, Becca," I told her firmly. "There aren't any crabs in Lusaka."

"There are, Grandma." Thandi's matter of fact voice brooks no arguing. "Even Mummy has seen them!"

This should have clinched the argument, yet I wasn't conceding easily. "You can't have crabs in a Lusaka garden and that's that," I tell them.

Now, in the darkness, I reflect, if a crab didn't bite Becca's toe, what did? A scorpion, ant, bee, worse, a snake? For sure she screamed loudly enough to shatter the neighbours' peace for a change, until we put 'pop-pop' on her sore foot and gave her a piece of orange to pacify her.

Becca looked at me with solemn, brown eyes. "It was a crab, Grandma, I saw it." Tomorrow Granddad must search for crabs in a garden in Lusaka.

This he does and finds a species of freshwater crab has also taken up residence in the sinkhole, swamp and perpetual stream that flows through the garden which leads us to conclude, it's time somebody did something about the situation.

However, another crisis takes precedence. On Wednesday evening Becca ends up in bed with me yet again. She may be missing Mummy, but she also has a temperature, sore throat, rash and appears floppy. She needs to see a doctor. Next morning, I bundle her in a taxi and head for the clinic.

Yet before leaving, every available bucket, saucepan and container in the house must be filled, because finally workmen are coming to dig up the garden. There'll be no water until they locate the problem. At this rate we could be bottling and selling genuine Lusaka spring water at the roadside before the end of the week.

Becca has a nasty strep infection. She sits solemnly beside me on the veranda, watching workmen digging up most of the garden to unearth (again no pun intended) the cause of the problem. It is not in the borehole pipes but in the municipal water supply that also runs through the garden. It's like Piccadilly Circus here, only with water pipes not traffic.

What's not so good, is leaked water has contaminated the house water making all drinking water hazardous. No wonder Becca is sick! From now on, all water must be boiled until new pipes are laid. In Zambia this could take until Christmas.

There is, however, one bright spot. Next door are moving out. Of course someone else will doubtless move in, but for the moment the squeaking door ceases. Even the frogs realise their courting nights in the swamps of Lusaka are numbered and make off in search of fresh mating grounds. *Ah bliss!*

On Friday, having been such an outstanding success with Becca's nursery class, we're invited to speak to Thandi's class, being the only people here ancient enough to remember life existed before computers, TVs, mobile phones and other gadgets without which nobody nowadays can survive.

The other excitement is that Ali is due back this evening. We plan a surprise dinner party to welcome Mummy back. The children don party dresses except that, having got hers on, Becca manages to fall into the bath water. But that's a minor hiccup, since what matters is, *"Mummy's back!"*

Normality returns, well not quite. Thandi also falls sick and has to go to the clinic and the men return to dig up yet more of the garden and turn the water off yet again.

"Thandi may need her tonsils out," says Ali when they return.

"So, will you bring her to the UK for that?" Hope, like water in the garden, springs eternal.

"Oh no, if I get the Mozambique job, I'll whip her down to Jo'burg and have it done there . . ." Pregnant pause. "But you're still up for helping us to relocate, aren't you?"

"What else would a mother do?" I say, more confidently than I'm feeling.

So ends another trip, with more uncertainties than ever before. Will we back? Will Starfish continue beyond this point? Will I keep my word to accompany Ali and the girls to Mozambique? Who knows!

CHAPTER TWENTY-NINE: ADRIFT ON A SEA OF UNCERTAINTY
2011

To my relief, Mozambique falls through. Phew, right from the start, it sounded way too uncivilised!

"So what now?" I ask Ali as Christmas 2010 comes and goes.

"The same organisation has offered me a video interview for a job in Tanzania, plus there's a job at the university in Baltimore I'm interested in."

I toss up the odds between Tanzania and Baltimore. I was once declared a prohibited immigrant thanks to a mix-up at border control between Tanzania and Kenya. Since I nearly ended up in prison there, the idea of Tanzania doesn't particularly appeal. As for Baltimore . . .

Yet these also fall through. The year is ticking by. Ali and the girls come to UK at the time of the royal wedding. Since Becca lives in a world inhabited by pink princesses, she's in seventh heaven. She now knows exactly how to become a real princess. Why, marry a real prince of course. And if she's lucky, there's still one on offer.

Watch out Harry!

While here, Ali learns the organisation that interviewed her for the job in Tanzania has put her forward for a similar job in Botswana, for which they think she's ideally suited. I know next to nothing about Botswana other than it's hot, it's dry and not that far from Zambia or Zimbabwe which, on the African scale of things, means actually about two thousand miles.

Oh, and Alexander McCall Smith has written a lot of books set in Botswana. All of which paint a picture of a nation at ease with itself and with a supposedly limitless supply of diamonds. Not only that, but its people are easy-going and delightful. If I am to accompany my family to a new life anywhere, it might as well be to Botswana.

Ali is out when a call comes through from the American aid organisation. Naturally they're not going to reveal anything to me, though they do say, "Tell Dr Cooke we have interesting news about the posting in Botswana."

In late April Ali accepts a posting in Botswana.

"So when is this likely to happen?" I'm envisaging late summer, time for one last visit to Zambia before she leaves.

"Actually, they want me as soon as," she replies.

"Surely you need to give notice on your present job?"

"They require three months' notice, but they also owe me one month's leave, so we're looking at the end of June."

So, no pressure then!

"So, that means you'd have a month to wrap things up in Zambia before relocating to Botswana in late July?"

"Not exactly. They want me to finish in Zambia at the end of June, then start in Botswana straight away at the beginning of July."

Whoops! The entire summer has just vanished faster than the white rabbit down a rabbit hole.

"So, are you still up for helping us out?"

"But when exactly?"

"Well, Botswana wants me there for an induction course before relocating there, so if you could possibly come out say mid-June to look after the girls while I'm . . ."

"Okay . . ."

"Then there's the house to pack up, since I'll be working right up till the time I leave."

"So, what you're saying is, I'd relocate to Botswana with you?" I can't even begin to imagine all the complications that's going to involve.

"Something like that."

"Then you want me to stay on in Botswana?"

"If that's possible. I'll need to find a house and furniture, a vehicle, a maid, oh and schools for the girls. If you could stay on, say for a couple of months?"

I allow time for all of this to sink in. It's on a scale of nothing I've ever done before, other than perhaps when Bob and I first went to Africa in the late 1960s and then again relocating to Rhodesia in the 1970s, on both occasions, not knowing anything about what we were letting ourselves in for. Maybe Ali imagines I'm some sort of expert at heading into the unknown and that's why she wants me along?

But where is Bob in all this?

"Are you sure you're up to this?" he asks when we're alone.

"I haven't a clue, but I agreed to it and now I must see it through."

"At least *you* get another spell back in Zambia," he says wistfully.

"Oh yes?" I retort. "What with packing, looking after the children plus sorting out a removal? If you imagine I'll be swanning around Zambia, you've got another think coming!"

"Maybe you'll find time to write a book about it," he jokes.

He is joking! What can possibly happen with a move from Zambia to Botswana that would provide sufficient material for an entire book? No, there are definitely no plans to write a fourth book, in particular about this escapade. Categorically not!

In mid-June, I board a flight to Zambia . . . *alone!* Ahead lies two weeks holding the fort in Lusaka while Ali travels to Botswana for an induction course into her new job. There's a house to pack up and travel arrangements to be finalised so that all four of us travel on the same flight to Botswana in two weeks' time. Then, at some as yet unknown date eight or ten weeks later, Bob will fly out via Jo'burg to join us in Botswana.

That is supposing by then we have a house to live in, a maid to do all the housework and a car to pick him up at the airport. Oh, and two girls happily settled into schools there. With me is a brand new net-book, mini laptop to the uninitiated, on which I can surf the internet, write emails and, most importantly, keep a journal of what happens over the next three months.

Good heavens, it'll be late August at the earliest before I see Bob again and mid-September before I see the UK again!

If this is not complicated enough, the two of us then plan to travel back up to Zambia, alone and rudderless, to wrap things up there. I hope British Airways and South African Airways get it right, because otherwise one or more of us might end up stranded somewhere along the line.

Oh dear, this is turning out a lot more complicated than anticipated!

The days pass quickly enough in Lusaka. Ali travels down and back from Botswana and seems to like what she sees, but then confesses, "Actually it's not all that like Zambia!" Which could be interpreted in more ways than one.

On Saturday July 2nd, after kisses, hugs and tears from Auntie Dora and Auntie Sandra, whose gutted expressions reveal the loss of two precious grandchildren all over again, albeit by adoption this time, we set off on a journey into the unknown. Two of Ali's Zambian colleagues appear unexpectedly at the airport to give her a rousing send off, before we board the flight to Botswana via Jo'burg.

"Shall we have a drink to celebrate saying goodbye to Zambia?" suggests Ali as the drinks trolley trundles into view. But no, by the time we arrive in Botswana, it will be late evening. With two tired children and a country and a language we neither know nor understand, maybe we need our wits about us.

Oh, did I forget to mention, unlike Zambia, English is not the first language of communication in Botswana, but something obscure called *Ttswana*? Maybe Portuguese might have been easier to contend with after all!

So we have soft drinks and watch out the window as the vast plains of Zambia fade away. For Ali it is definitely good-bye. She has no reason to return here, except perhaps to visit friends, though friends may well be attracted by whatever Botswana has to offer.

For once I'm at a loss for words. I couldn't express my feelings either in writing or speech, just a sense of enormous loss and the feeling that finally God has begun closing the door on Zambia. Yes, with good luck and good management, Bob and I will manage a couple of weeks back here in September. But will they indeed be the final goodbye?

Pass me a tissue, that wasn't my drink I spilt, but genuine tears of regret!

There is however one bright spot. The net-book has so far been put to good use. Over the past two weeks, each day, I've found time to keep a record of packing up my daughter's life in Zambia. To while away the time on the plane, I open it up now and type in: Part Two Botswana 2011 . . .

However, do not for one moment imagine this is the start of a fourth book!

Family - Alison and girls

Kalimba Reptile Park - crocodiles

Kumasamba – bridge to island

Mulungushi Dan

South Luangwa - elephants in camp

South Luangwa - 'heffalump' before breakdown

South Luangwa - Lion

African roadside market

PART THREE

THE LONG GOODBYE!

SEPTEMBER 2011 – OCTOBER 2013

CHAPTER THIRTY: THE UNITED COLOURS OF ZAIN
September 2011 – Part one

Unbelievably in September, we do fly back from Botswana to Zambia where this mammoth trip started many weeks ago. Except, with family no longer here, it's like sailing in uncharted waters. And, if we imagined immigration couldn't take as long after a short-haul flight, it can! Then there's the hassle of finding a taxi to speed us to the Protea Hotel for one night there costing more than is decent in a country still bedevilled by poverty.

Oh, and it's election time once again. Rupiah Banda's time as interim president is up and Sata's ready to step into his shoes. Election fever is running high.

Next morning a driver takes us to the home of the car hire company owner to arrange a deal. Apparently, we're now trusted customers, meaning owner, Rajesh, offers a bigger car for the same price as a Pajero and, because it's a gas-guzzler, knocks $10 off the daily rate. Yet since the driver's daily payment has increased, it works out more than we were paying before.

Ah Zambia, how we miss all your baffling ways!

In no time, we're speeding north to Kitwe for what must *surely* be the last time. And if the Zambian bush looks drier, dustier and hazier than ever, at least Zain, Zambia's newest cell-phone company, has been busy repainting buildings, formerly the hideous purple and green of Airtel, in Zain's equally hideous salmon pink. Phone companies must get through thousands of gallons of paint transforming the country from one lurid hue to another, though at least people get their houses painted for free.

Our driver, Oswell, seems competent if a bit fast. Certainly, he takes risks we wouldn't as he speeds us to Nobutula Lodge in Kitwe where we pray for an untroubled stay, free from the dreaded Aromat, which Bob swears almost killed him last time. So, no Aromat, no sprinkle, no spices, just plain food, please! But *with* mixed vegetables! Staff are keen to oblige, even ferrying vegetables along to the room for inspection. And could the security light be turned off outside our room. As ever, a good night's sleep in Zambia is never guaranteed . . .

The first night isn't great. Nevertheless, we arrive in the dining room at the time agreed for breakfast, except where is everyone? There's no sign of activity and no milk for Bob's cornflakes. Eventually, a sheepish waiter appears. "Ah sorry, milk will be three more minutes since I am trying to find a key to unlock the cupboard to get the milk."

People are scurrying everywhere in search of milk, until eventually two jugs of milk appear, just as someone dashes in carrying three cartons from the nearest shop. Meanwhile the errant key turns up.

Ah, the difficulties of getting breakfast in Zambia!

At least Oswell manages to find his way back to Nobutula. However, he came without a change of clothes and is still wearing what he wore yesterday. If we're here till next Monday, he could be humming by then. As ever the immediate challenge is maintaining sufficient cash not only to keep projects ticking over, but also because Rajesh doesn't take credit cards and, with election fever running high, there's no way we're risking a visit downtown to his sister's shop. This means almost daily changing money in crime-ridden Kitwe. Yet today, not only is the Post Office changing money, there's also no queue. Clutching more money than is decent, we dash back to the car before a street kid tries to mug us, then back to the lodge to await the arrival of Mr Mbai who, so far, is somewhat conspicuous by his absence. Is there something he's not telling us?

Twenty-four hours back in Kitwe and it's like we've never been away!

The second night is no better. Outside lights fail to go off so Bob pads outside in his pyjamas and switches them off, except lights elsewhere still bathe the room with light, banishing sleep. Just what we need before a trip to Kaputula!

Today Oswell appears wearing different clothes and Mr Mbai is on time. En route we stop to purchase salaula from the African Market. Mr Mbai leads the way in past stalls selling stinking dried fish which resemble dehydrated snakes, while we try not to step, worse fall into, stinking black pools of foetid water, since cholera is rife in there. Mr Mbai then negotiates the price, while we hide up an alleyway feigning interest in Nigerian-style flounced dresses, because market sellers hike up prices if they so much as smell a mzungu. Deal done and we've two bales of salaula costing £100 per bale, clothing which donors in UK imagine is *given* to poor people overseas.

Somewhere along the chain, someone's making a killing!

Today the Kaputula road seems worse than ever, especially in the back, sandwiched between two Zambians. Mrs Kauseni of Kafubu Baptist project also climbs in for a free ride to Kaputula and informs us the community are under the impression we're coming to build a teacher's house. Headteacher, Mr Mutale, still spends weekends travelling back to his family in Chambishi and, with six full time teachers, the need for teachers' houses is urgent.

The community members who have gathered propose that, if Starfish provides materials, they will do the job themselves. Yet the school account *still* worryingly only has the headteacher and staff as signatories which is unacceptable. Yet again we must leave disappointed faces, before bidding what must *surely* be a final farewell. No party, no streamers, not even a goat dead or alive, just the certainty this is the very last time. A door has finally closed and the only time we'll revisit Kaputula, scene of so much joy, so much laughter but also of many tears, will be in our dreams.

The emotional roller-coaster of parting leaves us completely at sixes and sevens. With two weeks of this trip left, over £1000 of Starfish money sits in my account, while another $1000 cash remains in the kitty here. And there's more in the UK bank account. Thus, a novel situation has arisen . . . *what to do with all this money?*

But there's always another meal to sort minus grease, fat, sprinkle, the dreaded Aromat, spices and onion, getting lights switched off for a decent night's sleep, providing dogs aren't barking, cats caterwauling or the man next door talking on his mobile phone or running a bath at midnight . . . Just how hard is it to get a night's sleep in Zambia? Answer, very hard!

Next morning is Chilumba day which could prove problematical, even though arrangements were confirmed on Tuesday. We will travel with Faith, while centre manager, Josephine, will have sponsored orphans waiting on site to be photographed. What could possibly go wrong? *Where Chilumba's concerned, quite a lot!*

The road there is notoriously bad, yet Bob confidently informs Oswell it's better than the road to Kaputula, perhaps forgetting the disastrous breakdown with the 'heffalump'. But no, he even indicates the exact spot. Arriving at Chilumba, younger pupils have already left the site, while older pupils attend Basic School one way and Secondary School the other way. Nevertheless, Josephine assures us they will appear in due course.

Meanwhile, over at the three classroom block, Mr Chama and his painters stayed overnight painting in time for tomorrow's launch ceremony. But what is this? Mr Chalwe has instructed the front wall of the head's office be painted *pink!* Did he perhaps get a deal on salmon pink paint from Zain? Apparently, there wasn't enough grey paint to paint the lower half of the wall grey all the way around, however they will paint the front wall of the office grey which may look slightly odd, but not as odd as if it was pink.

Seated outside, we only manage to photograph a dozen orphans. A few stragglers eventually appear, yet nineteen are missing making today a waste of time, effort and petrol, although more may appear tomorrow with the lure of sweeties and free drinks. We're just leaving when Dynass, the child who once asked if I would be her mother, races in. If Dynass had been informed we were coming, there's no way she'd would've risked missing her 'mother'.

After this fiasco, we're undecided how long to remain in Kitwe. Last night we were tempted to hand over materials for the teacher's house to Kaputula community and let them get on with it. Yet the cold light of dawn soon dispelled that idea. For the moment, what to eat tonight with a launch ceremony tomorrow? Definitely not Zambian chicken, which can have disastrous repercussions. Let's hope they put the lights out like last night, our first decent night's sleep since arriving here. For sure we need it!

The next day starts early with a visit to Mitanto Secondary School to learn grade twelve results for ex-Musonda pupils sponsored by Starfish. Provided we can find it, then reach it since the road there is closed for roadworks. Amazing that they're finally repairing Zambia's treacherous roads just as we're leaving. In the end we park, then walk down the road carrying all we possess . . . *in an African township!*

Mrs Tailash awaits at the school, but not any results. Someone 'interfered' with the slips, meaning every single one must be gone through for four pupils' results. They're not encouraging. Only one gained a full certificate, but with a weak pass. Two didn't pass sufficient subjects and were awarded GCE passes meaning little other than they completed secondary education. A fourth, because of illness, didn't present for the exam. Since nothing further can be achieved, Mrs Tailash escorts us back to our car, thus emphasising: *mzungus shouldn't go walking alone in townships!*

On to Helen Kaunda School and the office of the head teacher who is delighted to discover our daughter was 'the dear friend of her daughter'. She promptly embraces us both, before communicating this amazing fact by phone to her daughter while they also attempt to unearth results. Another disappointment, Brenda passed seven subjects but failed English, though she could re-sit next year if she applies early.

With no time left, we dash back to change before heading to Chilumba for the launch ceremony scheduled to start at 2pm. But first we must photograph more orphans, except only a handful more appear. Excuses vary from 'she is sick' to 'they have gone to Mufulira', even 'he refused to come' from older boys. This fails to dispel mounting disappointment and hammers the last nail into the coffin of our relationship with Chilumba.

But where are Faith and Mr Chalwe? I phone to check Faith is on her way. "Ah, Quistin did not tell you I am not coming?"

"Hardly, since Mr Chalwe's not here either!" Apparently, Mr Chalwe is collecting his father plus the chief. This could take some time since chiefs only come in their time. Meanwhile, over at the school, the pink office has been repainted grey. However, because of the pink underneath, it's turned out blue. Still, there are more blue than pink schools in Zambia.

Community members have begun gathering, but there's still no sign of Mr Chalwe nor the chief. Yet starting without them would so breach etiquette as to be unthinkable. Finally, at 3pm Mr Chalwe rumbles in on a truck carrying the aged chief complete with his fly whisk and an entourage of bodyguards, advisers and hangers-on. Everything is running late, so Mr Chalwe really needs to get a move on. Zambian roads are notoriously unsafe to travel on after dark because of accidents and armed attacks, in particular where the road crosses the railway line just outside Kitwe. Yet nothing with Mr Chalwe is ever brief. He begins by praying, then introducing everyone who must kneel and clap and greet the chief, though present company are excused the latter. However, we must not approach him or greet him or touch him, unless he indicates we may do so.

How then will we get a photo of him?

No launch ceremony is complete without speeches, starting with Mr Chalwe, followed by the chief, a councillor, child, community representative and finally us. Bob talks about talents and putting them to good use, while I talk about achieving the impossible with the help of God who used a small girl and her request for me to be her mother to enable this school to be built. Finally, the time arrives to inspect the new school. Naturally the chief goes first, yet progress is slow due to his extreme age and because he inspects every single room along with his entire entourage. No-one may precede him. Clearly satisfied, he would like his photo taken with his entourage, then with Mr Chalwe and finally with us. Hooray, we have several photos of the chief . . . *without addressing a word to him!*

After singing by Josephine and her girls, the ceremony ends and the chief processes to a classroom where refreshments await. One last task remains, handing out sweets and lollipops to children pushing and shoving and threatening to crush us. Older ones are grabbing treats willy-nilly, so we hand them over to Mr Chama and the other men for distributing.

"Why didn't you give them to me?" whines Josephine who's been pestering all day about refurbishing her house and why her daughter by her first marriage, has been removed from the orphan sponsorship scheme. Because Josephine, you have a house, husband, family and job. Besides, technically Sharon isn't an orphan since she has a mother and a stepfather. Not to mention being seventeen years old!

We return to Kitwe, hot, dusty, dirty and exhausted. But it's Friday night, so we head for a restaurant set in an oasis of peace and calm, there to indulge in poppadoms, onion bhajis and pakora, followed by chicken curry, prawn curry and ice-cream. And we don't have to drive back because outside, Oswell awaits. My last thought before sleep is . . . I hope the chief and his entourage returned home safely aboard the lorry.

The problem with overindulgence is the price to pay. Next morning, we're meeting the director of Chep along with Kai who co-ordinated the Musonda pupils' programme. Over the years, Kai has evolved like a butterfly emerging from its chrysalis into a gaudy butterfly, yet she still provides few answers. Meanwhile, the Chep director wants a full feedback even though, after years of partnership, not one Starfish project currently operates via his organisation. All we want is confirmation of results we've already obtained from another source. They're not encouraging, yet this prompts the director to *encourage* us not to get *discouraged*. At least all bar one pupil made it through secondary school, an achievement itself for such disadvantaged kids.

Finally, we've an appointment at Canon Zulu's home, where his wife insists on serving pizza at 10.30am. Still stuffed from last night, we force down pizza topped with chicken and minced beef, while making polite conversation about the forthcoming elections and wondering how soon we can escape. An hour feels about right . . .

"Let us go into the church and pray," announces Canon Zulu. What difference can five minutes make? We kneel in the Lady Chapel while Canon Zulu prays emotively and at great length for our continued good health and for Starfish's continued presence in Zambia.

When finally we make it outside, a senior church member rushes up to greet us, triumphantly waving two tickets. "Ah, you must come to our braai!"

The last thing we need is more meat. Nevertheless, we convey both of them to Kitwe Cricket Club where they're stoking up the braiis. The odour of charring meat is stomach churning. We're handed two braai packs each containing T-bone steak, boerwurst and a double chicken breast. We slap the meat onto a nearby barbecue, then consider abandoning it. Yet I hear a voice calling clearly, "Whose meat is this?"

And another voice answers, "It's the mzungus!" We are the only mzungus there. We eat what we can and sneak the leftovers to Oswell waiting in the car park. Yet disaster of gargantuan proportions looms and we must travel tomorrow!

Conversation is slow, until a church member, somewhat the worse for drink, spots our empty glasses and insists on sharing his bottle of wine. A tumbler full each . . . to wash down the meat. All hopes of sneaking away vanish when Canon Zulu requests a lift back to the church where he insists on 'a private word.' What can he want? Funds to complete their church plant at Chibuluma? But no, he wants Starfish to build him a retirement home. Yet had he requested money to complete Chibuluma, he might have got every last ngwee!

We really must leave, having agreed to meet Faith, despite her failure to turn up yesterday, to collect missing receipts. She is stressed at the non-appearance of a family of Canadian volunteers who have disappeared somewhere between Canada and Zambia. Meanwhile Mr Chalwe can't understand what the receipts are for or for how much. Did he drink too much chibuku with the chief yesterday? We don't hang around. It's been a long day and there are two days' journal to write up before the long journey tomorrow to Lusaka.

Not that writing today's journal comes easy. How to express our sense of failure at leaving Kaputula with no promise of teachers' houses and at leaving Chilumba orphan sponsorship programme in tatters. Without our presence, the latter will doubtless collapse. And Mr Mbai still isn't given clues as to what's happening at Salem, while relations with Chep have hit rock bottom.

At least let's rejoice Kafubu Baptist Church is thriving, while changes for the better at Kaputula are hopefully now permanent. With the education authority now in control, teachers' houses *will* one day be built. They just won't be built by us. Oh, and, the three classrooms at Chilumba are 'in the pink' *and* operational.

All that remains, is to survive the excesses of the past twenty-four hours, hopefully without any dire consequences, at the very least, live to tell the tale. Oh, and to escape the country before election results lead to full-scale riots.

CHAPTER THIRTY-ONE: THE SCHOOL WHICH NOBODY IS BUILDING!
September 2011 – Part two

Not surprisingly, the morrow starts explosively. How else after the weekend's excesses! And with someone new on duty in the kitchen, it doesn't bode well for a speedy get-away. Indeed, the waiter announces, "Sorry, there is a delay with the poached eggs."

"What, have they run out of eggs?" I ask.

There are eggs, simply a delay. Perhaps the new chef doesn't know how to poach eggs, or they've lost the egg poacher, or the cupboard is locked which contains the egg poacher and they can't find the key. I order boiled eggs instead.

"But what if my fry-up comes with boiled eggs?" Bob dashes through to the kitchen. No sweat, they're frying his eggs!

Yesterday the receptionist was most upset we were leaving and promised to have the bill ready this morning yet, even while we finish breakfast, the boss is totting up everything in kwachas, adding VAT and reaching a total far in excess of the agreed sum meaning . . . *if we were coming back, which we're not, we wouldn't stay here again.*

Finally, on the road, I glance back one last time towards Kitwe's smoke-shrouded skyline. Oh, how I shall miss it! Ahead lies a drop-off in Kabwe of rations for Kabwe prisoners, then Fringilla in time for lunch. Oswell must have heard us mention the meeting time because he sets off at a cracking pace. Not a great idea on a road notorious for accidents and where 4x4s like this travelling at high speed invariably roll right over if a tyre bursts.

In Kabwe, Father Benny Bohan, the prison chaplain, looks as dapper as ever. We hand over the usual oil, sugar and powdered milk along with rice and salt, mainly for prisoners with HIV Aids or TB, praying God will spare seventy years old Father Bohan for a while yet.

On to Fringilla for Sunday lunch where, unbelievably, after yesterday's excesses, we both order the traditional Sunday lunch of roast lamb and beef.

As we leave the waitress chirrups, "See you again soon!"

"I don't suppose so!" I respond, convinced this will be our last time here also, scene of so many relaxed family weekends.

Tonight, we're staying at a Lusaka guest house recommended by the Wixleys. First impressions aren't great. The room is dark and dingy with no sitting out area, though it does boast cooking facilities. The Protea Hotel this most certainly is not! Yet the one breakfast we order turns out massive enough for two and, since this place is reasonably priced, close to the airport, secure and hopefully well away from potential trouble-spots following an election, we book it again for our last night in Zambia. And the owner will arrange airport transfers.

Next day we're heading once more for Siavonga, though who knows whether we'll 'see-a-vonga'. Sorry, family joke! Three year old Thandi, tired of the long journey to Siavonga, once asked, "But Mummy, when am I going to 'see a vonga'?"

Oswell remains our driver along with the enormous 4x4 still guzzling petrol at an alarming rate. Again, he sets off at a cracking pace. Just as long as he realises, if *he* gets caught by a speed camera, *he* pays the fine. Yet he races round bends dropping down over the escarpment at such ridiculous speed, I'm forced to say something. He then slows to a crawl along the last straight stretch, even so almost taking out a young goat standing motionless in the middle of the road.

Arriving at Eagles Rest, we sit on the chalet veranda recapturing the many memories this place holds. It's forty years since we first came here, even occupying the same chalet which maybe has our number on it. Later we stroll over to the campsite to watch the sun setting in a spectacular Kariba sunset. But what to eat tonight other than Kariba bream, though crayfish tails are also on offer and even kapenta. Spoilt for choice for once!

Next morning waves lapping gently against the rocks on the shore below rouse us gently in time for a full fry up with toast and 'bottomless' coffee, after which Bob decides we need to change our schedule and go straight to Kiambi River Lodge from here, thus saving petrol by not going up and down twice to the Kafue turnoff.

No sooner is the booking changed than I realise, "Oh no, that means being in Choma over the election period!" Not a wise decision since Southern Zambia favours neither of the two main candidates but is going out on a limb for its own candidate, a local cattle rancher with an unpronounceable name.

We phone everyone all over again before Oswell appears to take us to Lake Kariba Inns where we would have stayed but they were full. There's only one problem, they're running out of food, though there's still the view to die for from the balcony and buckets of nostalgia to wallow in later as we laze beside the pool, recalling many times spent here with family, the girls shrieking and splashing in the water . . . The phone ringing shatters these reminiscences. Kiambi require email confirmation of the booking and they don't have credit card facilities. Just as well, for once, the Kitwe cashpoint came up trumps and we've sufficient funds to cover the cost.

Next morning heavy mist shrouds the lake. The sun has apparently forgotten to rise. Oswell arrives to drive us along the lakeshore to Sandy Beach Safari Lodge, a place we tried to reach once before but the diabolical road defeated us. Now it's improved thanks to ribbon development along the lakeshore including fishing industries to harvest Zambia's kapenta though, from the amount sold in markets in Kitwe and Lusaka, it's a wonder there are any kapenta left in the lake.

Everywhere is bone dry apart from a startling swathe of emerald green grass planted with trees in full leaf. Clearly someone with money, perhaps from selling 'salaula' at £100 per bale, is pumping water out the lake to create this verdant oasis. Also dotted along the shore are some of the most enormous baobabs, even one with a sign proclaiming 'Baobab Grocery'. Now what could it possibly sell?

Sandy Bay Lodge is a quaint place with yet another view to die for along with the eponymous sandy beach fronting the lake and a backdrop of wooded hills almost enclosing the bay. Sand stretches right up inside both bar and restaurant. The welcome is effusive. Even better, we can swim and have lunch at tables facing out onto the lake. Apart from crocs and hippos, we could be anywhere beside the sea in Greece or Turkey, not beside Africa's largest man-made lake.

Not another soul is around apart from hens scratching contentedly in sand underneath the tables. The food is worth the wait, while wine comes in the oddest glasses, heirlooms from Bavaria where the owner originated. Unfortunately, the bill is more than expected because of an extra dish costing as much as one three-course meal. The waiter cum chef claims this was for the fish. Not the fish in our curry, but Oswell's dinner. We remind the waiter we ordered a plate of chips.

The waiter looks abashed. "I asked him what he wanted and he said nshima, so I asked what he wanted *with* his nshima and he said fish."

Possibly because Bob keeps asking Oswell if he's had any Kariba bream yet!

Eventually the owner knocks Oswell's meal down, but then drinks rocket in price, because the man who served us didn't know the prices so guessed them. The proper barman and waiter who know the correct prices, have gone to a local football match, though where exactly that might be so far from anywhere!

Back at Eagles Rest the lake resembles a millpond, its surface a sheet of grey glass you could slice through with a knife. That and the treacle thick atmosphere. We stroll over to the campsite hoping to spot elusive hippos but, with water levels so high, they've gone elsewhere. Certainly, they need to get water levels down before the next rainy season, otherwise Nyaminyami could finally take his revenge, sweeping Kariba dam to destruction.

The night is not good. Yesterday's food leaves a nauseous aftertaste, while neighbours are socialising on their veranda till late. Then noisy kapenta boat engines roar off into the night, lights winking in a line along the horizon, fishing for fish that surely no longer exist.

Ahead lies a long journey to Choma to catch up on Simooya clinic project. Just as we're leaving, Bob spots the teenager from next door swimming out into the lake, clearly unaware signs on the lakeshore warning: *'Beware crocs!'* are not there for amusement. Since he may not survive a second foray into these waters, we feel obliged to warn him, then watch as he pales and quakes at the knees at his narrow escape from the jaws (literally) of death.

Today it's unbearably hot and sticky. The sun beats relentlessly on the vehicle turning it into a furnace inside. We reach Chisoboyo Farm hot, tired and thirsty. Our chalet is ready, but staff know nothing about a driver sleeping here. At least it's peaceful waiting as darkness falls until the Wixleys return. Oswell will sleep in the empty chalet next to us, however Elma's usual maid is on maternity leave and her replacement didn't understand instructions to make the room ready. We set to clearing out the chalet and making up Oswell's bed before joining Clive and Elma on their veranda for drinks. Later we stumble back across the grass to the chalet in pitch darkness praying none of the many snakes around here are out and about.

And there's still the squirrel rat that made off with my ring in the middle of the night last year. Fortunately, Elma has remembered a cool box to keep snacks safe. Meanwhile all jewellery is safely shut away in a toiletries bag inside a locked suitcase. Try getting inside that, then!

Day ninety-two since leaving UK dawns, the rising sun piercing through the curtains to wake us. Less than a week to go before returning to the advancing winter. This morning two community members accompany us to the DHO in Choma to chase up the so-far non-existent nurse for the completed health clinic. We ask for Mr Ngweni or Mrs Buluba, but no-one of that name works there, though there is a Mr Mweni and Mrs Mvula which sounds close enough. Mr Scouoni, with whom relations have previously been strained, also joins us, squeezed inside a small room crammed with settees, seeking answers as to why both a clinic and a nurse's house still stand empty six months after completion. Excuses fly around like angry bees: they've been stocking other clinics, one completed two and a half years ago. They're waiting for staff. They're waiting for transport to move a temporary nurse here, but first must await her replacement. Every excuse bar the real one . . . they can't be bothered to shift their butts!

Eventually, after much probing, they reveal that clinic registration is underway. Nurse Josephine Skwalanga will move here in two weeks' time after the elections are over . . . "Even she was in the office this morning and is right now in Choma," they let drop.

Well why didn't anyone mention that sooner?

Oswell and Mr Mweni are dispatched to fetch Nurse Josephine Skwangala here to meet two aging mzungus plus two community members who, for the first time today, are smiling. That she's getting on in years isn't mentioned. For now, she will go to Simooya along with drugs, duly followed by furniture and other equipment, though the precise date for these last two remains uncertain while an election hovers over everyone's heads.

Dropping Nurse Josephine back in town to complete her shopping, we head for the cashpoint still trying to amass sufficient cash to cover the car rental and to avoid going to downtown Lusaka the day after an election to pay by card at the shop of Rajesh's sister. Unfortunately, while getting cash, the two villagers escape into Spar leaving us stifling outside in the car waiting for them to reappear clutching their week's groceries.

We drive them over to the village, using this as an excuse to check out the nurse's house before this afternoon's meeting. All is more or less well, though in places daylight peeps through between roofing sheets. Also, they sprayed window ledges with a nozzle paint-sprayer instead of using a paintbrush spattering paint everywhere. Oh, and some window handles are back to front. Apart from that all is well. Solar electricity has even been installed courtesy of Milden's money raising; certainly, it wasn't from us.

It's sweltering at 2.30pm as we hump and bump our way back to the village to find not many villagers have gathered, possibly because of intense heat. "Let me show you the site where we hear you are to build a school," suggests Gilbert Palale, project secretary.

As yet, we've not committed to building a school here. Nevertheless, we visit the site located near to the clinic though still far enough to walk in blistering afternoon sun down a sandy trail to reach it. On site is a still smoking brick-making kiln which Gilbert reckons contains 20 000 bricks for the school which we're *still* not building! Besides, the bricks may not be good enough quality to build an entire school, plans for which are even now in my backpack. But, since we're not building it, Gilbert doesn't need to know that.

Back at the meeting place, a few more villagers have gathered, though not nearly enough to build the school no-one's building. Nevertheless, the community expects speeches. Bob outlines this morning's events, while I address misapprehensions as to why we're here and why there's no commitment to building a school. News of the nurse's imminent arrival goes down well, but the reality of a school *not* being built, at least not by us, is not quite so well received.

Back at the farm the day finally cools, though tomorrow will only be hotter, unless a sudden shower cools things off. Tonight should be our last night. There's nothing further to keep us here, except Kiambi isn't expecting us until Sunday. Oh dear, are we lingering under false pretences? Yet Chisoboyo is such a beautiful place to linger . . . All that justifies staying on for another day are a few bits and bobs in Choma and a last visit to the clinic and nurse's house.

It cools considerably on the morrow. Clouds appear and a fresh wind is blowing. We draw out another K1m to cover any shortfall in dollars for the car, then shop for food to last through Wednesday until the flight home on

Thursday. Once at the Lusaka guest house, we won't dare venture out in the aftermath of an election.

Next we need an internet café to pre-book seats together on the flight back to the UK. At the moment, we're on separate tickets so could end up at opposite ends of the aeroplane. Trawling the main street, a sign points up an alleyway, though maybe up alleyways in Choma are not the best place to be in the run up to an election. Yet the internet is surprisingly speedy. Seated at adjacent terminals, we attempt to click at the same time thus ensuring seats together, unless Bob gets bumped up into World Traveller Plus, since that's what he flew out on.

And wouldn't that just be his, or rather my, luck!

In the afternoon we repack suitcases with safari clothes ready for Kiambi, then count the steadily growing cash stash. We could drive over to the clinic to show them plans for a school, but don't want to stir up unrealistic expectations. In any case, the Wixleys may not wish further involvement while their own future is so uncertain. If Sata is elected, he's promised to kick out mzungus, starting with the Chinese. Having escaped Mugabe in Zim, the Wixleys could lose everything again here. Rumours abound of riots if people suspect election results are rigged. All we hope, is to escape before any violence erupts.

We share last drinks and dinner with Clive and Elma, the last ever if we don't return. They describe their on-going frustrations with locals who not only drive through their land leaving gates open allowing cattle to escape, but also drive down tracks Clive has blocked off when he's irrigating and smashing irrigation pipes in the process. Worst of all they steal his maize and wheat, fish his dam dry and are now shooting what little game there is. Next they'll be stealing his cattle. Yet if the tide of politics was to change, these same villagers would be first to claim his land from him.

The future for white Zambians right now is very uncertain. Yet for us at least, the time has come for more goodbyes before we move on yet again.

Postscript:
A four classroom school, funded by Starfish, was begun the following year and completed in 2013.

CHAPTER THIRTY-TWO: ZAMBIA DECIDES ITS FATE
September 2011

It's over two hundred miles from Choma to Kiambi River Lodge in Lower Zambezi meaning a journey of between four and five hours. We bid farewell to Clive and Elma, knowing that seeing them again lies in God's hands.

The huge orange ball of the sun is just rising at 7am as we drive out the gate. Already lorries from all over Southern Africa are thundering along the highway, yet for once Oswell keeps the speed down. En route we stop at Monze for yet more cash, still trying to amass a big enough stash to pay off the car in leftover dollars and kwachas. Yet filling the tank with petrol just about cleans Bob out, so it's back to the cashpoint again.

By the time we reach the road south towards the Zimbabwean border, it's getting warm. Oswell, however, spots it showered here in the night since footprints in the sandy earth are more clearly defined. It would also explain clearer skies today and an absence of the pall of haze and smoke that has hung over Zambia the past couple of weeks.

On down to Chirundu, passing lorries thundering up and down from Zimbabwe. Chirundu itself has grown, although the three miles long queue of lorries waiting to cross the border has lessened which means less custom for commercial sex workers here. Like any border town, it's not the most attractive of places. In the middle of town, Oswell turns left onto a dirt road. There's no sign indicating either Kiambi or Lower Zambezi, though it looks vaguely familiar from a trip here in 2005. Gosh, as many years ago as that!

Twelve kilometres on we reach the Kafue River to find the pontoon motionless on the far side of the river and no-one around to operate it. Eventually two guys stroll nonchalantly down on the other side. Immediately, people materialise from nowhere, all wanting to cross. The ferry chunters across and off-loads its cargo before taking us aboard. They insist we get out the car, but bizarrely must get back in again before it lands at the other side where nine kilometres remains to Kiambi, now clearly signposted.

The question is whether to keep Oswell with us here for two days doing nothing when he'd rather return to Lusaka to vote in the election and spend time with his family. Certainly, it would save on car hire plus his daily expenses, not to mention demolishing bream at restaurant prices. Against that is his petrol up and back from Lusaka plus two additional pontoon crossings. We let him go, praying he returns on Wednesday morning.

If not, we're stuck and not necessarily in seats 19A and B!

Our tented chalet isn't ready, so we wait in the bar overlooking the Zambezi River watching elephant on the opposite bank. The chalet enjoys a peep of the river but not a full panorama, though they promise to move us tomorrow. First impressions? Kiambi is rather more downmarket than expected, however the view towards the confluence of the Zambezi and Kafue Rivers *definitely* makes it worth it.

In the afternoon campers from the campsite commandeer the lodge pool, so we take over their pool, until it's time for a sunset cruise around a neighbouring island where crocodile and elephant abound along with more hippo than ever. Bob currently has his best lion shots ever, as well as his best elephant shots ever and so many photos he doesn't know what to do with them. As long as he doesn't delete them all by mistake!

Dinner is served outside under the stars beside a blazing brazier with ambiance present by the bucket-load. If only we could bottle it up and take it back to the UK. All we have are memories *plus 1001 photos!* Unfortunately, the food doesn't digest well, heralding a restless night. That plus anxiety that, in a fit of madness, I have agreed to a canoe safari, even though Ali's friend, the one whose boat overturned near here, once spent the night with her partner stranded on an island in the midst of these very croc and hippo infested waters waiting to be rescued the next day. *Oh joy!*

And no, the night is not great, but then getting a night's sleep in Zambia never has been easy. Nevertheless, I wake determined to get the canoe safari over with rather than spending another night worrying about it. Unfortunately, over breakfast, my beloved starts cracking jokes about pilots in wartime having two eggs on their plate before going out on death missions and would I like two eggs this morning? This isn't exactly encouraging.

Moreover, it promises to be scorching out in the middle of the Zambezi River. We don long sleeved shirts plus long trousers and hats and plastering on high factor sun cream. All I carry is one bottle of water. Bob, however, has a backpack with more inside than Dora the Explorer, but is made to stow it in a bucket. Not that that will save it if we overturn in croc infested waters.

At least the size of the boat is encouraging. *And* it has an engine plus two guides aboard. However, any relief is short-lived, since this boat merely speeds us to where a small three man canoe awaits which has no engine and must be paddled downstream . . . *for three hours in hippo and croc infested water.*

I murmur a prayer before pushing off from the shore, paddling down the mighty Zambezi River with me in the middle, arguably a safer spot than Bob who's in front. Meanwhile Jealous, our guide, is behind directing the canoe and steering us away from trouble. Jealous begins with a lengthy diatribe about tomorrow's elections, but soon calms down and begins pointing out hippo of which there are an inordinate amount in the river. School after school, or pod after pod, either term is acceptable, though terminology ceases to matter should they overturn the boat. Thankfully, most simply surface then sink, ignoring our passing boat.

Even so Jealous keeps a safe distance until suddenly we come face to face with a lone hippo standing on the river bank glaring down at us. Lone hippo pose a far greater threat than a whole pod or school together since they're always unpredictable. This one takes exception to our presence and makes a false charge to scare us off. Heeding this warning, Jealous gives him a wide berth and paddles on downriver.

Occasionally a croc appears on the riverbank, before slinking into the water and hanging suspended. Half way downriver, we pull onto a sandbank to drink water and relieve ourselves. Marking our territory, jokes Jealous, though he's a long time marking his. Meanwhile the man in the motor boat joins us, having followed at a discreet distance all the while. A relief to know, since the wind is now up and it's become very choppy mid-stream.

Nearing the end of the trip two elephant groups appear for yet more fantastic elephant shots to add to the best ever taken yesterday. Even better, these ones are mine, since I'm currently in charge of the precious camera while Bob takes his turn with the paddle, battling the mighty Zambezi. Even when one elephant feints charging into the water, I still capture a shot with ears flapping and trunk waving as it prepares to charge.

At the end of the trip, Jealous lands the boat on the Zimbabwean bank to transfer us to the motor boat for a swift crossing back to the lodge. The two Zambians watch bemused as I pocket a handful of Zimbabwean sand and stones to take home. How can they even begin to imagine the emotions landing in Zimbabwe arouses thirty-six years after leaving there!

We arrive back hot, tired and dehydrated after three hours exposure to full tropical sun. It takes coffee, a swim, several glasses of orange squash and lunch to restore anything approaching normality, difficult anyways with the thermometer hovering around forty degrees. After lunch, we collapse by the pool. Drinking gallons still isn't slaking the thirst, even after cups of tea followed by sun-downers watching the blood red sun sink and turning the river blood orange in its aftermath. Dinner is unexciting and tastes the same as last night's, either because of the same gravy granules or the dreaded Aromat, while dessert is merely chocolate gloop with custard.

"Is everything okay?" asks Janine who seems to run everything here.

"Not exactly," I tell her. "Everything contains either milk or cheese."

She promises to do something about it tomorrow. However, like changing chalet, it may never happen.

Another day gone and day ninety-five dawns. In four days we return to the UK where autumn is already advancing. The thought of a UK winter so soon after surviving a ferocious Botswana winter, fills me with dread. Let alone trying to settle back into the English way of life after the adventures of the past three months. Maybe there'll be an Indian summer!

Today is our last day at Kiambi. It is also election day when Zambia decides its fate for the next five years. A desire for change seems to be afoot, yet if the opposition isn't voted in, trouble is forecast. If they do get in, there could equally be trouble from out-going party supporters. It's vital we reach Lusaka quickly tomorrow, then stay holed up the rest of the day. As for today, nothing is planned other than to relax, since there'll be little enough time for that in the UK. Unfortunately, the pool is again commandeered by campers, mainly women and children basking under the full midday sun and drinking copious amounts of alcohol. The only option is the campsite pool again.

After lunch, we fall into conversation with three people who've also been involved in charity work here. However, their approach is somewhat different. They do absolutely everything for the school they've built, for which the lead woman raises over £50 000 annually, even painting classrooms themselves. Not exactly empowerment of the local community, but rather encouraging the dependency culture which was such a degrading feature of colonial times.

But who are we to judge? Maybe she's right and we're wrong.

We retire to the veranda for peace and quiet until sun-downer time, mingling with the throng on the patio watching the sunset turn the river to molten copper. Drums announcing dinner roll early tonight. Staff are eager to dash off to vote or celebrate, or simply run riot. Our last night eating out under the stars; there'll be no eating out tomorrow night and certainly no eating out under the stars back in the UK. We linger around the open fire along with the trio we met earlier, this time being careful what we say since our approach differs so much. Clearly, they're puzzled. Their leader confesses she's riddled with anxieties as to how long she can keep supporting the project. In the distance a bushfire shoots sparks into the inky blackness of the night sky, while music throbs from a neighbouring compound. Polls are now closed. Zambia has, for better or for worse, decided its fate. All we hope is to reach Lusaka safely, then be out the country before any real trouble erupts.

Oh, and that Oswell turns up to collect us after breakfast.

Next morning, Bob departs on a last photographic safari while I finish packing. Yet he again gets drawn into conversation with these other charity workers who reveal they run the whole project themselves with little community involvement. Since they even pay teachers' salaries, it's no surprise the education ministry has *demanded* they provide not only a head teacher for the school, but also a teacher's house. Unfortunately, Bob only adds to their disquiet by revealing more about how we operate: that is empowering the community to build the school themselves, then handing over the running of it jointly to the community and local DEB's office. He doesn't, however, reveal our first venture produced so much angst, an entire book was written recounting all the mistakes we made, proving it's always a minefield, however you go about it. Still, maybe he provides some food for thought.

Thankfully Oswell reappears as we're paying the bill with a mix of kwachas and dollars. For sure using a cashpoint is *definitely* off limits today. Oswell rings Rajesh to find out where we should drop the car, only to find Rajesh is waiting at his garage in the mêlée of the second class trading area. Today of all days, that's the *last* place we wanted to be! Thankfully there is less traffic about. Even so Rajesh is jumpy and has shut every single rental vehicle inside the garage and sent his entire staff home. We settle up quickly using the stash accumulated over the past two weeks. Even so Starfish is *still* left with a lot of kwachas.

Not much use if we're not coming back!

That done, Oswell drops us at the B&B before returning the car to be shut away at Rajesh's house, since not one more vehicle would fit inside the garage. We fill the afternoon repacking suitcases before tomorrow's flight. We've acquired several surplus items including a bushman's bow and arrow, a fistful of Zimbabwean sand and gravel and half a packet of soap powder, which may not help at check in tomorrow. However, Bob travelled out in World Traveller Plus, so is entitled to a second piece of hold luggage if needed.

That done we switch on TV for the election results, yet it's difficult to get an overview. Is Sata winning, or will Rupiah Banda hold his own? It would seem Sata is in the lead. However, one worrying factor emerges. Having thought we were ensconced in a safe area of town, we learn the presidential vote is being verified not five hundred yards down the road from where we're staying inside the Mulungushi Centre!

And that's it, apart from tomorrow's flight. Somehow, I've survived over three months in Zambia and Botswana. I cannot deny it hasn't been taxing both physically and emotionally. Yet sometimes, in facing up to your anxieties, you succeed in overcoming them. How well that will stand me for being back in UK, I don't know. There may not be crocodile infested waters or charging elephant and hippo, nor three weeks of watching every Barbie movie ever made, yet UK still holds challenges of its own and facing them can also sometimes create problems.

CHAPTER THIRTY-THREE: WALKING WITH RHINOS
October 2013

It's raining, one whole month before rains are due. Could that be because we've just arrived for our final visit? Okay, you've heard this before, yet this time it's for real. Age, health, finances, even British Airways have all finally got the better of us. The latter because, if we survive the next couple of weeks, we'll be leaving on the penultimate BA flight out of here.

We arrive as dawn is breaking. But heck, let's not wax lyrical about African dawns, even start getting emotional. Instead we disembark and race across the tarmac trying to be first in the queue for immigration. However, other passengers are equally savvy and we end up well down the line. Still, it could be worse, the immigration officer could suddenly pack up and go home.

Once out the terminal building we search for a driver bearing a card with our name on it. In fact, Daniel finds us because, being rather short, it's hard to spot him. Still, what he lacks in stature, he soon makes up for in knowing his way around Lusaka where traffic is worse than ever. It takes one and a half hours across town to reach the guest house in Makeni, which rules it out for a last night stopover, since we might not make it to the airport in time to catch the early morning flight. For the moment, it's a verdant oasis of peace and tranquillity amidst the hustle, bustle and sheer madness of Lusaka.

Next morning the gentle twittering of bulbuls outside the bedroom window, along with the sun poking its way through flimsy curtains, rouses us from slumber. By 9am Daniel is already outside the gate, eager to leave because of road-works and deviations between Lusaka and Kafue. It's a nightmare, single line traffic for long stretches, then just outside Kafue a lengthy crawl through a dustbowl around surrounding hills ending up only 500 yards from where we left the road.

The first thing Daniel asks is what speed are we comfortable with? Has someone told him . . . *these Cookes are difficult to please?* Unfortunately, he interprets our response rather too literally and travels 80kph most of the way. This, plus constant, mindless chit-chat between the two men in front, makes for a tedious journey, though at least Daniel drives more carefully than previous drivers.

He does, however, ask endless questions. Earlier he was probing about our charity work when I spotted a hoopoe, even as I was saying, 'God is currently pruning our vine.' Could spotting a sacred bird be significant? That God is indeed wielding the pruning shears, or he's changed his mind and wants us to carry on? Signs are all very well; understanding their significance would also help!

We arrive at Chisoboyo Farm to an effusive welcome from Clive and Elma. Sitting on their veranda overlooking the dam, Elma fills us in about what's been happening, while we fill them in on Bob's recent narrow escape from death . . . *caused by a sand-fly bite in Portugal!*

There's just time before dinner to relax in our usual chalet, now with a newly tiled roof replacing thatch which didn't survive the last rainy season. Is it too much to hope our old friend the squirrel rat has departed? Time will tell, for now all snacks are safely sealed inside a cool-box, while all jewellery will be locked away tonight.

Ken, a young man from South Africa, is also here harvesting wheat in an air-conditioned combine harvester which he drove all the way here from Livingstone. Over dinner there's the usual talk about the good old bad old days, swapping Africa stories which get taller by the telling as does inevitably Bob's tale of remarkable recovery from the jaws of death.

And so to bed, though my extra powerful, snake spotting torch, bought especially for this trip, has already packed up, meaning any midnight stirrings will be in total darkness. Let's hope nothing worse than a squirrel rat is keeping us company though, maybe, I'm too tired to care!

Next morning, the dawn chorus erupts before 6am. Yesterday I gave Elma a packet of Jungle Oats in the hope only cereals and toast would appear for breakfast each morning. But no, Elma's kindness knows no bounds, meaning porridge duly appears *and* bacon, sausage and egg. After a morning at the school site, there's meat again for both lunch and dinner. Three days into the trip, and dietary problems are resurfacing. And there are still two weeks to go!

However, things always look better next day when Bob announces confidently, "Today shouldn't be as exacting as yesterday."

What, in a country where everything can and does go wrong? At least a plain breakfast restores equilibrium before a day in town buying building materials. Since time is pressing, I travel back ahead in the car with Daniel, while Bob follows along with building materials in a hired truck. Except, I set off with Bob's passport in my handbag, forgetting immigration officials were manning roadblocks into town this morning trying to catch people without identification. And they're still there.

"Ah, no worries, I will explain that your husband is right behind." Daniel seamlessly appoints himself spokesperson, before announcing gleefully, "Even these people are building a community school here."

The police pounce faster than vultures on a kill. "So, you are working here? Then how is it you entered the country on a tourist visa?"

Things are looking bleak, yet how to shut Daniel up before he fuels the fire with yet more incriminating information that could land us in prison.

"We're merely staying with friends on their farm," I say, "and have bought some materials for a nearby community school."

Before I can say community school, both passports are snatched and taken across the road to a senior officer secreted inside a car. Meanwhile I sweat it out, muttering under my breath, "From now on, Daniel, I'll do the talking."

Yet, after a thorough vetting, back come the passports. "So how should we know your husband?" the police officer wants to know.

"He's seventy years old, grey-haired and travelling in a blue truck loaded with, er . . . *timber and roofing sheets.*" Silently I pray Bob offers the same story, otherwise they'll lock him up for sure.

Thus the first week passes and, even if Elma magnanimously stokes the furnaces because that's the South African way, we're with friends whose hospitality knows no bounds. And there's a weekend to look forward to at Livingstone and Victoria Falls, where there might even be fish.

First, we must get there . . . Theoretically it's 200kms from the farm to Livingstone, taking approximately two hours on a largely straight and empty road. But that's forgetting filling up with petrol and Daniel endlessly dusting the vehicle every time we stop. Plus both him and Bob needlessly fill the travel vacuum with nonsense about the royal family, witchcraft and other twaddle, causing Daniel constantly to reduce speed, the better to concentrate on what Bob is filling his head with, or the nonsense he himself is spouting.

"I am telling you, the coffin itself rose up out the ground and pointed out the one who had killed the person inside it!"

Or, "There was this man at Samfya who could turn into a crocodile and swim in the lake with other crocodiles!"

"What happened?" breathes my beloved, overawed.

"Ah, sadly that one is now late." *For late, read dead!*

I clear my throat loudly. "How much further is Livingstone, because it's taking a long time to get there?" Finally, they shut up and Daniel speeds up.

Livingstone, in October, is hotter than Hades. The last thing we need is a run-around because we can't find the Zambezi Waterfront Hotel. Did somebody move the goalposts in the intervening years, or have developers obscured it with yet more five star hotels? But no, the hotel still all but tumbles off the bank into the Zambezi River and we marvel anew at the view where elephant cross the river each evening at sunset.

At 4.15pm we report for a sunset cruise, though it's soon apparent not many of those aboard are there to see game or watch the sunset, but are there for free booze flowing faster than the Zambezi River and free food which appears like manna from heaven. They attack both with gusto. Not that it matters, since little game appears apart from hippo and two lone elephant. Still, this idle life compared to that of impoverished charity workers, has some bonuses. Back on dry land, we stagger up the gangway and head for bed reflecting, "Gosh, this *is* exhausting!"

Next morning is Victoria Falls day, except . . . *where are the falls?* Where have thousands of gallons of water that pour over the Falls daily all gone? On the Zambian side, nothing remains but mere trickles and one narrow waterfall. Vic Falls have all but dried up. Is what some are rumouring already coming true: drought-stricken Botswana is taking water from feeder rivers, thus causing the mighty Falls to dry up? Certainly, this morning, water bowzers were collecting water from a riverside parking place where normally no-one parks because of thieves and robbers.

Maybe thieves don't rob drivers of water bowzers!

For the first time, we can see the bottom of the Falls, where deep pools still linger until water-flow re-establishes itself. But that won't be until the rainy season is well advanced and water works its way down via Zambia's many rivers. Yet bizarrely, water still pours over Rainbow Falls on the Zimbabwean side. Have Zimbabweans discovered a trick to keep water flowing and tourists coming? Always supposing tourists don't topple over the edge onto rocks down below, since on the far side there's not a safety barrier in sight.

In the afternoon, it's too hot for anything but lazing around the pool, though it would take courage to plunge into its distinctly chilly water. Unlike over-landers from the nearby campsite who plunge straight in regardless. But they're half our age, we console ourselves, as another truckload rumbles in, to replace those making a racket last night till 2am. Still, listening to their chatter provides much amusement. They've all been there, done that, know all there is to know about Africa, take everything from it in experiences, yet give back nothing. Bob reckons their presence lowers the tone of the hotel, but these days there's more likely a market for youngsters on gap-years than for impoverished old-timers like ourselves.

Tonight, we eat under the stars on the banks of the Zambezi River, causing Bob to wax lyrical, "Ah, this is the life!"

To which I respond, "Get real, it's the end of the line, we're not coming back!"

However, after wine accompanied by tasty bream fillets, maybe that's not written in stone. Amazing what a turnaround sitting under a canopy of African stars achieves!

Only one day here remains. How best to fill it? Most activities are expensively geared towards tourists with more money than sense. However, we have the advantage of both a car and driver, so we head for the Crocodile Park run by the family that formerly ran the lodge in Choma.

Inside pens and enclosures are crocs of varying sizes. Females have recently laid eggs and are feeling both territorial and aggressive. Our guide is either very brave or very foolhardy. He climbs into a pen and sits on the back of an immense crocodile, then clambers into another and beats the water with a stick to rouse an ill-tempered croc named Godzilla to leap out the water threatening to gobble him up. Finally, he lifts out an eight months old croc for us to hold, but we decline. Catch hold of even a young one the wrong way and it'll take a finger off.

From crocs to snakes, generally of the deadly variety. Not over-joyed to see us, they hiss, spit and shoot venom against the glass cages. Unmoved by these heroics, crocs and snakes remain my prime enemies in Africa.

We're just leaving when Mr Brookes junior appears. He informs us his wife still has her parrot sitting on her shoulder and old Mr Brookes senior is still alive. Meanwhile he's content here in Livingstone surrounded by crocs and snakes. Contrary to most black Zambians, he prefers snakes alive rather than dead and would happily tolerate a brown house snake or boomslang slithering around his house to keep down vermin. Myself, I err on the side of most Zambians for whom the best snake is a dead one.

This afternoon, in spite of intolerable heat, an ever darkening sky and the threat of rain, we head for Livingstone Game Park. Inside, we immediately come upon elephant, closely followed by buffalo, zebra, giraffe, impala, baboons and warthog. Sticking closely to River Drive, we meander along the Zambezi River since everywhere away from the river is sere from lack of rain, meaning any animals are sticking close to water.

We asked the guard on the gate where to see rhino, so he's directed us to guards at the far end of the park. There a cheery chap toting an AK-47 greets us and announces, "Ah, you will not find these rhino yourselves." He allows this to sink in before adding, "However, myself, I can take you to them."

Not rocket science where this is leading. "You mean, if we give you something for taking us there?"

"Ah, there is no charge," he assures us. "However, if you give myself and the guy guarding them a little something, that would be most welcome."

And if that's not paying, I'll eat my safari hat!

We set off with him up front beside Daniel and with his rifle disconcertingly pointing ceiling-wards. Meanwhile he buries his head in Daniel's newspaper, only raising it to direct us out the park, along the main road and into another part where the public isn't generally allowed. There we find another guard with another rifle.

"Okay, now we get out the vehicle," announces the guide.

What better, when eight rhinos, two of them with young, are patrolling somewhere around here. I position myself behind the man with the biggest gun, confirming in a whisper, "There are actually bullets in there?"

He assures me also in a whisper, "There are!"

We edge forwards, all the while glancing warily around for charging rhino. In an open space five rhinos graze placidly. All the more amazing since, what we will pay to experience this, is a fraction of what hotels would charge.

"Okay, so we can go now." A note of panic enters the guard's voice as two rhinos the size of armoured tanks lumber into view.

"Even we are feeding these rhinos with Lucerne," reveals one guide.

"And this lucerne comes in large white sacks," adds the other glancing my way. "Maybe, madam, the rhinos think your white T-shirt is a bag of food."

Meanwhile two armoured tanks plod ever nearer. We beat a cautious but not too hasty retreat. If charged by rhino, it's best not to run away, rather to dodge from side to side or hide behind a tree. They're no good at changing direction, yet can accelerate rapidly from 0 to 40mph when charging.

Back in relative safety beside the vehicle, we tip each guy K20 which puts a smile on their faces, telling them to guard their rhinos carefully and not let any Chinese near, for whom powdered rhino horn is a powerful aphrodisiac. As we near the gate, three elephant cross back over the river from the island and emerge right beside us. What a visit! This may be Zambia's smallest game park, yet it's provided some of the best game viewing ever!

CHAPTER THIRTY-FOUR: THIS TIME IT'S FOR REAL!
October 2013 continued

All too soon we're back at the farm near Choma where, not long after arriving, we spot an immense, hairy spider on the veranda. Bob reckons it's a deadly trapdoor spider. What with spiders and spitting cobras, one of which crawled up their daughter's leg in the living room, plus tales of a puff adder in Elma's office, all this is not conducive to a first night's rest.

Besides, did we perhaps dominate conversation this evening, even boring the pants off the others? Maybe we need to talk less and listen more. However, Elma is curious about all things British and Bob is happy to satisfy this curiosity. Yet, surely Clive and Ken would prefer man to man conversation about farming or sport? Besides, Clive rises at 5.30am, so why are we keeping everyone up till 9.30pm? Tomorrow night I'm keeping schtum!

To this end, I plonk myself between husband and Elma, then craftily steer conversation by asking questions of the others. Yet I still fear they're tiring of our voices. At least they now have the thought . . . *these Cookes will be gone forever the day after tomorrow!*

Indeed, next morning finds us in Choma's one garden centre searching for a suitable plant as a gift to remind Clive and Elma of us. We purchase a bushy alamander, nick-named the custard plant because its flowers smell like custard. Perhaps years hence Clive and Elma might one day look at it and wonder . . . *whatever happened to Bob and Moira?*

Back at the farm, bags must be unpacked and repacked. But what's this? Two cockroaches plus two fat white grubs in larva stage have taken up residence inside our cases. Hopefully a pregnant cockroach didn't lay more eggs even now hatching into grubs. The last thing we want is a cockroach infestation back in the UK!

For the last time, we gather on Clive and Elma's veranda for drinks, struggling over with the plant which looks a little wilted because the salesperson forced its roots away from another plant. However, Elma's green fingers will hopefully revive it. We are truly sorry to say goodbye to this couple who have welcomed us into their hearts and homes, but does Bob have to keep telling everyone he categorically does *not* want to return to the UK.

What does he have in mind, a life out here? No response!

Next morning, determined to depart early, Daniel is outside at 6am flapping his duster against the sides of the car, running buckets of water, revving the car engine and finally singing.

Okay Daniel, we get the message, time to go!

We enjoy one last hearty breakfast, before it's goodbye to Elma and Clive who comes in especially from the fields.

"For sure, I know it, you'll be back," says Elma.

"No," I tell her, "this time it's for good, I feel it in my bones."

Ahead lies a long journey to Gwabi River Lodge on the confluence of the Kafue and Zambezi Rivers. Apart from distance, there are road-works and off-road diversions in the stretch before dropping down over the Zambezi escarpment. Here drivers of huge lorries frequently misjudge both speed and steepness of the gradient, then lose control and career off-road, over-turning their vehicle. Finally, there's a treacherous potholed road to Chirundu, before a last stretch over sand and dirt to Gwabi.

Before leaving, Elma warns Daniel about hazards ahead, urging him not drive too fast. Does Daniel heed her advice? Not one jot, when he's determined to knock seconds off her three hours record to reach the T-junction, then he rattles over the temporary road surface at break-neck speed. Even worse is the speed at which he drops down over the escarpment, always a danger because there's no way of knowing what hazard lies around the next bend. Since Bob says nothing, I ask Daniel to slow down. Yet ignoring both this and Elma's words of caution, he hammers over the potholed stretch and dirt to reach Gwabi in under five hours.

First impressions? The view from the pool area is as stunning as we remember. However, from our 'luxury riverside chalet', the river must be here *somewhere* . . . if only we could see it, because the view is strangled by a large tree festooned with creepers.

"Sorry, there is no electricity," reveals a guy who shows us to our room.

"There was electricity in the bar area," I point out, but apparently, the generator isn't big or powerful enough to supply the expensive chalets, which situation persists until evening. As it darkens, Bob goes over to request candles and hot water to make tea. Eventually someone appears with one candle so we send him straight back for more. The room is not only expensive but also very large.

"And there's no mosquito net either," I call after him. But then there's no hook to attach one to anyways. The list of all that's wrong here is too long to write everything down.

"Did we mistakenly check into Fawlty Towers?" I mutter across the shadowy darkness.

We stumble over by torchlight for dinner. Everywhere is in darkness, except for candles on tables littered with empty bottles and ashtrays. There's no sign of waiter or barman. Nobody seems to be doing anything or to be in charge. Worse, the generator has now run out of diesel and packed in.

"Moses number one has gone to Chirundu to fetch diesel," they tell us.
"And Moses number two?"
"Ah, that one knocked off at 2pm and nobody has seen him since."

The boss isn't here either, otherwise chaos might not be reigning. But wait, lamb chops are on the menu, which we order with plain chips and veg plus a couple of glasses of wine. Two slowly sipped glasses later and no food has arrived. Other people are also waiting. First one goes to the kitchen, then another. One man, who knows the owner, demands his food comes *now* or he refuses to pay the bill.

At this point we discover we're paying K40 per glass for wine which, in real money not rebased kwacha, is more than in central London or Lusaka where wine's only K18 per glass. But this is beyond whoever the one person on duty is. We tell him, since we're paying for it, just leave the bottle!

One hour and forty minutes later food arrives . . . *pork chops!* I could scream. So I do, joined by the man from the next table hollering that the boss will hear about this fiasco when he returns from wherever, before adding we're not paying for food we didn't order, nor that we waited so long for!

We stumble back to the chalet in the dark, yet at 9pm power is miraculously restored. Lights come on, but not the air-con, located *behind* the bathroom wall, not in the bedroom where it's needed. We collapse sweltering into bed with the question looming large whether to stay a second night or up-sticks in the morning. For sure, we're not paying full price for this shambles.

Next morning breakfast fails to dispel mounting dissatisfaction. We check Daniel is on hand before calling Lake Kariba Inns at Siavonga to see if we can arrive a day early. Firstly, they claim they're fully booked then, since we didn't pay a deposit, decide we don't have a booking, even though we have email confirmation. They offer Lake Safari Lodge instead. I inform them through gritted teeth we don't want Lake Safari Lodge . . .

All this in the car park at Gwabi, the only place where there's a phone signal. Since it looks like we're stuck here, we head for the swimming pool which today is pea-green in colour. One more thing to add to the list of complaints. And, since all sunbeds with umbrellas have been nabbed, we sit under a tin roofed veranda on hard metal seats. Ambience score zilch!

Lunchtime is approaching when suddenly the phone rings, Lake Kariba Inns have a room for three nights from tonight. We inform Moses one or two we're leaving, then sling belongings into suitcases, before arguing the bill. Moses has charged the lower rate for the room, but full for last night's meal: £112 for twenty-four hours without lights, power, air-con and either the wrong or not enough food. If I never see this place again, it'll be a day too soon.

But since we're not coming back, that's not likely to happen anyways.

It should take one and a half hours to reach Siavonga, except last night Bob had a quiet word with Daniel about his driving. Now we wend our way to Siavonga and sanity, ironically on one of Zambia's straightest and safest roads, at a snail's pace, finally rolling into Siavonga, where not a vonga is in sight. (Sorry, family joke!) It's so good to be at Lake Kariba Inns, in a room with not only a view to die for out over the lake towards the distant hills of Zimbabwe, but more importantly with a mosquito net. What else to do but sit back and enjoy the view, before dinner on the veranda along with wine costing a mere K10 per glass.

"Ah bliss!" the first thought on wakening. "Thank goodness we decamped here!"

"Better still if we weren't flying back to UK on Thursday!"

A whole day to relax lies ahead, so we immediately exhaust ourselves walking downhill to the lakeshore in overwhelming heat. Struggling back uphill we meet an irate gander walking his wife and goslings to the lake. We give him a wide berth. Not wishing to exhaust ourselves further, we flop by the pool before a light lunch *and* we don't wait an hour and forty minutes for it to arrive!

A party of VIPs and NGOs from around Zambia has also arrived for a conference, here to live the good life on overseas donor money. The last thing any of them wants is to solve Zambia's problems, since that would do them out of a job and the wonderful perks that go with it.

Bob fancies a boat trip, but I'm not keen. However, urged on by, "Oh come on, our last trip out on Lake Kariba," I allow myself to be persuaded. If I'm never coming back, how can I miss one last trip on the lake, one last Kariba sunset? I then spend the next hour worrying about being out in a small boat on a vast lake doubtless without a life-jacket since we've never ever been offered one here. Quite possibly there aren't any on the boat.

Even as we set off, my worst fears are realised. There's an enormous swell on the lake causing the boat to thud down alarmingly as huge waves continuously smack against its sides. No worries, there *is* a life-jacket on board, but unfortunately only one. At least this boat has a proper engine and seats, not plastic chairs balanced on a platform as on previous trips.

Kelly loops around various creeks past kapenta fishing boats before crossing the mounting swell to reach the dam wall and Zimbabwe. A large sign nailed on posts now sticks up out the water, warning against entry beyond this point. Zims and Zams don't take all that kindly towards each other, due to disputed fishing rights and an uneasy marriage based on shared electricity, meaning Zims don't want Zams getting too close for comfort.

Thankfully the wind lessens and the swell reduces making it less of a white knuckle ride, though it's still a small boat on an immense lake. Leaving the dam wall, the sun is sinking as Kelly heads out towards islands where he lands on an isolated stony shore. Phew, the relief of a pit stop before the customary sundowner, alone on an island in the middle of the lake, watching the sun go down.

Putting the icing on the cake, Kelly announces, "Even we are right now in Zimbabwe!"

Albeit illegally! After fifteen minutes of bliss, we head back to the Zambian mainland, though Zimbabwe has never quite felt so tantalisingly near as we wallow in buckets of emotion before facing the uphill climb to the hotel with the gander still vociferously objecting to our presence.

"Oh dear, this last trip's rapidly disappearing!" sighs Bob as we retire.

"Hmmm, did I really say I wasn't coming back to Zambia?"

"To Africa, or just to do charity work?" asks Bob.

Actually, there are shades of differences, which could provide a get out clause. And know what, I might just need one!

Next day we urgently need to book accommodation in Lusaka for our last night. However, deals at the Protea Hotel are no longer available and there's no budging them on price. We need a rethink . . .

Yesterday Daniel had a day off, as much to give us a break from his incessant twaddle. Today he's back, albeit still on a go-slow to a petrol station on the road we're taking tomorrow. However, they've run out of diesel and I only just manage to stop Daniel from driving over a hundred miles to reach another filling station.

Today we're off to paradise, Sandy Beach Safari Lodge, though Sandy Beach Shack might be more accurate. Nestling in a sandy bay surrounded by undulating hills, one could almost imagine oneself in Greece. Except today, one most definitely is not. A gale is blowing and the pool looks far from inviting even in tremendous heat. Management assures us it's only sand blown in by the fierce wind, not mud, worse a straying hippo's calling card! Yet even the assurance they've put chemicals in the water doesn't convince me.

We head for our favourite table, last in line, looking out over the water. But what's this? Daniel has already settled himself there for the day. Previous drivers have always maintained a low profile, but not Daniel. He slips off shoes and shirt and sets off striding along the beach firstly in one direction and then back along the other.

"What on earth is he up to?"

Bob also is puzzled. "He seems to be looking for something."

Since there's not much we can do about his bizarre behaviour, we order drinks and food, telling the waiter Daniel can choose between sausage and chips or a toasted sandwich, though the waiter can't actually ask him because Daniel's vanished from sight.

"He's probably stripped off and is swimming in the water," decides Bob.

"Like the man who turns into a crocodile?" I joke, yet in Zambia stranger things have happened.

By the time food arrives, Daniel has reappeared, settling himself like King Canute on a white plastic chair on the water's edge and dabbling his feet in the water.

"Do you suppose he's been drinking?"

"More like Lake Kariba reminds him of Samfya and he's homesick!"

Eventually Daniel emerges from the water long enough to demolish sausage and chips, before roping Bob into conversation while I withdraw a discreet distance, feeling somewhat under-dressed in a swimsuit.

Back at Lake Kariba Inn, the pool area is being set up for a grand finale BBQ for charity guys approaching the end of their jolly. If they weren't fat before they arrived, they are now. Some are so overweight, they can hardly walk, yet they've demolished three buffet meals a day and are just setting off on a sunset cruise laden with booze and softies and with music blaring. And on this dear reader, a large proportion of overseas donors' money goes!

This evening it clouds over and becomes sticky, even looking like rain, which might put a damper on the BBQ. As soon as I taste the meat, it's obvious it's been doused in the dreaded Aromat, cause of Bob's near demise one time in Kitwe. Should I say anything and risk Aromat fuelled rage or keep schtum? But he notices anyways and takes it more calmly than anticipated. Besides, there's chocolate cake for afters to drown any aftereffects.

And so to bed where, even here, the air-con is not working properly. Inside the mosquito net, not a breath of cool air stirs. Oh well, this time next week, doubtless we'll be complaining about the cold.

And so finally . . . Doubtless I had every intention of writing an entry for our last day, except it never got written. Thus, what follows is a cobbled together version some two years later of what we recall of our last day ever in Zambia.

We leave Lake Kariba early, since we're still unsure where we'll spend the last night. Do we attempt once more to knock Protea down or admit defeat and settle for the guest house in a concrete yard with zilch atmosphere? Remembering also we need transport to the airport tomorrow.

Perhaps sensing his time is nearly over, Daniel heads for Lusaka at a reasonable speed, not stopping until Kafue where Bob makes one last attempt to bag a room at the Protea Hotel. This time he's lucky, probably because management realises any booking is better than no booking and agrees a reasonable rate with breakfast in time to catch tomorrow's flight.

Buoyed with success we crawl the last few miles between Kafue and Lusaka, stopping off at the garage in the second class trading area to pay for the car with a mixture of kwachas and dollars, before Daniel drops us at the hotel. Over all, he's been safer than previous drivers, yet his incessant twaddle has proved wearing. Would we have him again? Since we're not coming back, the question doesn't arise. Maybe, maybe not.

Though if the Wixleys *ever* receive improved phone connections courtesy of whoever Daniel swears he knows in Zamtel, I shall eat my hat!

Or turn into a crocodile and swim away in Lake Bangwuelu!

The Protea Hotel is an air-conditioned oasis amidst the furnace that is currently Lusaka. But there are things to be done, namely a painstaking haircut that will last months, then complete the flight check-in. After a previous shambles when someone offered to do this for us and almost cancelled our booking, we complete it ourselves in an internet café.

Just time to relax before dinner and no, we're not swimming in the Protea Hotel pool which, even in the height of summer, is bone numbingly chilly. We toy with a last supper at Rhapsody but, having been satisfied with Ocean Basket in Livingstone, choose the same in Lusaka. Is the wine rougher? Have they added Aromat to the food? After the first few mouthfuls, our moods plummet downhill by the forkful. By the end of the meal we're barely speaking. And this as the end is finally reached. In stony silence we head back for our last night ever in Lusaka, our last night ever in Zambia. What, no fanfare of trumpets, no swansong, just overwhelming sadness our time here is finally all over. Tomorrow we catch BA's penultimate direct flight between Lusaka and London, the final nail in the coffin that has terminated our time here. And not even an upgrade, since the flight is heavily booked as everyone tries to escape on the last but one direct flight from here to UK.

How to describe our feelings? Sad yes, but also empty that what has filled such a large part of our lives for twelve years will no longer be there. As we wait out on the tarmac, I recall that last flight out of Rhodesia in August 1976, the sorrow then that it was all over.

Oh heck pass the tissues somebody, please, these tears are for real!

For sure, there's still Botswana where a whole new country awaits discovery, but whether we return to Zambia is another matter. Our work here is finished and no plans exist to take on anything new, even though more could still be done at each project, so maybe the work never is truly finished just passed into the hands of others.

For the past couple of years, God has steadily pruned every last branch of our vine in Zambia. But could that be because he has something greater in store, greater fruitfulness in another vineyard? Well for that, we'll just have to wait and see.

Chilumba launch ceremony - chief second from left. Messrs Mbai and Chama to Bob's right

Kiambi - pontoon crossing

Kiambi - canoe trip

Kiambi - hippo up close

Livingstone Game Park – rhino

Vic Falls – dry season

Sandy Beach Lodge

Simooya Clinic Nurse Josephine Skwalanga and first baby born there

GLOSSARY

'A Heart for Africa': second print book about work of Tanworth Starfish Fund in Zambia, available on Kindle as 'A Heart for Zambia.'

Alex: former street kid

ARVs: anti-retroviral drugs for management of HIV Aids

Baas: 'boss' hangover from colonial days

Baobab tree: also 'upside down' or 'bottle tree.' Supposedly tree angered God who uprooted and planted it upside down.

Bata: shoe shop chain

Bemba: one of largest Zambian tribes mainly in Copperbelt region

Bilharzia: parasitic infection, flukes carried by water snails, causes internal bleeding, kidney failure, brain damage and death if not treated

Blixen, Karen: author of 'Out of Africa'

Boerwurst: blood sausage much favoured by Afrikaaners

Botswana: country bordered by Zambia, Zimbabwe, South Africa, Namibia and Angola. Formerly protectorate, *not* a colony

Braii: barbecue

'Bwanakula Thandi': first print book about work of TSF, available only on Kindle as 'The story of the Building of Kaputula School'

Cellphone: mobile phone

Cerebral malaria: form of malaria affecting brain, fatal unless caught early

Chalwe, Mr Quistin: assistant director of Faith Orphanage Foundation and co-ordinator for Chilumba project

Chama, Mr Wilson: building supervisor for most TSF building projects

CHEP: Copperbelt Health Education Project, TSF partner organisation

Chilumba (Orphans' Centre): Faith Orphanage Foundation project for OVCs

Chingola: mining town in Copperbelt region

Chipata: provincial capital of Eastern Province

Chipotoyo, Mr Mwansa: chairman of building committee and foreman for construction of Kaputula School

Chisoboyo Farm: farmed by former Zimbabweans, where we stayed while completing Simooya project in Southern Province

Chitenge: colourful patterned cloth worn as wrap-around skirt

Choma: provincial capital of Southern Province

Chondoka, Mr: Chep adviser for construction of Kaputula School.

Copperbelt Region: in northern Zambia bordering DRC

Dambo: marshy area in Copperbelt Region often used for vegetable plots.

Damson: former member of Chep staff

Deet: repellent effective against malarial mosquitoes

DOOM: kills insects in seconds, and anything else as well!

Duiker: small antelope

Dung beetle: large, black beetle that collects dung, rolling it along, then laying its eggs inside

Extended family: system whereby every sister of child's mother is also its mother, every brother of the father is its father, thus no child is ever without family. Due to HIV Aids, system on verge of collapse leaving many orphans.

George: former high court judge turned chef at Kumasamba Lodge

Go-way bird: hornbill, call sounds like 'Go-way, go-way!'

Guavas: small pear-like fruit, inside resembles tomato but tastes like strawberries

Harare: formerly Salisbury, capital of Zimbabwe.

HIV Aids: 'full blown' Aids, when HIV virus enters its most virulent form. Nowadays, with ARVs and healthy diet, victims can live for many years.

HIV+: HIV positive ie body contains virus but not yet in most virulent form

Hungry Lion: fast food restaurant and take-away chain

Independence Day: celebrated 24th October

Iwe: 'You!' 'Here you!' or 'Come here, you!'

Jungle Oats: South African traditionally milled porridge oats

Kabwe: town midway between Kitwe and Lusaka

Kafubu: rural town en route to Kaputula where TSF managed building of Baptist Church funded by Hockley Heath Baptist Church UK.

Kafushya: former member of IT staff at Chep

Kalingalinga: one of Lusaka's largest high-density townships

Kalulushi: municipal centre of Lufwanyama District, location of town clerk's offices, district offices plus education board.

Kapenta: small sardine type lake fish, fished nightly from Lake Kariba.

Kapiri Mposhi: town between Lusaka and Kitwe

Kaputula: rural community in Lufwanyama District where TSF completed seven classroom school in August 2006

Kitwe: Copperbelt town where most TSF projects were located

Kopje: small hill or rocky knoll

Kwacha: Zambia's official currency, re-based 2012 though $US widely accepted and exchanged

Kushuka: Bemba name, meaning 'lucky one', of goat given to Kaputula community.

Livingstone, David: explorer who discovered Victoria Falls, though presumably Zambians knew they were there!

Luapula Province: located in northern Zambia

Lufwanyama District: rural area north and west of Kitwe, location of Kaputula, Kafubu and Chilumba projects

Lusaka: capital of Zambia

Maputo: formerly Lourenço Marques, capital of Mozambique

Mbai, Mr Mwape: project manager of TSF projects in and around Kitwe, former ED of Salem Centre for Street Kids

Mealies: corn on cob

Mosi: Zambian beer

Mufulira: Copperbelt mining town where we lived Dec 1968 -> August 1971

Mugabe, Robert: president of Zimbabwe

'Mulishane!' 'Bwino mulishane?': Bemba greeting 'How are you?' 'Fine, and how are you?' Considered rude to forego proper greetings

Musungaila, Mrs Nkazwe: former head of accounts at Chep.

Mwinilunga: town as far north-west from Lusaka as it's possible to travel

'mzungu': literally foreigner, more generally white person

Ndola: provincial capital of the Copperbelt Region

Nkana mine: copper mine in Kitwe

NGO: non-governmental organisations generally with charitable basis and self or overseas funded

'nsaka': open walled thatched rondavels for meetings or talking

'nshima': thick, white porridge made from maize meal, staple of Zambian diet

Nyaminyami: river god said to have inhabited Zambezi river gorge prior to construction of Lake Kariba. It is said he will one day seek revenge.

Orphans: numbers close to 1m in Zambia. Single orphans have lost one parent; double orphans have lost both. Formerly cared for by extended family, now often in child-headed families or living on streets

OVCs: orphans and vulnerable children, vulnerable because of poverty, disease or status, sometimes all three.

Patricia (1): former maid at self-catering flats in Kitwe, now supervisor

Patricia (2): in charge at Gwembe Lodge, Choma

peer educators: workers trained to disseminate health education to colleagues

Pin: originally 1 pin = K1 000, now 1 pin = 1 re-based kwacha

Pit toilets: pits latrines in rural areas varying from basic holes to brick lined cavities with concrete reinforced floor and breeze block shelter.

Poaching: for game meat, elephant tusks, rhino horns, latter used in Chinese medicine.

Rhodesia (southern): now Zimbabwe

Rhodesia (northern): Zambia before independence

Riverside: low-density suburb of Kitwe

Rogue: ie rogue hippo or elephant, generally lone male driven out in dominance dispute, often aggressive, dangerous and best avoided.

Rondavel: circular hut with thatch or tin roof providing cheap accommodation

Salem (centre for street kids): on outskirts of Kitwe, provided safe accommodation for former street kids, also large community school for OVCs

Salisbury: former capital of (Southern) Rhodesia, now Harare, capital of Zimbabwe

SDA: Seventh Day Adventist Church popular in Zambia

Secondary Certificate of Education: school leaving certificate after five years secondary education

Shoprite: supermarket chain

Simooya: rural settlement near Choma, Southern Province, where TSF completed rural health clinic, nurse's house and three classroom school

Solankis: Mufulira clothing and haberdashery store in 1960s & 1970s

Spoor: tracks or droppings by which wild animals can be identified

Starfish story: written by Loren Eiseley and told by Nicky Gumbel as part of Alpha course, inspiration behind setting up of TSF

Tanworth Starfish Fund: registered charity set up in 2002 to assist OVCs plus needy individuals and communities as result of HIV Aids crisis in Zambia.

Tembo, Mrs: former head teacher of Kaputula Community School

Tonga: language and people of south-western Zambia

Tresford: former part-time gardener and HIV Aids counsellor, TSF paid Tresford's treatment until ARVs became freely available in health clinics

UCZ: United Church of Zambia

Village marriages: informal marriage ceremony in rural areas, legal status is debatable.

Vlei: open grassland

Voortrekkers: early settlers who trekked from South Africa to settle in Northern Rhodesia (Zambia) and Southern Rhodesia (Zimbabwe).

VSO: Voluntary Service Overseas, provides opportunities for voluntary work for people of all ages in third world communities

ZESCO: company providing electricity in Zambia, or not as case may be!

Zim: familiar name for Zimbabwe

ZNBC: Zambian National Broadcasting Corporation